Roots of Country

Roots of COUNTRY

The Story of Country Music

BEKKER ★ GRAVES ★ HAGER ★ NELSON
PASTERNAK ★ SEYMOUR ★ SPENCE

FRIEDMAN/FAIRFAX
PUBLISHERS

A FRIEDMAN/FAIRFAX BOOK

© 1996 by Michael Friedman Publishing Group, Inc.

Library of Congress Cataloging-in-Publication data available upon request.

ISBN 1-56799-376-1

Editor: Nathaniel Marunas
Art Director/Designer: Lynne Yeamans
Photography Editor: Wendy Missan

Color separations by Ocean Graphic International Company Ltd.
Printed in China by Leefung-Asco Printers Ltd.

For bulk purchases and special sales, please contact:
Friedman/Fairfax Publishers
Attention: Sales Department
15 West 26th Street
New York, New York 10010
212/685-6610 FAX 212/685-1307

Visit the Friedman/Fairfax Website:
http://www.webcom.com/friedman

*This book is dedicated to all of the talented men and
women who brought country music to life.*

Acknowledgments

The editor would like to thank the many people, in no particular order, who made this book possible: all of the hardworking employees of the Michael Friedman Publishing Group, especially art director Lynne Yeamans and photo editor Wendy Missan, both of whom are extraordinarily talented and wonderful to work with; the extremely knowledgeable and dedicated Nick Shaffran, senior A&R producer at Sony Music; writer and historian Ronnie Pugh, who conducted invaluable research for this project at the Country Music Foundation in Nashville; all of the writers who agreed to share their thoughts on the history of country; and everyone else who lent their time and efforts to making this project a reality.

About the Authors

Peter O.E. Bekker is currently a multimedia producer for the Microsoft Network (MSN). Formerly a freelance journalist, writer, editor, and computer consultant, Bekker was also music critic for the CBS-owned radio stations during a fourteen-year career with CBS News. He is the author of several books on music, including *Gospel* and *Country*, two titles in the Life, Times & Music series. Bekker lives in Issaquah, Washington.

Anna Graves has been working in the music industry in various capacities for many years. She holds a bachelor's degree in American studies from Yale University and is an authority on the history of American music. Graves is also the author of *Folk* and *My Boyfriend's Back!*, two titles in the Life, Times & Music series. A native of Tennessee, Graves now makes her home in Brooklyn, New York.

Andrew G. Hager is a freelance writer, playwright, and specialist in twentieth-century music. He received a master of fine arts degree from New York University's Musical Theatre Program and is a Jan Peerce and Yip Harburg Fellow. A country music reviewer for *Island Ear*, Long Island's music magazine, and *Country Beat*, Hager is also the author of numerous books on music, including *Women of Country*, *Satin Dolls: The Women of Jazz*, *Outlaws of Country*, and *Southern Fried Rock*. In addition, Hager wrote the liner notes for the best-selling boxed book-and-CD collection *Elvis: His Life and Music*. Finally, Hager is the guitarist and lead singer for the band Big Iron Skillet.

David Nelson is the editor of *Living Blues*, the bimonthly magazine of the African-American blues tradition published by the University of Mississippi's Center for the Study of Southern Culture. He also hosts a weekly blues radio program on a public radio station in Mississippi. A native of Chapel Hill, North Carolina, Nelson holds a bachelor's degree from the University of North Carolina and a master's degree in Southern Studies from the University of Mississippi. Nelson makes his home in Oxford, Mississippi.

Judith Mahoney Pasternak, a freelance editor, writer, and print and broadcast journalist, is a self-taught expert in American music, particularly in the fields of folk and jazz. She has written about the arts for local and national newspapers and magazines and was Director of Women's Programming at listener-sponsored WBAI-FM from 1983 to 1985. Based in New York, Pasternak is also the author of *Ludwig van Beethoven* and *Dixieland: The Birth of Jazz*, two titles in the Life, Times & Music series. Pasternak lives and writes in New York City.

Chris Seymour is a journalist and folk singer who lives in Brooklyn, New York. Seymour has written on such diverse subjects as music and politics for numerous national and local publications. He performs traditional and contemporary folk music, accompanying himself on banjo and mountain dulcimer. Seymour is also the author of *Bluegrass*, a title in the Life, Times & Music series.

William Spence is a freelance editor and writer who lives in New York City. He has written and edited liner notes on a variety of musical topics, from contemporary to classical, for several recording companies. As an editor and consultant, Spence has worked on numerous books and articles about the history of music, including several titles in the Life, Times & Music series.

Contents

Foreword

The nineteenth century had just ended when Oscar Wilde died, a little more than a decade after Thomas Alva Edison had devised what many people consider to be the inventor's only original creation: the phonograph. Edison's high, reedy voice reciting "Mary Had a Little Lamb" presaged great things, though at the time the recording device was little more than a novelty. What it needed, of course, was an application, and soon enough people began finding many uses for the remarkable contraption. This in turn fueled technological improvements, the end product of which is today's dazzling array of recording techniques and equipment. The key to understanding Wilde's quip is that he was referring to live music, which is entirely of the moment; the arrival on the scene of sound recording and reproduction technology in a sense changed this fleeting quality.

One of the applications found for the technology was, naturally enough, recorded music. In the 1920s, when the phonograph became widely available to a large number of people, it was discovered to the pleasant surprise of many entrepreneurs that recorded music was an eminently marketable commodity. These entrepreneurs were even more surprised to find that music of many different sorts—not just music from the Western classical tradition—sold rather well. In retrospect, they shouldn't have been

so startled; the experiences and ethnic and socio-economic origins of North America's settlers were too diverse to expect a narrowly focused music, imported from Europe (from where many people had fled), to appeal to everyone. Of course, it didn't take long for the recording companies to realize that the music that had been percolating throughout the New World for decades upon decades was the music people wanted to hear.

On the shoulder of those revelations and with the aid of the new technology, the recording industry was born. Many different kinds of music from around the continent began to be recorded and sold—including the outpourings of the rural peoples of the Appalachians, the "hillbillies." Over time, this "hillbilly music" would come to be recognized as one of the major threads in the fabric of what is known today simply as "country," a name that is used rather freely to describe an incredibly varied collection of musical genres. Little has changed as far as the names by which country has gone is concerned: for much of the history of recorded music, the naming of regional music was undertaken by (northern) recording companies and not surprisingly reflected their supercilious urban attitudes.

What is important to note is that country music—despite the common perception of its audience and its roster of performers as conservative

and homogeneous—was from the beginning one of the most inclusive genres, incorporating various strains of music from around the world that had come together in the North American continent. It was this willingness to mix and match that gave country its vitality for so many years. If country music is to continue to grow it needs to maintain the curiosity and inclusiveness that served it so well in the past.

This book is a celebration of country's diversity. It goes without saying that the eight essays and assorted biographies are inadequate to the task of telling the history of country in a comprehensive manner, but we hope it will give the reader an idea of the scope of the music's rich history. If it inspires some readers to seek out some of the other wonderful books about this topic (many of which are listed in the bibliography) it will have accomplished enough. If the book inspires indignation in other readers because it commits the inevitable sin of omission, then perhaps those readers will become the historians of the future. And most importantly, if it inspires people to go out and listen carefully to some of the magnificent but too often overlooked country music of the past, then people will be talking about good music for a long time to come.

—Nathaniel Marunas, Editor
New York City, 1996

Chapter One

They Called It Hillbilly Music

A Regional History

by Andrew G. Hager

Until relatively recently, Old World dreamers in search of a New World made their way in a torrid rush to New York City, the gateway to the promised land known as North America. The city's ports, which welcomed vessels of every description from around the world, were the conduit for these refugees, who sought to carve out a portion of the "untamed" North American continent for themselves. Not surprisingly, Manhattan's international significance as a port—and a center of commerce—made it the trusted source for news throughout the enormous continent.

Before the advent of the teletype and radio, much of the information that made its way to the Big Apple from around the vast country was vague or embellished—if not wholly inaccurate—having made its way, one storyteller at a time, across the great frontier. Once the news had reached the desks of New York reporters, it faced its ultimate refashioning in the name of popular consumption.

The result of this kind of media generalization and hyperbole was the birth of a New World mythology. Tales of men like Daniel Boone, Paul Bunyan, Johnny Appleseed, and Davy Crockett gave the United States its first generation of popular myths. By inspiring ambitious men and women who wanted to participate in the formation of a New World nation, these tall tales—disseminated to a large degree by the New York media—served in turn to fuel the great migration westward toward the Pacific Ocean.

Thanks to the corralling nature of the northern media in the early to mid-twentieth century, the nation shared one set of eyes—located in the northeastern corner of the United States—through which the world was viewed.

The tendency of New York City's newsmakers and businesses to ascribe identities to people and places outside the city's geographical and cultural boundaries had its negative effects. News of the South, for instance, has, over the majority of the twentieth century, often been tainted by the emotional and political after-effects of America's bloody Civil War. A continual focus on southern racial prejudice has fueled an international perception of white southerners as universally racist, which is in and of itself prejudicial (not to mention inaccurate).

So too the history of rural southern and western white music has been riddled with evidence of New York image tampering. The term *hillbilly*, which was used by New York phonograph producers and field agents to describe the people and music of the South (in particular the southern Appalachian mountain range), rather blatantly belied the northern belief that all things that lay beyond the Big Apple suffered from a rolling, provincial sameness. It's hard to believe, now that the recording and distribution of country music (the modern descendent of "hillbilly

music") is a multibillion-dollar international industry, that some early record producers initially assumed that nobody would buy recordings of these "crudely constructed" southern songs—not even the southerners who had penned, performed, and grown up listening to them.

Evidence of how wide of the mark this theory was had actually surfaced almost a decade before massproduction of the phonograph had even begun. *Spirit of the Mountains*, a collection of essays printed in 1905 by the waifish but strong-willed Emma Bell Miles, ignited a national fascination with the music and culture of the Appalachian Mountains. In turn, what would become a voracious appetite among Americans for all kinds of southern music was awakened.

The daughter of a Presbyterian minister, Emma Bell spent her childhood learning the niceties of Victorian ladylike behavior. People of good breeding, it was believed, avoided whenever possible contact with the "great unwashed." The men, women, and children who lived off the rich resources of the Cumberland Mountains were considered by Chattanooga society, from which Emma Bell Miles' family came, just the sort of undereducated heathens a well-bred person should steer clear of.

Despite her early instructions in proper behavior, however, Emma strayed far enough from her home by her early teens to become familiar with the lifestyle of the mountain dwellers. The flora and fauna, the mist that settled slowly into the valley, and many other aspects of the surrounding natural environment soon inspired her to write poetry and to begin painting what she saw. In turn, this deep respect for the majesty of the rugged natural environment drew her closer and closer to the people who lived in the mountains and depended upon them for their livelihoods.

By the age of nineteen Emma Bell had met her soul mate, a soft-spoken mountain man by the name of Frank Miles who shared her passion for nature and art. Frank introduced her to songs written and performed by the men and women of the communities around him. Their two-year courtship finally led to marriage and, not suprisingly, to Emma's disinheritance from her family.

During the long, difficult winters, Emma Miles made her way from her mountainside shack into the city to earn money by giving lectures and selling paintings to the city's socialites. Slowly but surely, Emma began to enlighten southern aristocrats regarding the humanity of the mountain people. Thanks to her early education in the ways of polite society, she was able to play a crucial role in breaking down the barriers between the aristocracy and mountain folk.

The impact on northern readers of the publication of her first book was overwhelming. Thanks to mass production, Emma's mission to break down barriers soon included the destruction of some of the divisions between the North and the South. As a result of her success as a cultural intermediary, northern musicologists began to believe that they too could participate in reuniting the nation.

The contribution of these musicologists to the post–World War I dialogue, however, was limited. Since their outlook was not, as Miles' had been, forged from a lifelong relationship with two worlds, their perspectives often proved more harmful than healthy. Less enlightened pundits even went so far as to announce that the Victorian ethic, which was the mainstay of the northern aristocracy (and the epitome of cultured society worldwide), was apparently meaningless to those people in the mountain communities. To urbane Victorian northern minds, rural southern women—who averaged eight children and sang not only of church and familial duty but also of sex and death—were no better than any woodsdwelling animal. Although Emma Miles had made some cultural headway, prejudicial media generalizations continued to cast the southerner in a negative light.

Had it not been for the money-making potential of marketing phonograph records, northern consumers would most likely have not heard from their rural counterparts again for a long time. A search for broader economic markets within the phonograph industry, however, inevitably led to a reconsideration of the southern population. Though early results from mass distribution of the phonograph suggested that the South wasn't very interested in the product, a few producers were convinced that it wasn't that southerners were opposed to the phonograph itself but rather that the music being printed on the records at the time simply didn't appeal to the southern population.

So with crude recording equipment in tow, northern entrepreneurs from the big record labels—OKeh, Victor, and Paramount, to name a few—went south to search for music that would prove correct the theory that southerners would purchase records if those records contained southern music. Ralph Peer made his way to the Appalachians on several occasions in the 1920s, perhaps most notably in 1927. That year, hundreds of performers, drawn by the offer of fifty dollars a song, made their way to Bristol, Tennessee (or Virginia, depending on which side of town you're standing on), with the hope of catching Peer's ear. Although early sales of the first recordings from these Bristol sessions seemed to prove him wrong, Peer's investment eventually proved a gold mine— commercially and musically. Among others, the legendary Carter Family and the Father of Country Music himself, Jimmie Rodgers, became nationally recognized figures thanks to the Bristol sessions.

The advent of the radio and phonograph did much to diffuse Manhattan's cultural stranglehold, and both quickly came to be considered necessities in households across the United States. It is estimated that by 1929 every third home had a radio—an astounding figure considering the fact that the radio industry itself was only nine years old at that time. Not surprisingly, the fact that they could reach a third of the population of the United States with the existing equipment inspired in the early captains of the recording industry the dream of one day becoming a ubiquitous presence in the American household. As a result, radio stations, able to reach across great expanses of land and into every home, became the focus of burgeoning businesses of all sorts.

To better promote their goods and services, many large companies, from insurance agencies to clothing chains, began to buy up America's airwaves. Atlanta's WSB, the first high-powered southern radio station, heralded the beginning of a new age not only

Above: *Upon hearing (left to right) Maybelle, A.P., and Sara Carter performing their "mountain music" for the first time, producer Ralph Peer suggested that the trio perform only square dance music. A.P. flatly refused because dancing was against his mother's religious beliefs.* **Right:** *Although recognized as the Father of Country Music, Jimmie Rodgers performed with a variety of musicians, including Lil and Louis Armstrong, who backed him on "Blue Yodel #9."*

Although everyone is aware of the impact that the barn dance had in Nashville, few Americans are aware of the impact that radio barn dances had on northern urban culture. Sears' Chicago-based radio station—WLS (for "World's Largest Store"), broadcaster of the first "Barn Dance of the Air," which later became *The National Barn Dance*—was home to the most popular radio entertainers of the 1930s and 1940s. Thanks to the exposure she got on WLS, for instance, Lulu Belle (Myrtle Eleanor Cooper)—a vaudeville-style musical comedy performer who was teamed with Scotty (Scott Wiseman)—drew more

votes in *Radio Guide*'s 1936 fan poll than any other actor, jazz singer, or Broadway entertainer of the day.

Lulu Belle's brash behavior, which stood in stark contrast to Scotty's own bashful, southern nature, proved so successful that their brand of musical comedy became a standard for many other husband-and-wife teams to come (most notably influenced by them were George Burns and Gracie Allen and, a decade later, Lucille Ball and Desi Arnaz). Their routines also set a precedent for comedy in country music that would survive in ensuing generations in the stylings of Minnie Pearl, Homer and Jethro (whose novelty song "[How Much Is] That Hound Dog in the Window" was a best-selling record in 1953), and even the ensemble cast of the long-running country variety television show *Hee-Haw*.

With the marriage of Lulu Belle and Scotty in 1934, the media began referring to the radio couple as "The Hayloft Sweethearts" and "The Sweethearts

Above: *Lulu Belle and Scotty, the most popular entertainment couple (largely because of Lulu Belle) in the United States during the 1930s, appeared in a total of seven feature films, the most notable of which was* **Shine On, Harvest Moon.** **Inset, right:** *"Coming to you from the WLS hayloft in the Eighth Street Theatre, Chicago,"* The National Barn Dance *was a northern show that disseminated southern rural sensibilities throughout the United States. This is the cast in 1936, the show's twelfth year.*

in technology but also in American music. Audience response to WSB's time-filling local talent show began to shape rural music as a healthy commodity. One radio station after another, popping up throughout the United States and Canada, began to air hillbilly music. Accordingly, singers and comedians willing to be labeled hillbillies in return for media exposure began crawling out of the woodwork. Although only a small percentage of the performers actually lived in mountainside shacks, thousands of southerners—many of whom were urban professionals—assumed the label used in the industry to refer to undereducated pickers and strummers.

George D. Hay

The Solemn Ol' Judge

George D. Hay was remarkable in recognizing the potential of the radio to spread the rural music he had come to love.

It was a newspaperman from Indiana who founded, built, and shaped the Grand Ole Opry, country music's most prestigious stage and a radio broadcast that in more than sixty years has featured every great name in the field.

George Dewey Hay (1895–1968) was in his early twenties when he moved from his hometown of Attica, Indiana, to Memphis, Tennessee, to take a reporting job on the *Memphis Commercial Appeal* newspaper. At the time commercial radio was in its infancy, and the *Appeal,* like many newspapers, had invested in a station of its own, mostly as a tool to sell newspapers. Fascinated by the new medium, Hay took a job as an announcer while continuing to work as a reporter. Soon afterward, having established himself in radio and deciding he liked the work, Hay moved to Chicago, where he was hired as an announcer at WLS, a 50,000-watt powerhouse whose signal still blankets most of the Midwest.

One day an idea was hatched at WLS to invite amateur musicians into the studio for a "Barn Dance of the Air." Those live concerts gobbled up quite a few hours of broadcast time, and soon the barn dances could be heard, morning, noon, and night. Public reaction was immediately favorable and, because of its powerful signal, the nighttime barn dance show on WLS was quickly renamed *The National Barn Dance*, and Hay was installed as master of ceremonies. Not particularly musical, Hay played no instruments and never sang or wrote a song. But he had always loved the informal hoedowns that were put on by local pickers in the Ozark mountains and in other places he traveled. He was tremendously impressed with the energy of the music and the joy that it brought the players and their audiences. He was the perfect choice for ringmaster of the WLS program.

It was on *The National Barn Dance* that Hay began developing the "Solemn Ol' Judge" character that later became his signature as host of the *Grand Ole Opry*. The Chicago show featured string bands, square dance callers, and fiddlers, and it eventually branched out to include "singing cowboys" such as Gene Autry. As time went by, mainstream pop singers and balladeers were also featured. Much later, WLS became one of the first stations to adopt the records-only Top 40 format, and *The National Barn Dance* moved to another Chicago powerhouse, WGN, remaining on air there until 1968.

Hay hosted *The National Barn Dance* only until 1925. As the Solemn Ol' Judge, he blew a steamboat whistle to kick off each segment of the program and otherwise did his best to assure that the folksy, "barn dance" flavor was maintained.

An offer from the National Life and Accident Insurance Company lured Hay to Nashville in 1925. The firm owned WSW there, a low-power station with a fifty-mile (80km) range, and Hay was hired to run it. At first this seemed like a step down. Nashville was a much smaller city than Chicago and WSM was a tiny station compared to WLS, which could also be heard in Nashville, hundreds of miles from Chicago. But Hay was inspired by the challenge of directing the new station, and one of his first suggestions was for a barn dance program like the one that he had emceed in Chicago. It was not an easy sell, for the station's owners were hoping to develop a more sophisticated image, but Hay ultimately prevailed.

The *WSM Barn Dance* went on the air on November 28, 1925. The Solemn Ol' Judge held forth as master of ceremonies, but it was an unspectacular debut. The only performers to appear on the maiden broadcast were an elderly fiddler named Uncle Jimmy Thompson and his niece, a pianist named Eva Thompson Jones. Within weeks, however, WSM was deluged with requests from local amateurs for a shot at some radio time. Hay would anoint the performers who had been chosen to appear on the show with such down-home names as the Possum Hunters or the Clod Hoppers.

WSM carried a number of programs, including a New York City classical music broadcast that sometimes preceded the barn dance. It is said that one night as he opened his show, Hay bellowed, "Folks, you've been up in the clouds with some grand opera...now get down to earth with us...in a shindig of Grand Ole Opry!" Whether or not this story is true, by 1926 the WSM show was being called the *Grand Ole Opry*.

In 1932 WSM raised its power to 50,000 watts. With the station's signal loud and clear throughout the Mississippi Valley, along the East Coast, and into Canada, the influence of the broadcast grew significantly. The vigilant Hay continued to serve as master of ceremonies until 1956, determined that the *Opry* remain true to its to its roots as down-home, folksy entertainment. The show stretched to three hours in length, and portions of it were networked to the rest of the nation over NBC. As the *Opry* grew in stature, its importance to the increasingly powerful Nashville music industry also grew. But of course its homespun appeal couldn't last. During the late 1950s, the *Opry* was transformed into a slick, structured showcase for Nashville's burgeoning music machine.

Hay retired to Virginia, returning to Nashville in 1966, ten years after leaving the *Opry*, to be inducted into the Country Music Hall of Fame. His death on May 9, 1968, was first announced over WSM in a special tribute to one of the station's earliest employees and the founder of the longest-running program on American radio (it can still be heard every Saturday from Nashville).

—P.B.

Roy Acuff

King of the Hillbillies

If he had not been dangerously susceptible to sunstroke, Roy Claxton Acuff (1903–1992) might have pursued a career in professional baseball instead of becoming a pioneer in the efforts to make country music an internationally recognized art form.

Augmenting Acuff's impressive credentials as a showman is his legacy as a major force in the business of country music. He was also an unsuccessful Republican candidate for governor of heavily Democratic Tennessee, and for twenty years was a perennial on the USO circuit. Roy Acuff was elected in 1962 to the Country Music Hall of Fame—the first living performer to be so honored.

The son of a fiddle-playing Baptist minister in Maynardsville, Tennessee, the young Roy Acuff showed almost no interest in music—but this is not to say he was not expressive. Acuff was a gregarious youngster who enjoyed acting in school plays. After high school, Acuff won a minor league pitching position with the New York Yankees. It was during his brief tenure with a Yankees farm team that Roy discovered the susceptibility to sunstroke that would force him to give up baseball and nearly every other outdoor activity. While recuperating from sunstroke, Acuff taught himself to play the fiddle by listening to some of his father's recordings.

Acuff was able to put his burgeoning talents as a fiddler and his stage experience to good use when, at age twenty-eight, he signed on with a neighbor's traveling medicine show. As a member of "Doc" Hauer's troupe, Acuff helped hawk a patent medicine (called Moc-a-Tan) by entertaining impromptu audiences with songs and musical sketches. It is not clear what benefits Moc-a-Tan promised, but Acuff benefited from its existence in at least two ways: he learned how to charm even skeptical audiences and he more than likely developed his booming singing style trying to reach those pre-amplification audiences.

In 1932, Acuff formed the Tennessee Crackerjacks. He soon renamed them The Crazy Tenesseans, and was on his way to stardom. In 1936, after three years of playing local venues, American Records in Chicago offered The Crazy Tenesseans a chance to record a number of songs. One of these was the Carter Family's "The Wabash Cannonball," sung during the sessions not by Acuff but by Sam "Dynamite" Hatcher. It became a regional hit in 1938. (The 1947 recording of "Cannonball" features Acuff's vocal. It became a much bigger hit than the earlier recording.)

Another song put to wax in that 1936 session was "The Great Speckled Bird," an enigmatic and mystical gospel song based on a quote from the Book of Jeremiah. Its quirky appeal, and a lucky break, soon brought Acuff to the stage of the Grand Ole Opry, a platform he did not relinquish until his death.

Acuff had already failed three auditions for the Opry when, in 1938, fiddler Arthur Smith was suspended by the management. Acuff and his group were summoned as a last-minute replacement, bickering right up until showtime about the best way to capitalize on their unexpected big break.

Despite the quarreling among the band members and the studio audience's polite but muted response to the outfit's debut performance, Roy Acuff left the stage a star.

At the time, Acuff told reporters that he was not comfortable with his performance and that he felt he may have blown his big chance. But over the next several days, thousands of letters praising Roy Acuff arrived from listeners, and the *Opry* promptly invited him to become a regular. Throughout his prolific run, Acuff's roots remained firmly planted in the mountain and folk music first popularized by the original Carter Family, whose themes were steeped in spir-

Before fiddler Roy Acuff (standing) joined the Grand Ole Opry and became its most popular spokesman and performer, he and his group the Bang Boys (by the time of this photo they were called the Crazy Tennesseans) performed mostly songs with tawdry lyrics.

ituralism and pathos. Although Acuff eventually changed the name of his backup band from the Crazy Tenesseans to the more dignified Smoky Mountain Boys, he reveled in the moniker "King of the Hillbillies." As his stature and popularity grew, "King of the Hillbillies" was changed to "King of Country Music."

This name was apt in more than one way. Acuff and songwriter Fred Rose—through their Acuff–Rose Music—laid the cornerstone that eventually transformed Nashville from an informal gathering place for musicians into a booming center of musical commerce. Acuff–Rose became a multimillion-dollar business that published sheet music and songbooks; operated its own recording studio and record company, Hickory Records; and booked tours, represented talent, and operated an overseas office. It remains one of the world's foremost country music publishing companies.

Acuff is remembered as an honest, down-to-earth man whose onstage antics included balancing his fiddle on his nose and showing off his vast collection of hand-painted ties. In 1974, when the Grand Ole Opry relocated (from Ryman Auditorium to the Opryland USA complex), Acuff amused millions by trying to teach President Nixon to use a yo-yo during the opening ceremonies.

Roy Acuff was an archtraditionalist who strongly resisted the appearance on the *Opry* of nontraditional songs and instruments even though his own debut had ushered the *Opry* into the era of the solo performer and away from its roots as a showcase for string bands and other multimember outfits. Acuff was criticized for stifling the growth of country music by resisting the appearances of honky tonk performers and other talents whose style was at odds with Acuff's ideal. Quite a few performers either were denied access to the *Opry* or quit because of Acuff's dislike of electrified and other nontraditional instruments.

Roy Acuff was honored on many occasions during his lifetime. In addition to his 1962 election to the Country Music Hall of Fame, in 1987 he received a Lifetime Achievement Award from the National Academy of Recording Arts and Sciences, the organization that presents the Grammy Awards. In a 1991 televised ceremony from the Kennedy Center in Washington, D.C., Acuff was honored for his contribution to the performing arts. That year he was also presented with the National Medal of Art.

Roy Acuff died of congestive heart failure at Baptist Hospital in Nashville on November 23, 1992.

—P.B.

of Country Music." The birth of their first child, Linda Lou, two years later again boosted the couple's already tremendous ratings. So popular were the duo over the next decade that Linda Lou's high school prom was even decorated in a "hillbilly hoedown" motif in honor of the teen's famous parents.

The success of Lulu Belle and Scotty's radio show was due not only to the couple's quirky compatibility but to their success with younger audience members. Family entertainment had become the standard of broadcasting, and the radio began to be considered the great American baby-sitter. Children sat and listened to the vacuum tube–powered boxes for hours without being exposed to the seedier side of life. (As much as television has become the baby-sitter of today, it cannot promise the same sort of sanitized family fare.)

In order to maintain this level of acceptability, the radio industry gave many of America's earliest recording stars an ultimatum: change their lyrics for propriety's sake or be forbidden from the airwaves forever.

Jimmie Davis, the four-term governor of Louisiana and author of the much-recorded "You Are My Sunshine," had begun his musical career penning tawdry ditties like "Tom Cat and Pussy Blues." But after the success of the radio barn dance, the politically ambitious Davis spent the rest of his life playing down these early exploits. Even Roy Acuff himself, the pride of the Grand Ole Opry, played fiddle early in his career for the notorious hillbilly outfit the Bang Boys (an ensemble known for its suggestive material) before he too was made aware (mainly by George Hay, the founding father and watchdog of the Grand Ole Opry's radio broadcast) of the error of his ways—and of the considerable rewards to be reaped from mending them.

Many urban music lovers (both southern and northern) weren't so entranced by hillbilly music, however; an urban fondness for nighttime entertainment nurtured the growth of a music unique to the city—jazz. The love child of the blues, French marches, barrelhouse, African-Caribbean rhythms, and (a little later) European song form, jazz became a national sensation around the same time the first hillbilly acts were becoming popular.

The southward search from Manhattan for new hillbilly acts ultimately exhausted the hills where billies were to be found and reached the Gulf of Mexico and New Orleans, the home of Dixieland jazz. Although hillbilly music and jazz had always been implicitly linked (through the country blues that had influenced both), comparisons and cross-nurturing between the two began to occur with the search for new rural music. The northern perception of the South as the milieu of the goofy hick was shattered by the likes of New Orleans natives Jelly Roll Morton and Louis Armstrong, entertainers who were sophisticated, engaging, and—unlike many of the early hillbilly performers—virtuosic musicians. More and more, northern markets were demanding to hear the sounds of such smooth southern performers; whether the hillbillies liked it or not, a new standard for popular American music had been set.

Rural southern music faced the tremendous possibility of being permanently upstaged by those city slickers from the South, but a westwardly change of focus from Louisiana to Texas quickly brought rural music back to the forefront. By being able to distance itself geographically from the nexus of hillbilly music, Texas was able to reinvent the hillbilly. Assimilating the jazz musician's sharp dress—satin took the place of cotton, rhinestones replaced wooden buttons, and slacks supplanted overalls in the cowboy's wardrobe—and the jazz combo's more diverse instruments and arrangements, Texas refashioned hillbilly music. In doing so, the Lone Star State began to reshape the northeast's perception of the "West."

Texas, being the largest state in the continental United States—and nearly dead-center between the nation's two coasts—could have been considered any number of things, geographically speaking. El Paso is, in fact, pretty far west, but Brownsville is the southernmost point in the nation. And Amarillo is so far north that it's part of the Great Plains, and therefore technically part of the Midwest. As a result the word *Texas* itself came to signify developments in the evolution of country music. The history of rural folk music throughout the twentieth century has been reshaped time and again in deference to the northern perspective of the great migration southward and westward from Manhattan. The change of apparel effected by Texan musicians was only half as shocking as the refashioning of the music itself. The first dramatic change that occurred is credited in part to sometime Texan Bob Dunn, who was among the first musicians to include the Hawaiian pedal steel guitar in rural American music. The roots of Dunn's offering began in 1917, when he heard a performance by a Hawaiian group that featured a steel guitar in the World War I boomtown of Kusa, Oklahoma. Dunn wanted to learn how to play this homespun style of twangy steel guitar (and eventually became a gifted player, going so far as to amplify his instrument in 1934, making him perhaps the first country musician to plug in his guitar). By 1927 Dunn had joined the Oklahoma-based group the Panhandle Cowboys and Indians, an early practitioner of the "western swing" sound. Ultimately Dunn rode the wave of the pedal steel to its inevitable glory, his talent on the instrument coming into full blossom with his becoming a featured member of Milton Brown's Brownies.

The blending of country songs and sensibilities with the soloistic improvisational techniques and instrumentation of jazz known as "Texas swing" or "western swing" (both of which terms suggest the northeastern perspective)—began its rise to international stardom thanks to another Texan, Bob Wills. He and his orchestra are credited with many incremental changes to the music, including the popularization of the drum set, which was theretofore unheard of in rural music. Thanks to hits such as "Texas Playboy Rag," "Take Me Back to Tulsa," "San Antonio Rose," and "New San Antonio Rose," Bob Wills and the Texas Playboys remained on the charts for nearly a decade. Wills, the group's "breakdown" fiddler, is also credited with the earliest beginnings of the "Austin sound," which would emerge more fully some thirty years later.

Demand for word from the West quickly mounted in the Northeast, and country songwriters in New York's Tin Pan Alley and in Nashville's growing music community supplied the rest of the nation with many songs "from the prairies." The once-popular hillbilly, as defined in the eyes of the market-con-

Left: *Bob Wills, one of the founding fathers of western swing, began his music career as the fiddler for the Light Crust Doughboys, which promoted Light Crust flour on the radio. The group's duties also included the delivery of their sponsor's flour to Dallas-area stores.* **Below:** *Gene Autry (right) proved to have one of the great business minds in country music; by the 1960s he had invested in several concerns, including television and radio stations and a major league baseball team. Here, he and his Cass County Boys perform a ballad for radio's* **Gene Autry Show.**

trolling Northeast, was removed from his mountain trappings, dressed anew, and removed to the West. In terms of the songs' imagery, mountains were replaced by plains, valleys were turned into canyons, and deer were supplanted by buffalo and cattle. And the word *hillbilly* began not to apply as well to these well-groomed buckaroos; instead, popular rural music went by the name *western*.

The first true "musical western" star, Gene Autry, was originally a radio and recording artist from Oklahoma. As legend has it, Will Rogers heard Autry perform while visiting Oklahoma and told him to head to—where else?—New York City. Thanks to the Great Depression, Autry had enough time on his hands to make the journey northward. After several successful recordings and continued success in radio, Autry finally took his chance and moved to California in 1934 to become a silver screen cowboy. Autry's success was meteoric and permanent. Although Ken Maynard is generally acknowledged as having been the first cowboy to sing on film, Autry will always be remembered as "America's number one singing cowboy."

Most Oklahomans who made their way to California during the Great Depression, however, were not, like Autry, welcomed with open arms. Of the 750,000 residents of the Great Plains, half of them picked up stakes and moved out West during the Dust Bowl (a term that perfectly described what Oklahoma had become after a four-year drought and poor farming techniques combined to destroy 150,000 square miles [388,500 sq km] of topsoil).

In California the "Okies" were treated as unwelcome guests and often turned away at a city's limits. The local movie theater in Bakersfield in fact had a sign on its doors that read "Negroes and Okies Upstairs."

The Oklahoman migrants who were allowed to settle in Bakersfield, California, were relegated for the most part to sharecropping. Under the worst of working conditions, the displaced farmers kept hope and memories of their home alive by playing the music that they had brought with them. Though many of those singers and songwriters were enormously talented, the majority of them weren't heard outside of the cotton fields for almost a generation, doomed as they were to obscurity by the prejudicial attitudes of the people in their adopted state and the immense popularity of Hollywood's singing westerns.

Of those early Okie talents, only one musical group made it out of Bakersfield and gained national attention. The Maddox Brothers and Rose worked vigorously to project the western image that had been popularized by Hollywood while maintaining an equally vigorous musical integrity. The key to their prosperity and success lay in their ability to rise above their economically depressed upbring-

Rose Maddox

Sister Rose

Taking second billing to the band she was lead singer for, Rose Maddox (b. 1925) helped bring her family to the forefront of country music. The Maddox Brothers and Rose quickly grasped national attention, billed as "The Most Colorful Hillbilly Band in All the Land."

In 1933 the Maddox clan left their home in Alabama, migrating as part of the Okie rush to California. Holding on to the memories of their Alabama home through song, brothers Cal, Henry, Fred, and Don played the guitar, harmonica, mandolin, and double bass, respectively, while the pure church choir voice of Rose soared above the rhythmic sounds her brothers produced. The family took to wearing loud costumes and depended on brother Cal to tell jokes to warm up their growing audiences.

Before two of the brothers were drafted for service during World War II, the family played regularly in Modesto, California, on KTRB, and at night traveled from rodeos and honky tonks to piece together a living. After the brothers' army tours were over, the band began a ten-year recording career with Columbia, Decca, and the notorious 4 Star recording companies. Their greatest single success came with the recording of Woody Guthrie's "Philadelphia Lawyer." In 1949 they claimed their second national success with the rowdy "Mamma Says It's Naughty," and in 1952 had another major hit with "Old Black Choo Choo."

With the help of KWKH's *Louisiana Hayride*, the Maddox Brothers and Rose continued to capture the hearts of Americans until they broke up in 1956.

Rose pursued a solo career during the 1960s, producing many hit songs, including "Gambler's Love,"

"Sing a Little Song of Heartache," and "Down to the River," each recorded for Capitol Records. She also sang with Bill Monroe, Red Smiley, Buck Owens, and Donna Stoneman of the Stoneman Family Revival.

In the 1970s Rose Maddux decided to retrace the path she had taken and return to her roots in country music, recording with specialist labels Takoma and Arhoolie. In the 1980s Rose Maddox began appearing in concert and recording with a couple of musical outfits, including Vern Williams' bluegrass group (performing in California), Merle Haggard and the Strangers (with Emmylou Harris, on an album called *Queen of the West*), and with Glen Glenn, a rockabilly artist (in London, on an album called *Rose Maddox Sings Bluegrass*).

—A.H.

The Maddox Brothers and Rose made their way from Oklahoma to Bakersfield, California, with their parents by stowing away in westward-bound boxcars.

ing: raised on a Farm Services Administration Camp in abject poverty, the Maddox family musical troupe nonetheless became known for their energetic stage presence, flashy colorful costumes, and comedic sketches between numbers.

The celluloid image of the Old West as perpetuated by the Hollywood establishment, however, soon lost its luster. Rural American music started to be weighed down by the dying western and its Tin Pan Alley soundtrack. The industry scrambled to refashion the music in the image of the times. *Billboard* magazine (at the behest of the Texas troubadour Ernest Tubb) led the way in 1946 by establishing the country chart, thereby giving the music a new name.

White teenagers throughout the South, a significant portion of what had suddenly become the nation's largest block of music consumers, were still not satisfied with the boundaries of their parents' music. Unlike the generation before them, the teens of the 1950s were primarily born into urban centers and hardly identified with the rural existence. A bicoastal United States with sprawling communities from east to west was no longer a dream but fact; accordingly, the younger generation began to demand music that reflected the mechanized, fast-paced environments in which they were growing up.

The idea of revolution, a stepping away from the past into a new and very real other world, seemed inevitable to the young and wholly dangerous to the ideals and values of their parents. The presumptions of these teenagers quickly brought about the concept of a nation of two primary cultures: the young and the old.

Whether by accident or sheer genius, their revolution began in Tennessee, the heartland of hillbilly music. Tennessee parents faced the tremendous dilemma of either accepting the younger generation's seemingly pagan music or squaring off against it. The options for the state's burgeoning music industry were a little more complicated: rise up against rockabilly (and lose any stake in the craze) or quietly profit from it. Oddly enough, Nashville's music producers were able to make a lot of money off the newest sensation while they pretended to be vehemently against it.

The subject of sex, a topic that had been banned from country music by the radio industry almost a generation before, had again reared its prurient head. The mixture of hillbilly and rhythm and blues that made up rockabilly gave parents across the country interracial nightmares about a modern-day Sodom and Gommorrah. The wiggling and jiggling of its performers inspired visions of America's children engaging in premarital sex. The veritable panic that ensued led many members of the conservative, older generation across the country to believe that, even if the nation's ethical culture survived (and how could it?), country music was definitely on its last leg.

For the first time, all children of the era, no matter their heritage, heard the same songs on the radio and saw the same images—through the wonder of television—as did the next kid, whether black, brown, or yellow. The new, self-described rockabilly artist (and sound) was the product of a collective aural-driven society, a conglomerate of local and national influences (although, of course, it took a white man who sang like a black man to make the new sounds commercially viable). The King of Rock and Roll, Elvis Presley, was the first and greatest example of a new consensus on reality among young Americans. Raised on Pentecostal church hymns and country music, Elvis strayed from tradition in his teenage years and began listening to what his mother, as many mothers did, termed the devil's music. The African American rhythm and blues that Elvis was listening to spoke honestly and unrelentingly of many social matters and was backed by locomotive rhythms that reflected the pace of modern life.

The Nashville movers and shakers, though fearful of the response country music's reactionary audience might have, claimed Elvis as a member of the establishment (as indeed he was). It was, after all, the Tennessee country music industry, headed by Chet Atkins, that helped make Elvis an international star. Although his rhythm and blues vocalizing and dancing helped point the way to rock and roll, the sound of his band was pure Nashville Sound. Furthermore, all of the players that backed Elvis—throughout the entirety of his career—were Music City country

musicians. Finally, let us not forget that *Billboard*'s country charts list eighty-four Top 100 hits sung by Presley.

Also, although Nashville had helped to create rock and roll, the industry elite were justifiably afraid that they had created their own worst enemy. Country's image, the captains suspected, again needed refashioning. Their response was to ditch the cowboy hat and make the music more pop-oriented. (By 1964 almost none of the male country stars of the day—including Johnny Cash, Hank Snow, Eddy Arnold, Jimmie Dean, and Marty Robbins—regularly sported a Stetson.)

The most drastic change in country music during this time, however, was the emergence of the Nashville Sound. The brainchild of Music City producers, specifically RCA executive and guitarist extraordinaire Chet Atkins, the Nashville Sound was a blending of high-tech recording techniques, jazz-influenced studio musicians, flawless choral work (such as that exemplified by the Jordanaires), and the outpourings of a stable of slick songwriters focused on the concept of small-town values. By updating the sound of the music, Nashville took the torch from the West, once again becoming the capital of country music. As a result, country music and Nashville continued to thrive. The music power brokers of the city—who had witnessed country music's power base blossom, fade, then flourish again—had the growing sense that it was both their responsibility and right to mold the future of country.

Even though Music City had made a gesture toward the kind of change America's music consumers were in search of with the removal of the cowboy hat, fans felt that it just wasn't enough. Certainly, the music itself had become, if anything, homogenized by the pervasive Nashville Sound. The time was right for the Okies who had been honing their skills in the honky-tonks of Bakersfield to be heard from.

The rise of Buck Owens, Bakersfield's first superstar, apparently left Nashville a little miffed. Owens had not waited his turn in the Tennessee pecking order—nor had he even said "please." Although Owens was the most consistently success-

Elvis Presley

The Hillbilly Cat

Like Hank Williams, Elvis Aron Presley (1935–1977) did not have to learn about the blues because he grew up with them. Born in the poorest neighborhood in East Tupelo, Mississippi, Elvis was exposed to the blues from the start. In fact, his musical style and eclectic tastes were shaped by the racial diversity of the neighborhoods he and his family lived in. Like most of country music's stars, Presley learned at an early age that success in music is often the only way out of desperate circumstances.

Elvis' father, Vernon, was rarely employed during his son's childhood and spent much of his time trying to acquire money the old-fashioned way—by stealing it. Unfortunately, Vernon's luck as a thief was no better than his luck as a laborer. He spent time in jail in Tupelo for petty crime, and ultimately the Presley family's move to Tennessee was the result of a failed check-writing scam. Rather than put the head of the Presley family household in jail and thereby place young Elvis, and his mother, Gladys, in permanent jeopardy, a benevolent Tupelo judge decided it would be best if the Presley family just got out of town.

Once in Memphis, Elvis began spending time in the African American business district near his family's new Memphis home. It was there that he bought his first records, the works of Big Bill Broonzy and Arthur Crudup, then the two biggest musical influences on Elvis' life. He also became enamored during this time with the flashy clothing, the boisterous collage of color and designs, that was sold on that side of town. Until his overwhelming success, these acquired tastes became a danger to his life. In fact, Presley's lifelong bodyguard Red West made himself invaluable to Elvis during those years by defending Presley against white teenage thugs who found the would-be King's hipster clothes, long hair, and sideburns offensive.

Elvis' first break in the recording industry came when he went to Sam Phillips' Sun studio to record a birthday gift for his mother. As legend has it, Phillips had been searching for a white boy who could sing like a black one and found Elvis to be the perfect blend. Over a year's span, Phillips cultivated that African American–influenced style of singing carefully.

Phillips wisely hired two musicians, bassist Bill Black and guitarist Scotty Moore, both members of the country band Doug Poindexter's Starlite Wranglers, to play on Presley's first single, "That's All Right." The audience response to the first play of the single on WHBQ radio was so overwhelming that the trio soon recorded four more singles together. Widespread national success then brought Elvis to the attention of his lifelong manager (and exploiter), Colonel Tom Parker, who soon after brought the King to RCA.

The concept of blending sounds of country music with Presley's blues-influenced style was taken one step further by RCA producer/guitarist Chet Atkins, who had begun experimenting with the blending of jazz orchestrations with the simple melodic structure of country music. Atkins, now fondly remembered as the father of the Nashville Sound, helped to make Elvis an international superstar with the aid of Music City's finest musicians: the famous country singing group the Jordanaires performed with Presley for the majority of his career, and pianist Floyd Cramer, saxophonist Boots Randolph, and drummer D.J. Fontana—all Nashville legends—were regulars on the King's finest recordings with RCA.

Originally known as the Hillbilly Cat, the once and future King of Rock and Roll, Elvis Presley, left his fingerprints all over the history of country music.

Elvis Presley died on August 16, 1977, of heart failure that may have been brought on by a massive dose of sleeping pills.

—A.H.

Buck Owens

The Baron of Bakersfield

While almost all the country musicians who strived for popularity and financial success in the entertainment industry submitted to Nashville's whims bowing and scraping, Buck Owens (b. 1929) doggedly fought his way to the top of the charts from his home in Bakersfield. Known as the "Baron of Bakersfield," Alvis Edgar Owens, Jr., paved the way to success outside the confines of Music City for other country performers.

Buck Owens must have annoyed the power brokers in Nashville because he didn't receive any awards for his contributions to country music until 1975, some twenty-five top ten hits after his first success (of those twenty-five songs, twenty went to #1 on the country charts).

Owens' family, who lived in Sherman, Texas, at the time of Buck's birth, moved to California during the Great Depression to work as sharecroppers. En route to California, their truck broke down in Arizona (where Buck would remain with his family until 1951). With the Owens' luck going from bad to worse, Buck was forced to quit school at the age of thirteen to help support his struggling family.

It was during his rough teenage years that Buck Owens took up singing and playing the guitar, studying the performance styles of many country performers. Like many country music artists, Buck realized that his way out of the fields was through music. By the age of sixteen, he had worked up enough material to host his own radio show in Mesa, Arizona.

When Buck was old enough to drive an eighteen-wheeler, he took a job hauling produce from Mesa to the San Joaquin Valley in California. Enamored by the sprawling beauty of the valley, Buck made the move to Bakersfield in 1951, joining his uncles, who already lived there.

Owens was soon playing guitar for celebrity acts such as Wanda Jackson, Faron Young, and Sonny James, all of whom made their way through Bakersfield on tour. His

band, for which he played guitar, had also begun working regularly at many of Bakersfield's famous honky tonks. Buck's career as a singer officially began one evening when the band's original lead singer canceled and Buck went to the microphone. The audience's response to his performance was good enough to launch his career.

In 1957, six years after his move to California, Owens got his first major recording contract, and two years later he entered the charts with "Second Fiddle." National recognition finally came about for him when his songs "Under Your Spell Again" and "Excuse Me (I Think I've Got A Heartache)" both reached #5 on the country charts.

Buck Owens' first string of #1 hits began in 1963 with "Act Naturally" and ended in 1972 with "Made in Japan." Although he is best known for his work in the eighteen-year run of the television country variety show *Hee Haw*, Buck's first success in television was during the

late 1960s with the *Buck Owens Ranch Show*, which aired from Bakersfield.

Owens retired from the music industry in 1984 to run a string of successful businesses, which included radio stations, real estate, and a publishing house. Then in 1988 he was approached by Dwight Yoakum to record "Streets of Bakersfield," which became a #1 hit. His former label, Capitol, offered him another record deal and later that year he released the album *Hot Dog*.

—A.H.

Buck Owens (right), pictured here with country musician and sausage impresario Jimmie Dean, picked cotton with his family in Mesa, Arizona, from the age of eleven to the age of sixteen, when he turned to music as a profession.

ful country recording artist of the early to mid-1960s and had starred not only on his own California-based television country music show but also on *Hee Haw*, Owens didn't receive recognition from the Nashville music industry until 1967—some eight years after his first chart-topping single, "Second Fiddle." (In fact, if it hadn't been for pop-music maestro Dick Clark's Academy of Country Music, many so-called outlaw artists from California, like Owens and Merle Haggard, might have never received institutional recognition for their musical accomplishments.) Thanks to the likes of Buck Owens and Merle Haggard, America's thirst for news from the western frontier had again been quenched.

Like the teenagers of the 1950s had, teenage fans of country music during the early 1970s craved revolution. Although acid rock provided classic music-to-be-a-teenager-by, southern high schoolers and college students felt that their own musical needs had not truly been spoken to. Much as it had done for rural white music in the 1930s through native sons such as Bob Wills, Texas once again took the reigns and guided country music's course for a spell.

With the return of prodigal son Willie Nelson from Music City to his home state, Texas began to seem to many country musicians a safe haven from the Nashville machine. Nelson practically single-handedly anointed Austin the headquarters of this revolution, a place whose allure lay in its continually growing national reputation for good times and good music. By throwing the first of what was to become his annual (and legendary) Fourth of July picnics on the Nelson ranch near Dripping Springs (a small town outside of the state's capital), Willie became a local and national hero.

One of country music's most beloved performers, Willie Nelson also has a flair for storytelling— he once said of his life with his first wife, Martha, a full-blooded Cherokee Indian, that "every night was like Custer's last stand."

Willie Nelson

The Red Headed Stranger

Willie Nelson's career has taken many bizarre and sometimes dangerous twists, but "The Red Headed Stranger" has survived them all to emerge as an immensely popular icon in American entertainment. His achievements in songwriting are considerable, his appeal as a recording artist and performer is legendary, and his appearances in movies and on television are as convincing and amiable as his beloved down-home personality.

As a boy in his hometown of Abbott, Texas, Willie Nelson would tune in to the *Grand Ole Opry* to hear the hillbilly music of Roy Acuff, the driving bluegrass of Bill Monroe, and the satisfying picking and singing of the many other *Opry* stars. In the cotton fields near his home he would listen to the cotton pickers singing "call back" blues—a line sung in one part of the field was answered by a picker in another part, and the exchange would continue, evolving into an impromptu song. Nelson's earliest desire was to become a musician.

Nelson's first experiences with music-making occurred while he still lived in Abbott, where he played guitar in a polka band and also in a western swing band. But the obstacles to an authentic career in music seemed insurmountable in his tiny Texas outpost.

Nelson then joined the U.S. Air Force, only to be discharged with a back injury. He returned to Texas and married a waitress named Martha Matthews, with whom he soon had three children. He worked many daytime jobs to support the family, including selling Bibles door to door and performing in bars and clubs at night. Nelson was also writing songs. In 1959 he sold the rights to a tune called "Family Bible" for fifty dollars. It became a top ten hit the following year for singer Claude Gray. He also sold the rights to "Night Life" for a hundred and fifty dollars, and this has since become a country classic, been recorded by more than seventy artists, and appeared on nearly thirty million records over the years. Because he had transferred

all rights, Nelson didn't see another dime from either of these compositions, but with the hundred and fifty dollars he had been paid for "Night Life," he bought a car and moved his family to Nashville.

Nelson's reputation as a marketable songwriter had already been established and Nelson continued to pen such hits as "Crazy" for Patsy Cline, "Hello Walls" for Faron Young, and "Funny How Time Slips Away," which has been recorded by more than eighty artists since. But Nelson wanted to become a recording artist himself. While he managed to record two albums, and had a minor hit (a duet with his second wife called "Willingly"), Nelson was told over and over again by record company executives that his performance style wasn't nearly commercial enough and his voice was simply too odd. He continued to work as a musician, playing bass for several years in Ray Price's band. (Price was one of the Nashville stars who had a major hit with Nelson's "Night Life.")

A near-tragedy in 1969 again changed the course of Nelson's life. A fire destroyed his home in Nashville, and he decided the time was right to head back to Texas, as Austin had become a musical refuge for Nashville's dispossessed. It was there that he teamed up with Kris Kristofferson, Waylon Jennings, Leon Russell, and other musicians and cultivated the anti-establishment brand of country music that came to be called "outlaw."

The transformation worked. Nelson's 1971 album, *Shotgun Willie*, and the subsequent releases *Phases and Stages* (about the break-up of his marriage) and *Red Headed Stranger* found a huge audience of country music lovers who had become bored with the pop leanings of Nashville. Nelson also tapped into a new, urban audience of counterculture types who were intrigued by the bandanna-wearing maverick from Texas and his rough-riding cohorts. The 1976 release of *Wanted: The Outlaws* was such a spectacular sales success that even the Nashville

establishment showered the twangy-voiced, smiling renegade with nearly every honor on the shelf.

Nelson's run as an outlaw was brief. He began recording songs in a number of styles and genres, shocking his public most with the album *Stardust*, produced by Booker T. Jones, a collection of jazz classics crooned by Nelson, backed with an intimate session band. The songs from this period include "Somewhere Over the Rainbow," "Georgia On My Mind," and "Blue Eyes Crying in the Rain," all of which won him vast new audiences because of the warm appeal of his voice, the very instrument the Nashville sages had warned would sink him.

In 1979 Nelson began a movie career, appearing in *The Electric Horseman* with Robert Redford. Subsequent films included *Honeysuckle Rose* (1980), *Thief* (1981), *Barbarosa* (1982), and *Red Headed Stranger* (1986). During this time, he also continued to put out hit songs, including "Mamas, Don't Let Your Babies Grow Up To Be Cowboys," "On the Road Again," and "You Were Always On My Mind."

Willie Nelson has been instrumental in several high-profile causes, including the Farm Aid concerts, which were organized to help the economically pressed owners of small farms to survive. In an unprecedented "self-help" campaign, and to the amusement of his millions of fans, who probably appreciated the gesture's outlaw flavor, Nelson released an acoustic album (available only through the mail) to raise money to help pay the millions of dollars he owed the IRS in back taxes (his bills were fully paid). In 1991 he married Annie D'Angelo, with whom he has begun a family.

A unique figure in music who has defied every convention, Willie Nelson has managed to win and satisfy listeners in unthinkably broad categories with his warm and appealing voice and his obvious love for and dedication to his craft.

—P.B.

Not since Bob Wills, Nelson's music idol, had Texas musicians incorporated so many of the state's disparate musical elements and by doing so captured the hearts of so many American music lovers. The German polka, Mexican mariachi music, Texas blues, and Dixieland jazz found a common home in Austin music halls.

The "goat-roper-turned-hippie" image that was Nelson's and Waylon Jennings' calling card became a popular model for urban Texans. Musicians like Michael Martin Murphey and Jerry Jeff Walker began their rise to popularity during this period perceived, as were Nelson and Jennings, as Austin's "bad boys done good."

Only hours, or so it seemed, since mending its wounds from the scrap with Bakersfield's honky-tonk heroes, Music City began another battle for control over the future of country music. This time the battle-ground was the capital of Texas. The Austin Sound, which had so clearly been its own, singular phenomenon, began to be coopted by the Nashville Sound machine. Many of Twitty City's performers—like Travis Tritt and Marty Stuart, with their long hair and electric guitars—owe their success directly to the forefathers of country music.

Why then has Austin not been able to survive, even nostalgically, within popular music of the 1990s? Outside of the Texas state capital's poor odds of winning against a musical Goliath like Nashville, Austin has done little economically to brace itself for battle. While the *Grand Ole Opry* uses its international recognition among music fans to build an economic defense against the whimsy of the music business, *Austin City Limits*, a local music television program viewed by twenty million music fans around the world every week, has remained saddled with the burdens of a nonprofit organization. Its budget, only $180,000 a year, is regularly barely met. The battle for the world's attention is an expensive publicity campaign that Austin (known to locals as "the Velvet Rut") has shown little to no interest in staging.

The next noteworthy rise in country music popularity was spawned by the work of none other than northern matinee idol John Travolta. Thanks to the movie *Urban Cowboy*, not so surprisingly set in

Texas, every city slicker acquired the right to wear boots, a bolo tie, and the long-defunct cowboy hat. Musically speaking, these urban rednecks generally craved songs about eighteen wheelers. Technologically speaking, their relationship with old-school good ol' boys was limited to arcane chat on CB radios.

The Nashville music industry raised its stakes during the 1980s, when the country music audience grew to include urban music lovers, by grooming singers and songwriters who showed potential as crossover artists. The result, as evidenced in the work of such artists as Barbara Mandrell and Kenny Rogers, was the breeding of an entertainer whose music was secondary to his or her merchandising efforts. Museums and gift shops exploiting the image of Nashville's most recent stars began popping up throughout Tennessee. And television, which had been a marketing tool for country artists since the boob tube's creation, became the custody of Music City and the national pulpit for the promotion of its product. The Dolly Doll, the Gambler Doll, and the Mandrell Sisters doll collection (each sister sold separately) made their likenesses wealthy as mainstream audiences were bathed in the glow of a widespread marketing blitz.

Since then, country has moved in several different directions, both geographically and musically. The Information Age has brought new levels and new forms of dissemination (The Nashville Network and sites on the World Wide Web being just two examples), leaving the United States as only one of many country music markets, a subset of the global market as a whole. New York City has lost the pull that once enabled it to prescribe the national perception of country music; instead, international demand (and the powerful Nashville establishment) determines what the supply lines carry. It's strange to think that Japan, Ireland, England, and Europe in general now have as much say in the direction of American music marketing as the United States.

The fallout from this audience expansion is palpable. Artists like Garth Brooks have changed the image of country music possibly forever through

their success with non–United States music lovers (he pulls in ten percent of his label's annual income). Driving rock guitars and classic rock–style, high-tech stadium presentations are two of the elements that Brooks has incorporated into country music thanks to his overwhelmingly large and loyal global audience.

The nostalgic, eastwardly review of country's post-western heritage has not been completely lost. Many American observers interested in the history of country music have directed their attention, once again, toward the Atlantic seaboard. Not surprisingly, these observers have seen that what was once the purview of the hillbilly has become (at least in part) the domain of the college-educated songwriter/performer.

The rise of the urban intellectual is one of the most recent developments in popular country music. The immensely talented and successful Mary Chapin Carpenter, for instance, is a graduate of Brown University and the daughter of a *Life* magazine VIP. Other contemporary artists, such as k.d. lang, Lyle Lovett, and Rosanne Cash (a Manhattan resident), sing from a more worldly sociopolitical outlook than have the country artists of previous generations.

As all art tends to, country music has been most successful when it speaks honestly about real issues that concern real people. Country songwriters in the final years of the twentieth century are lyrically hovering over a United States fully explored, clearly parceled out, and as easily accessible from one coast to another by plane as it is by fax and electronic mail.

It is apparent that country music faces its greatest challenge to date: outside of what has been preserved in the amber of nostalgia, is there a rural American lifestyle left to be sung about? If sales figures are any indication, country music is more successful than all other American music genres combined. No doubt the music will continue to thrive, with or without a realistic conclusion to that looming question, but the search for and discovery of popular country entertainment continues vigorously at the dawn of the Information Age just as it did at the dusk of the Industrial Age.

Chapter Two

Yodel Number One

The Legendary Bristol Recordings

by William Spence

On the first four days of August 1927, Victor Talking Machine Company talent scout and field recorder extraordinaire Ralph Peer conducted a series of recordings in a slap-dash studio in Bristol, Tennessee, that launched the careers of two of the most influential forces in the development of American music: Jimmie Rodgers and the Carter Family. It was also perhaps the most seminal event in the evolution of country music, not to mention a major turning point in the history of recorded music in general. The by-now-legendary Bristol sessions were important for a variety of reasons, but two reasons—which on close inspection seem inextricably intertwined—in particular seem worth noting.

of the New World had inspired the "hillbilly music" of the day. The Carters' songs also inspired the countless artists who were exposed to the music of these Clinch Mountain natives through the miracle of radio. In general, the Carters were the wellspring from which the more traditional forms of country music would flow. In particular, they were the direct ancestors of bluegrass and folk. To give just one example, "Little Darling Pal of Mine," one of the sides recorded in Camden, New Jersey, at the Carters' second Victor session, became a bluegrass mainstay and was also the melodic basis for Woody Guthrie's "This Land Is Your Land," a song that would go on to be immortalized by numerous artists, including Pete Seeger and others of the folk revival.

The music of Jimmie Rodgers contained plainly audible examples of a variety of influences, including vaudeville, "hillbilly music," and, most notably, many African American forms of music, pointing the way to many of the country music stylings of the mid- to late twentieth century. Rodgers was a free-wheeling romantic whose unique "blue yodel" and tendency to hybridize various strains of music would set the stage for the most dynamic forms of country music to follow, including bar-room boogie, honky-tonk, rockabilly, and country rock. His legacy as a rambling musician would become an archetype in country music; this legacy was carried on not only by Hank Williams (if in a more dissolute fashion), who was the direct inheritor of Rodgers' style, but by countless others in a long line of performers—Jimmie Davis, Hank Snow, Lefty Frizzell, and Merle Haggard among them—that extends into the present day.

Above: Ralph Sylvester Peer was one of the visionary field scouts who pioneered the recording of the early legends of rural American music. Right: The tiny town of Bristol, which was home to the seminal recordings that brought the Carter Family, Jimmie Rodgers, Uncle Dave Macon, and other "hillbilly" talents into the national spotlight, is part of both Virginia and Tennessee—depending on which side of State Street you happen to be on.

First, with the commitment to wax of a smattering of songs by the Carter Family and Jimmie Rodgers—even though those first few songs were not overwhelming best-sellers (the Carters' "Simple Girl, Married Girl" proved to be the biggest hit)—an archival effort was (perhaps unconsciously, considering the sessions were at their core a commercial effort) undertaken that would expand to provide posterity with an invaluable record of the major

musical influences that continue to inform country music even today. The "hillbilly music" that these men and women played is itself an important link in the evolution of country and popular music, but it also cataloged the sources from which country music stemmed and pointed the way to the future.

The music of the Carter Family showed how various Scottish, Irish, English, and other European traditions that had traveled with the original settlers

Jimmie Davis

The Governor

Former Louisiana governor and country singer-songwriter James Houston Davis (b. 1902) has nearly faded from the memory of country music fans, even though he once yielded a great deal of political and musical influence.

Like many of country's early performers, Davis was the son of sharecroppers. He was born in the small town of Whitman, Louisiana. As a child, he attended a one-room schoolhouse known as the Beech Springs Consolidated School, from which he graduated in a class of three.

After graduation and a brief stint working at a sawmill in his hometown, Davis attended a New Orleans business school. He later received a bachelor of arts degree from Louisiana College and a master of arts degree in music from Louisiana State University—Baton Rouge. Davis got his first taste of success as a professional singer with a popular college vocal group called the Tiger Four.

Davis later became a faculty member (he taught history) of Dodd College in Shreveport. He resigned his position after three years and took a job as criminal clerk for the Shreveport City Courthouse. It was during that time that Jimmie Davis' career as a singer really began to take hold, beginning with regular appearances on KWKH radio station (the future home of the *Louisiana Hayride* barn dance program).

A week after his twenty-seventh birthday, Davis was approached by a Victor talent scout who was impressed by his radio performances. The scout flew him to Memphis for a series of recording dates. The four songs from that session were so well received that Victor signed him to a more extensive contract. Between his first recording date on September 19, 1929, and the year 1933, Jimmie put more than sixty-eight singles on shellac.

Davis' style drew heavily on Louisiana blues. His earliest recognition came in March 1932, with "Tom Cat ·

and Pussy Blues," a suggestive number about the pursuit of physical love. Davis continued to record that type of "love" song for the next five years.

By 1934 Davis had become so popular that he was courted by a new and larger label, Decca Records. With the change of contract, Davis began to direct his material more toward a mainstream audience, and by 1938 he had abandoned sexually explicit songs. His attention turned toward crooning.

Davis had his greatest success in 1939, with "You Are My Sunshine," which he cowrote with Charles Mitchell. Peer International Corporation (the company founded by legendary talent scout Ralph Peer), which published the song, claims that it is the single most valuable copyright in country music history.

In 1938 Davis became the State Public Service Commissioner of Public Safety in Shreveport—an office once held by Louisiana's notorious governor Huey Long. Aware that Jimmie could win any popularity contest, the Democratic Party of Louisiana offered him the nomination for their party's bid for the governorship. With "You Are My Sunshine" on his side, Davis won the seat hands down (even though his opponents had led a smear campaign using his early lewd songs as a weapon).

After Jimmie Davis' second term ended in 1948, he did not run for governor again until 1960, when he won

One of the early stars of rural American music, Jimmie Davis (left), standing next to one of the greatest country legends of all time, Hank Williams.

without a struggle on his segregationist platform. Between those two stints in office, Davis spent the majority of his time recording sacred music for Decca/MCA. After his third term was up in 1964, he continued recording with Paula Records in his home town of Shreveport.

—A.H.

Left: *Vernon Dalhart (whose recording of "The Prisoner's Song" eventually sold more than six million copies and helped cement "hillbilly" as a commercially viable form of music) was born in Texas but made his career in New York, where he began by singing opera.* **Above:** *Brooklyn-born Hank Snow was among the many early "hillbilly" stars who owed their inspiration to Jimmie Rodgers' yodel and guitar style; in fact, not only did Snow come to be known as the "Cowboy Blue Yodeller" and "Hank the Yodelling Ranger," he also named his son Jimmie Rodgers Snow.*

The second reason for the Bristol sessions' importance was the degree to which the recordings of Rodgers and the Carters struck a chord in audiences in the United States (and eventually around the world) as measured in dollars and cents. This demonstrated that with the right material, recording companies could realize considerable profits through the marketing of "popular" (in this context perhaps "populist" would be a better word) music. By the late 1920s, recognizing the mass market for such music, many labels had begun successfully marketing vaudeville, jazz, "race music," and other popular forms of music. Some labels had even had runaway best-sellers with such music, starting with OKeh's million-selling recording of Mamie Smith's landmark "Crazy Blues" in 1920.

In fact, "hillbilly music" was much in demand when Ralph Peer conducted the Bristol sessions. The success of the 1922 recordings Peer had made of Fiddlin' John Carson's "The Little Old Cabin in the Lane" and "The Old Hen Cackled and the Rooster's Going to Crow" (considered by many to be the first country recordings ever made) had drawn the Victor A&R man back to the Appalachian region on a number of occasions since. Above all, he no doubt hoped to duplicate the meteoric success of Vernon Dalhart's 1924 recording of "The Prisoner's Song," which was the first million-selling country single.

All things considered, Peer couldn't have been luckier than he was those four fateful days in August

1927: within the first two days he had met and recorded the Carters, and by the end of the second two days he had met and recorded Rodgers. The subsequent recordings that Victor would make with both Rodgers and the Carters following the Bristol sessions made the company a good deal of money, particularly since (or perhaps despite the fact that) the label had proffered royalty arrangements of about a half-cent per record.

Jimmie Rodgers and the Carter Family were by no means the only acts to show up for the auditions in Bristol. On the contrary, Peer's advertisements, which promised fifty dollars for every song recorded for Victor, attracted performers from several regions around the United States (the most notable, besides the Carters and Rodgers, being banjo demon Uncle Dave Macon, whose humor and songwriting abilities led to his becoming the *Grand Ole Opry's* first full-blown star). To the people who responded to the advertisement, that sort of money was unheard of in that day, especially when it was offered in return for songs that many of these musicians were performing for their own pleasure anyway.

That Rodgers and the Carters were the artists who emerged from the pack and ultimately left their stamp on the history of recorded music is due to the fact that in many respects they and their music reflected the nation at large: the Carters because they were unassuming people and sang about a simpler, more rural way of life that was swiftly evaporating before the advancing fires of technology, and Rodgers because he was a charming performer and a talented songsmith who sang about the randier elements of human society in a way that showcased his indomitable lust for life (a particularly endearing quality in a man who spent the majority of his days among the living in a losing battle with tuberculosis).

These country music primogenitors were also so warmly embraced, of course, because they were wonderful songwriters (and sometimes, particularly in the case of A.P. Carter, transcribers) and solid musicians whose homespun, heartfelt music touched and even changed the lives of millions of people.

Born in Maces Springs in 1891, Alvin Pleasant Delaney "Doc" Carter was a child of the Clinch Mountains of western Virginia. His upbringing, like that of his neighbors, was founded in religion and (mostly religious) music. Like everyone in the area, his family lacked many of life's luxuries, but the community was strong, and music—both inside the church and out—played a large role in holding it together. A.P. Carter got plenty of singing practice from his early childhood on and was exposed to a swirling mixture of music, which had roots in European folk and sacred music. In such communities as Maces Springs, slightly isolated from the rest of the swiftly industrializing United States, time

Right: *Born in 1870, Uncle Dave Macon was a living link between the vaudeville tradition (which infused his banjo playing and singing) and the popular "hillbilly" music of the 1920s and 1930s, of which he recorded more than 170 examples.* **Below:** *The Carter Family—from left, Sara (with autoharp), A.P., and Maybelle—performed songs that mirrored the beauty and earthiness of their Clinch Mountain home.*

moves a little more slowly; as a result, the cultural trappings that had traveled with the original settlers of these regions had been preserved—though not unchanged—in the rarefied atmosphere of the Appalachian Mountain range. A naturally inquisitive person, A.P. Carter was always combing the region looking for new material to adapt for his purposes. As fate would have it, this insatiable curiosity made A.P. one of country music's most important archivists, particularly of "hillbilly music."

Johnny Cash

The Man in Black

Probably the best-known country performer in the world today, Johnny Cash has had a long, diverse, and eventful career. As a musical performer, he has sung country, gospel, folk, and the blues; he has performed and recorded with talents as diverse as Carl Perkins, Jerry Lee Lewis, Roy Orbison, Bob Dylan, Merle Haggard, Waylon Jennings, Tom Petty, and George Harrison. He married June Carter, a daughter of the original Carter Family's Maybelle Carter. He has acted in feature films and television movies, and he has written soundtracks for a number of films. Cash is rightly considered both a pioneer and a great contemporary innovator of country music.

Born on February 26, 1932, in Kingsland, Arkansas, Cash was the fourth of Ray and Carrie Cash's seven children. When Johnny was three, the family moved to Dyess, Arkansas, where they eventually bought and operated a cotton farm. The Cashes were charismatic Christians; relatives on both sides were Baptist preachers or missionaries, and there was a family tradition of gospel singing. There was also a fondness for traditional songs, especially as rendered by the Carter Family, whose records and performances the Cashes heard on the radio.

Cash evidently decided early on that he was not meant to farm cotton; he left Dyess soon after graduating high school and worked briefly in an Arkansas oleomargarine factory and then in an automobile plant in Pontiac, Michigan. He joined the U.S. Air Force in 1950 and served four years in Germany, where he began playing the guitar and transforming poetry he had written into songs, and later, composing songs outright.

After he was discharged in 1954, Cash settled in Memphis and married a woman named Vivian Liberto (they were divorced in 1966). He sold electrical appliances door to door and also formed a small gospel group with two friends, calling it Johnny Cash and the Tennessee Two. Their music-making was informal until 1955, when Cash worked up the courage to approach Memphis record producer Sam Phillips for help. With his Sun Records label, Phillips introduced the world to such rockabilly acts as Elvis Presley, Jerry Lee Lewis, Carl Perkins, and Roy Orbison. Phillips' advice to Cash was: drop gospel, think commercial.

Cash took this advice to heart, returning several months later with new material that impressed Phillips enough for him to offer the young man a contract. The Sun Records track "Cry, Cry, Cry" was a regional hit in 1955, and was followed the next year by "Folsom Prison Blues" (released again in 1968) and "I Walk the Line." Johnny Cash was on his way to superstardom.

The Grand Ole Opry invited Cash to become a member in 1956, and he gladly moved to Nashville, where he spent the next two years writing, recording, and performing on WSM's most famous broadcast. Then, in 1958, Cash resigned from his regular *Opry* appearances in favor of hitting the road with his own traveling show, accepting frequent requests to make television appearances. Professionally, this decision paid off. Cash's road show toured the country through the 1960s, causing a great deal of excitement wherever it went. His television appearances eventually led to his own weekly network show on ABC from 1969 to 1971. By then Cash had mostly conquered his serious drug addiction, which had begun in the early 1960s, when he frequently took amphetamines and barbiturates to make life on the road easier. His carousing in Nashville with contemporaries Waylon Jennings and Willie Nelson is the stuff of legend.

Surprisingly, drugs did very little outward damage to Cash's career. During the 1960s, he began expanding his repertoire, writing and performing folk- and blues-based music and "plight" songs (songs about Native Americans and prison inmates, for example). He recorded regularly and brilliantly, and he kept his road show intact and functioning smoothly. His 1968 appearance at Folsom Prison in California, and the subsequent release of "Folsom Prison Blues" recorded there live, took him to #1 on the charts.

Johnny Cash was one of the talents ushered into the major leagues by Sun Studio maven Sam Phillips, who encouraged Cash to go commercial; the result (by Johnny Cash and the Tennessee Two) was "Hey Porter" b/w "Cry, Cry, Cry," the latter of which was a #14 hit on the country charts in 1955.

In 1968 Cash married June Carter, who, with her mother and sisters, had been a fixture in the road show, and whom Cash credits with being instrumental in helping him overcome his addictions.

Cash has appeared in feature films and made-for-television movies, among them *A Gunfight* (1970), *Pride of Jesse Hallam* (1981), and *Stagecoach* (1986). He has written soundtrack music for *The True West*, *Little Fauss*, and *Big Halsy*, and *Pride of Jesse Hallam*. He was the producer and cowriter of *The Gospel Road* (1973) and he has written an autobiography, *The Man in Black*, and a novel, *The Man in White*, about the conversion of the apostle Paul. Despite heart bypass surgery in 1989, Cash continues to perform and record regularly at this writing. He recorded several albums in the 1990s, including *Highwayman 2* (1990) with Waylon Jennings, Kris Kristofferson, and Willie Nelson, *The Mystery of Life* (1991), and the best-selling *American Recordings* (1994).

Cash's discography is vast; the best estimates peg his record sales to date in excess of fifty million. He has had more than 130 songs on the country charts, and nearly fifty on the pop charts. Johnny Cash was elected to the Country Music Hall of Fame in 1980.

—P.B.

When he was twenty-four, A.P. married a woman named Sara Dougherty. Sara was fluent on several musical instruments (including the guitar and auto-harp) and together she and A.P. would sing and play the songs that were popular in their region, mostly folk songs that had circulated in the community for untold generations. They were joined by Sara's cousin Maybelle Addington (who eventually became a Carter when she married A.P.'s brother Ezra), who played guitar.

It is important to note here that the Carters' music did not only point backwards in time to country's past, though in large part that is true—it also changed the future course of country music. Although Maybelle was by no means a technical wizard, her unique style of playing the guitar—which came to be known as the "Carter scratch" or "Carter style"—would have ensured the Carters' place in history all by itself. She revolutionized the approach to the instrument by playing the melody on the bass strings with her thumb while strumming the accompanying chords with the backs of her fingers. Many of the musicians who grew up listening to broadcasts of the Carters on XERA radio out of Villa Acuna, Mexico (across the Rio Grande from Del Rio, Texas)—from folk godfather Woody Guthrie to the leading architect of the Nashville Sound, Chet Atkins—learned to play guitar at Maybelle's feet.

Chet Atkins was a guitar wizard (who owed his early inspiration to Mother Maybelle's "scratch") and production impresario who revolutionized country music with the "Nashville Sound" in much the same way that Phil Spector revolutionized R&B with the "Wall of Sound."

Furthermore, Maybelle tuned the strings on her Gibson L-5 down from the standard tuning, and this arrangement became standard for many of the blue-grass performers who followed.

In response to Peer's 1927 advertisement, the Carter threesome traveled by car to nearby Bristol to try to peddle the material they had been performing. Ralph Peer bought six of their songs and would soon be asking for more (beginning a musical odyssey that would span several generations of Carters and intertwine with the history of many of country's greatest stars, including perhaps the most widely known and loved of the contemporary pantheon, Johnny Cash). It is to Ralph Peer's credit that he was able to recognize the value of the Carters' output. Their music does not by any means jump up and grab the listener with its rhythmic flash or lyrical audacity (both of which were features of the popular and often best-selling "race records," usually blues recordings, of the 1920s). Instead, the appeal of the Carters' music lies in its simplicity, its spirituality, and in the way it resonates with the collective cultural unconscious (the legacy of the pre–New World ancestors of many of the peoples of the rural United States).

In direct contrast, Jimmie Rodgers' music probably did jump up and grab Ralph Peer, who recorded a few of the Blue Yodeler's numbers at the Bristol sessions. Whereas the Carters' music was a reassuring balm, Rodgers' material was full of fire both musically and lyrically. From a more varied background and perhaps more naturally inclined to an adventurous life, Rodgers sang about many day-to-day issues and events—including many of the vicissitudes of life, a theme on which he could speak with authority—in a frank and sometimes sly way that was usually found only in the music of contemporary bluesmen.

The son of a railroad worker, James Charles Rodgers was born on September 8, 1897, in the town of Pine Springs, near Meridian, Mississippi—located just outside the musically fertile Mississippi Delta (which is often cited as the birthplace of the blues). After his mother died (probably from tuberculosis) Rodgers went to live with an aunt, Dora Bozeman, an

Jimmie Rodgers, the Singing Brakeman, was one of the most beloved of early performers. His first wife, Sandra Kelly, from whom he separated after only a few months of marriage, said that he was a sweet man but "would strum away on some instrument and fool away his time and his money."

of fourteen, Rodgers was living the life of a rambler, frequenting pool halls and barbershops (and even performing a little music along the way), when his frustrated father gave him the option of either returning to school or going to work.

The physically slight Rodgers left school forever to follow in his father's footsteps and went to work on the Mobile and Ohio Line—and later on other rail lines—in various capacities, ultimately working as a brakeman (hence his sobriquet "The Singing Brakeman"). His early decision to pursue a career as a railroadman is indicative of his adventurous spirit and the thirst for new experiences and sounds that would help shape his music. At heart an experimenter and in temperament open-minded and generous, Rodgers was always prepared to try something new and was a regular collaborator with musical talents in many genres (the most famous of whom were probably trumpeter Louis Armstrong and his pianist wife, Lillian Hardin Armstrong, on a couple of tracks, including "Blue Yodel # 9").

After just over a decade working on the railroads, Rodgers was forced to quit the profession due to his increasingly poor health, which was daily worsened by the demanding labor and omnipresent soot and grime of railroad life. The tuberculosis that would eventually cut short his remarkable life caused him to change his metier, ironically benefiting the rest of the world in the process. In 1924, by which time doctors had diagnosed him with the disease, Rodgers was already splitting his time between the railroad work that kept his family alive (he had already married twice) and performing music. By

1927, when fate finally knocked on Rodgers' door in the form of Peer's Bristol sessions, he had given up railroading forever and was working at various jobs, from taxi driver to janitor, to keep his family afloat while he played music.

It is crucial to note that the simultaneous rise of his music career and decline of his railroad career played a central role in creating the bluesy flavor that his music would always have. Indeed, the material he had been exposed to while riding the rails was fresh in his mind as he began performing more and more often in the late 1920s. While on the railroad, Rodgers had been working side by side with numerous African Americans, many of whom were musicians. (At this point in history, the railroads employed many black people; indeed, the railroad provided some of the better job opportunities for African Americans, especially those who were trying to escape from the racist and economic nightmare of the Jim Crow South, where sharecropping had come to represent an updated and insidious form of slavery.)

In his travels, Rodgers had picked up quite a lot of musical instruction from these black men. In fact, he had accumulated a wealth of material and learned to play both the guitar and the banjo in the course of his tenure as a railroadman. Thus, it should not come as too great a surprise that as his career riding the iron horse was in decline he was working as a blackface performer on the medicine show circuit. In late 1924 and early 1925, when Rodgers was embarking in earnest on his musical career, black and white performers alike performed on the medicine show circuit, which was the crossroads for many forms of music, from vaudeville to spirituals to operetta. (At the time, however, even African American performers had to appear in blackface, the makeup serving to dilute the "blackness" of the musical experience by inserting a simultaneously actual and symbolic barrier between the audience and the artists.) In 1927 Rodgers was the headman for and performed banjo in the Jimmie Rodgers Entertainers, a blackface troupe that toured the South playing all sorts of different material and hawking patent medicines.

educated woman who very well may have been his first musical inspiration (though she was unable to keep the boy off the streets, where he loved to roam). Eventually, his father retrieved him but could give the boy little supervision because the railroad kept the elder Rodgers away from home. So at the tender age

When the siren's call of Peer's advertisement beckoned to Rodgers, the ex-brakeman traveled with his band to Bristol but wound up recording solo following a dispute about how the band would be credited on the record label. (The group recorded at least one song at Bristol as the Tenneva Ramblers.) As he had with the Carters, Peer recognized almost immediately that the raw material he heard the charismatic Rodgers perform, characterized by a delightfully pure tenor yodel and eclectic style, was special. The songs that Peer wound up purchasing were "The Soldier's Sweetheart" and "Sleep, Baby, Sleep." Although the record of these two songs was not a blockbuster, upon its release in October 1927 Rodgers traveled to New York with almost no money, booked himself in at a hotel by lying about being a Victor recording star, and lucked out by convincing Peer to record him again (in Camden, New Jersey). This launched the final, hectic stage of Rodgers' brief but meteoric career.

Rodgers began recording and performing furiously over the next six years, a period during which he knew little rest. The year 1929 saw his greatest popularity; indeed, he was in such great demand that year that, despite his fragile condition, he was constantly either in the studio (in February alone he sat in on eleven sessions) or on the road. Although he had become country's first superstar and was by this point in demand even in England, Rodgers had little money and was struggling to support not only his current family but also his ex-wife and first child (the two had surfaced demanding child support when the Singing Brakeman had become a national personality). But Rodgers' music was always strong—even when his health weakened his voice and ruined his stamina—and his devotion to it unflagging. If anything, Rodgers' great sensitivity to the spirit of the blues kept the music vital despite his failing body; his 1931 recording of "T.B. Blues" and the courageous 1932 recording "Whippin' That Old T.B." illustrate how music was an integral part of his life—and helped him fend off death.

Realizing he was deathly ill and concerned for the future welfare of his family, Rodgers persuaded Peer to speed up his recording schedule in 1933, pushing a series of sessions back to May. In order to complete his final recordings, Rodgers had a cot set up in the studio on which to rest between takes. One of the final numbers he recorded was "Mississippi Delta Blues," which reveals (in both lyrical and musical content) perhaps more than any other his debt to the blues tradition. On May 26, 1933, America's beloved Blue Yodeler was dead, having drowned in his own blood as a result of a pulmonary hemorrhage.

On June 10, 1931, Jimmie Rodgers and two of the Carters (Sara and Maybelle) had a reunion of sorts, staged by Peer for Victor. By this time, both Rodgers and the Carter Family were in considerable demand as artists, having risen to stardom playing their music around the country. (What could be more fitting, then, that they should unite on record?) They laid down a few tracks together in a studio in Louisville, Kentucky, including the songs "Why There's a Tear in My Eye," "The Wonderful City," and a couple of novelty items, "Jimmie Rodgers Visits the Carter Family" and "The Carter Family and Jimmie Rodgers in Texas" (comprising both music and dialog), bringing to a close the circle they had been describing since their historic (though separate) participation in the sessions in Bristol, Tennessee, in 1927.

The Bristol sessions laid the foundation almost entirely upon which the country music edifice would be erected, in the process helping to further establish the recording industry as a mass producer of popular entertainment product. If the irony of the latter aspect is that more music is available to the world through the enrichment of major recording labels, it is an irony we can well afford.

Together, Jimmie Rodgers (left) and the Carter Family (from left, Maybelle, A.P., and Sara) were the founding fathers and mothers of modern country music; through them, diverse rural performance styles and lyric idioms were gathered, augmented, and recombined to produce the wellspring for one of the most powerful strains of American music.

Chapter Three

Back in the Saddle Again

The Singing Cowboys

by Anna Graves

In March 1993 an artist named Toby Keith went to the top of the *Billboard* country charts with a song he wrote entitled "Should've Been a Cowboy." The lyrics of Keith's hit single express his longing for the bygone days of the American West, with references to Marshall Matt Dillon, a fictitious character from the television show *Gunsmoke*, and other well-known cowboys who seem to have served as role models for Keith:

I should've learned to rope and ride   *Just like Gene and Roy*

Wearing my six-shooter   *Singing those campfire songs*

Riding my pony on a cattle drive   *I should've been a cowboy.*

Stealing a young girl's heart

During the 1930s and 1940s, song folios such as this one featuring stars Gene Autry, Roy Rogers, and Tex Ritter helped to popularize the romantic image of the singing cowboys, who were more appealing to the public than the hillbilly performers who had emerged in the 1920s.

From a musical standpoint, "Should've Been a Cowboy" is closer to pop than country; however, its lyrical content recalls a significant period in the history of country music—the era of the singing cowboy. Throughout the twentieth century, the cowboy has been one of the most romanticized figures in American popular culture. Starting in the mid-1930s and continuing into the 1950s, the singing cowboy (as portrayed by Gene Autry, Roy Rogers, and oth-

ers) acquired a massive following through radio, movies, and television. When cowboys began singing in the movies during the early 1930s, the public developed a particular visual image of the western songster, and soon the mythology of the American cowboy was inextricably linked with the image of men harmonizing while riding the range or strumming guitars around campfires.

Ironically, as a former rodeo hand from Oklahoma, Toby Keith may have come closer to being an actual cowboy than some of his fellow country music performers who have sung about western life over the past six decades. Nevertheless, his nostalgia for the make-believe cowboys of film and television demonstrates the way in which the mythical cowboy singer has largely obliterated the real history of cowboy songs and those who sang them. Authentic cowboy songs have long been considered a staple of American folk music, and when they were performed and recorded by artists of the 1920s they became part of the burgeoning genre of country music, which was then labeled "hillbilly music." As country evolved in the 1930s, it came to be known as "western"—a term that was less derogatory than "hillbilly"—and eventually it was referred to as "country and western." Following in the footsteps of the singing cowboys of the silver screen, numerous country singers of the Depression era adopted fancy western attire. Although cowboy singers were becoming less common by the mid-1950s, the western culture that spawned them had unquestionably made its mark on country music. For a better understanding of how this happened, it is necessary to go back in time to the days when real cowboys rode the range.

According to one historian, the term *cow-boy* was first used around the time of the American Revolution to describe outlaws who stole cattle, among other things, from colonists and sold the

stolen property to British troops. The word did not take on its common historical meaning—a hired cattle driver on horseback—until shortly after the Civil War. Between 1867 and the end of the 1880s, countless cowboys (previously called "drovers" or "cowherds") were responsible for moving large herds of Texas livestock great distances to such cities as Abilene, Kansas, where they could be transported by train to Chicago and other northern markets. Toward the end of the nineteenth century, as the cattle industry dwindled, the number of cowboys diminished as well, and within a relatively short time period the trail-riding cowhand of the American West was virtually extinct.

The cattle are prowlin' and coyotes are howlin'
Way out where the dogies bawl
Where spurs are a-jinglin', a cowboy is singin'
This lonesome cattle call
—"Cattle Call," Tex Owens, 1934

By most accounts, the cowboys of the late 1800s rarely carried musical instruments along on cattle drives. As a result, much of their singing must have been a cappella. Guy Logsdon, an authority on authentic cowboy music, notes that the fiddle and the banjo were probably the most common instruments present in cow camps; guitars and harmonicas were for the most part "twentieth-century romanticized adaptation[s] imposed on the cowboy." The image of cowboys singing as they sat around a campfire might be another popular misconception. Historians agree that cowpunchers often sang to the cows while herding them on horseback, especially at night. The singing helped to pass the time and supposedly calmed the cattle, reducing the likelihood of a stampede. Ramon Adams, who has written extensively on cowboys, remarks, "The practice [of singing to the stock] got to be so common that night herdin' was spoken of as 'singin' to 'em.'" In his autobiography, *We Pointed Them North: Recollections of a Cowpuncher*, Montana cowboy E.C. "Teddy Blue" Abbott explained how "the two men on night guard would circle around with their horses at a walk,...and one man would sing a verse of a song, and his partner on the other side of the herd would sing another verse; and you'd go through a whole song that way...." The folk songs sung by these cowhands were uncomplicated, often poetic, and occasionally vulgar, addressing the daily concerns of cowboy life.

Even before singing cowboys became a part of American popular culture, interest in the music that came out of the Old West could be found among a small number of song collectors who worked independently to gather and preserve old-time cowboy material. Around the turn of the century, few well-known cowboy singers existed; however, a wealth of western songs was available to those who knew where to look. In 1889 and 1890, Nathan Howard "Jack" Thorp, a cowboy who later became a rancher, traveled fifteen hundred miles (2,415km) on horseback throughout New Mexico and Texas in an effort to obtain cowboy and western songs. His endeavors resulted in the first collection of such songs, published in 1908 under the title *Songs of the Cowboys*. The fifty-page book, which Thorp sold for fifty cents a copy, consisted of the lyrics to twenty-three songs, including "The Cowboy's Lament," a song originally derived from a British ballad "The Unfortunate Rake" that can be found in hundreds of different forms (the most commonly known version is "Streets of Laredo"). Thorp gave no credit to the authors of the songs (except for "The Cowboy's New Years' Dance," an obscure song he attributes to Mark Chisholm), but later admitted that he himself composed a few of them, such as the popular ballad "Little Joe, the Wrangler." Scholars have been able to determine who wrote some of these traditional cowboy songs, but many of the people who created the western songs that were passed on orally for years before being transcribed remain unknown. The cowhands who sang the songs often altered them, adding new verses they created themselves. The presence of numerous variations of the best-known songs made it even more difficult to trace the origin of a particular composition.

In 1910 ballad hunter John Avery Lomax published *Cowboy Songs and Other Frontier Ballads*, the best-known compilation of cowboy music and the first collection of American folk material that

Music scholar John Lomax's collection of western songs, **Cowboy Songs and Other Frontier Ballads,** *published in 1910, became the best-known and most widely circulated cowboy songbook in the United States. With the help of his son Alan, Lomax went on to collect and record a vast amount of folk material.*

included musical transcriptions for some of the songs. Endorsed by former president Theodore Roosevelt, this anthology was reprinted several times before being revised and enlarged in 1938. In 1919 Lomax put together a follow-up collection, *Songs of the Cattle Trail and Cow Camp*, consisting of the work of western poets without any music. Cowboy song scholar John I. White notes that "many of the poems [in the Lomax collection] probably never had actually been sung by cowboys or anyone else." In

regard to *Cowboy Songs and Other Frontier Ballads*, White points out that Lomax has been criticized for combining lines from different versions of a particular song, as well as for cleaning up the language used in the cowboy songs. However, Lomax defended himself by reminding purist scholars that "the volume is meant to be popular." Meanwhile, Jack Thorp produced an expanded version of his cowboy songbook in 1921, containing 101 songs. In 1940 Thorp's essay "Banjo in the Cow Camp," detailing his adventures riding the trail in an effort to hunt down authentic cowboy songs, appeared in *Atlantic Monthly*.

As the public was beginning to show interest in the popular versions of the folk songs of the cowboys presented by Thorp and Lomax, early recording artists offered listeners some of this material over radio airwaves and on 78 rpm phonograph records. Concert singer Bentley Ball recorded two songs he learned from the first Lomax anthology, "The Dying

Cowboy'' and ''Jesse James,'' for Columbia in 1919, and Charles Nabell recorded three cowboy songs for OKeh in late 1924, including ''The Great Round Up,'' which uses western metaphors to stress the importance of embracing religion. Like so many other authentic cowboy compositions, this song can be found in a great many forms, including one that appeared in Thorp's collection called ''The Grand Round Up,'' with instructions to sing it to the tune of ''My Bonnie Lies Over the Ocean.'' In 1925 Carl T. Sprague, the son of a Texas cattleman, traveled to the Victor studios in New Jersey to make the first commercially successful western recording, ''When the Work's All Done This Fall,'' the tragic tale of a cowpuncher who dies in a night stampede. Written in 1893 by D.J. O'Malley, a Montana cowboy, this song had been recorded for OKeh under the title ''Dixie Cowboy'' by a southern folk artist known as Fiddlin' John Carson a year earlier, shortly before Nabell's sessions. Although Carson and Ball predate him, Nabell is generally considered to be the first commercial cowboy recording artist, perhaps because he had a western background.

Sprague's cowboy hit sold more than 900,000 copies, earning him the title of ''the Original Singing Cowboy'' and proving that a market for western music existed. ''When the Work's All Done This Fall'' became so popular that over the next fifteen years it

Early southern hillbilly musician Fiddlin' John Carson (above, left, who had a hit with "The Little Old Cabin in the Lane") and western entertainer Otto Gray (above), who toured the country with his cowboy stage show in custom-built Cadillacs, were both commercially successful performers in the 1920s.

was recorded by nearly thirty other performers. Other western artists followed Sprague's lead, such as Jules Verne Allen, a Texas cowhand who became known as a radio performer in his home state and in California. He is remembered today for the Victor recordings he made in 1928 and 1929, which included such traditional songs as ''The Cowboy's Dream'' (a version of ''The Great Round Up'') and ''The Dying Cowboy,'' which is better known as ''Bury Me Not on the Lone Prairie.'' Allen also recorded the classic ballad ''Home on the Range,'' the origins of which can be traced back to Kansas in the 1870s. Pioneer hillbilly recording artist Vernon Dalhart had been the first to record this

particular song, along with several other cowboy standards, in 1927.

Other cowboy performers who emerged in the 1920s included John I. White, who was often called ''the Lonesome Cowboy,'' and Otto Gray, who became the first western artist to be featured on the cover of *Billboard*. Born and raised in Washington, D.C., White developed an interest in cowboy songs after visiting an Arizona dude ranch in 1924. Two years later, while living in New York, he began performing western material on the radio. He eventually recorded several hillbilly and cowboy tunes, such as the popular ''Whoopee-Ti-Yi-Yo (Git Along, Little Dogies)'' and Carmen William ''Curley'' Fletcher's epic ''The Strawberry Roan,'' for the American Record Company (ARC) with producer Arthur Satherley. From 1930 to 1936, White sang western songs on the weekly radio program *Death Valley Days*. Although he was by no means a real cowboy, White put a great deal of effort into tracking down genuine cowboy folk songs to perform on the show. In 1975 he published his research under the title *Git Along, Little Dogies: Songs and Songmakers of the American West*.

Otto Gray was an Oklahoma rancher who joined a string band named the McGinty Cowboys in the early 1920s. He restructured the group, which had originally been made up of bona fide old-time cowboys, and renamed it Otto Gray and His Oklahoma Cowboys. During the late 1920s and early 1930s, they established themselves as show business professionals, performing cowboy and popular songs on radio stations throughout the country and recording for a variety of labels, including OKeh, Vocalion, and Columbia.

In addition to writing the folk hobo songs ''Big Rock Candy Mountain'' and ''Hallelujah, I'm a Bum,'' Harry ''Haywire Mac'' McClintock was known as a singing cowboy on California radio during the mid-1920s. In 1928 he became the first artist to record several classic cowboy and western tunes. Among these were ''The Old Chisholm Trail,'' ''Sweet Betsy from Pike,'' and ''Get Along, Little Dogies,'' all released on the Victor label. Another western performer, Goebel Leon Reeves, known as ''the Texas Drifter,'' also performed cowboy and hobo songs,

Gene Autry

Public Cowboy No. 1

Through his considerable talents as a singer, songwriter, actor, and businessman, Gene Autry (b. 1907) became the most beloved singing cowboy in the world. Over a career that spanned the majority of the twentieth century, the affable Oklahoman appeared in innumerable western films, wrote and recorded several million-selling singles (many of which are now country standards), hosted his own radio and television shows, and brought joy to countless millions of country fans around the world.

Orvon Gene Autry was born on September 29, 1907, in Tioga, Texas, the son of a poor itinerant farmer who moved the family several times during Autry's childhood, eventually winding up in Oklahoma. Autry's grandfather, a Baptist minister, taught the young boy to sing and Autry's father taught the boy to ride; when he turned twelve, Autry got his first guitar, making him a veritable singing cowboy in training. At the age of seventeen, Autry set out to make a living, first as a medicine show performer and soon thereafter as a telegraph operator for the Frisco Railroad in Chelsea, Oklahoma. It was at the latter job where he was discovered singing and playing guitar by none other than Will Rogers, who suggested the young man make his way to New York City and pursue a career in music.

Autry tried unsuccessfully to start his music career in New York and returned to Oklahoma, where he soon landed a spot on radio station KVOO as Oklahoma's Yodeling Cowboy. Modeling his style somewhat on Jimmie Rodgers', Autry made a few recordings for RCA Victor, then for Art Satherly's American Record Company, and finally for Sears' Conqueror label in Chicago. In 1931 he cowrote (with Jimmy Long) and recorded what he later claimed was his favorite song, "That Silver Haired Daddy of Mine" (which became his first million-seller),

and began appearing on a couple of Sears' radio shows, most importantly as a guest on the *National Barn Dance* (broadcast on WLS).

By 1934 Autry was well known as a music personality because of his recordings and radio appearances, and was being promoted as a singing cowboy. Determined to become a singing cowboy of the silver screen, Autry headed to California. He landed a small part in the Ken Maynard oater *In Old Santa Fe* (in which he was teamed up with Smiley Burnette, a comic cowboy who would be Autry's sidekick in many subsequent films), which led to a role in the twelve-part serial *The Phantom Empire*, a science-fiction western. In 1935 Republic Pictures signed Autry to a contract and his rise to megastardom began with the movie *Tumbling Tumbleweeds*. Between then and 1942, when he enlisted in the U.S. Air Force, Autry continued his entertainment efforts, touring widely with his show when not filming or recording. During this period he recorded many of his greatest tracks, including his hallmark "Back in the Saddle Again" (written by the smooth Ray Whitley, a member of the later generation of singing cowboys).

Following his return from the war, Autry continued to record and to make movies, eventually producing several films himself with Gene Autry Productions (a film-production company he started in 1947). In the 1950s Autry turned his interest to the business end of the entertainment industry and bought several radio and television stations. He produced several television shows, including *The

Shown here in his first feature-length film, **Tumbling Tumbleweeds** (*Republic Pictures, 1935*), *Gene Autry eventually became known as "the Nation's Number One Singing Cowboy," inspiring a host of imitators.*

Gene Autry Show* (which ran for ninety-one episodes) and *The Adventures of Champion*, which starred his famous horse Champion (actually, by that point it was Champion III). In the 1960s Autry expanded his empire by buying the California Angels baseball team.

Over his lifetime, Autry made many friends and impressed everyone who worked with him as a charming and easy-going man with a sound business grounding. He also earned countless accolades for his singing, songwriting, and acting: in 1969 he was elected to the Country Music Hall of Fame and in 1980 he was inducted to the Cowboy Hall of Fame of Great Westerners. Autry's contributions to country music and to the musical western are immortalized at the Autry Museum of Western Heritage in Griffith Park, Los Angeles.

—W.S.

some falsetto vocal embellishment in their cattle calls, the use of yodeling in western music came from Jimmie Rodgers." Rodgers spent part of his life in Texas, and he adopted its western heritage, sometimes posing for publicity photographs in cowboy outfits. His songs "When the Cactus Is in Bloom," "The Cowhand's Last Ride," and "Yodeling Cowboy," among others, undoubtedly influenced many of the singing cowboy performers of the late 1920s and the 1930s.

increasingly well-polished, resembling the pop music of the period. The more authentic cowboy singers who had established western music's popularity in the 1920s were soon to be displaced, as the singing cowboy craze continued to flourish with the emergence of the musical western.

My business is singing. I sing about horses, sunshine, and the plains.
—*Gene Autry in* **The Phantom Empire**

Toward the end of the nineteenth century, at about the same time the historical cowboy began to disappear, the fictional cowboy sprang up in popular dime novels and touring "Wild West" shows that featured such stars as Buffalo Bill Cody and Buck Taylor, King of the Cowboys. These figures were the predecessors of early movie cowboys, who first appeared in silent screen adventures in the early 1900s. Bronco Billy Anderson, who starred in hundreds of serial westerns, was the first Hollywood cowboy, and he was followed by Harry Carey, Hoot Gibson, William S. Hart, Ken Maynard, and Tom Mix, among others. Many of these celluloid cowboys successfully made the transition to talkies (movies with sound), and B-movie westerns, also referred to as "oaters" or "horse operas," remained popular throughout the 1920s.

After the introduction of sound, however, the public's interest in westerns began to wane, since cowboy movies relied more on action than dialogue to hold the audience's attention. In 1929, however, Ken Maynard became the first cowboy to sing on screen, performing traditional cowboy songs in *The Wagon Master*. Maynard's self-described "nasal-soundin' Texas voice" may have left something to be desired, but the concept of the singing cowboy gave new life to the western genre. A few years later, a professional cowboy crooner named Orvon Gene Autry made his motion picture debut with a small role in a 1934 Maynard vehicle entitled *In*

Above: *Ken Maynard had a long career acting in westerns, including* **In Old Santa Fe,** *the first movie to feature Gene Autry in a singing role. Smiley Burnette appeared in the movie, singing his "Mama Don't Allow No Music," and Maynard also had a couple of songs (though the voice audiences heard actually belonged to Bob Nolan of the Sons of the Pioneers).* **Right:** *William S. Hart was a Shakespearean actor who became famous for his portrayals of cowboys on the silent screen.*

sometimes using a distinctive yodeling style. According to country music historian Bill Malone, Reeves claimed he taught Jimmie Rodgers his yodel around 1920 in New Orleans. A former railroad worker nicknamed the "Singing Brakeman," Rodgers is generally considered to be the father of country music. Western music expert Guy Logsdon notes that "while there is little evidence that cowboys used

Rodgers' music also signified a new trend in western music, which was moving away from the traditional cowboy songs of the 1800s. As interest in cowboy singers grew, artists and the public began to show a preference for romantic cowboy songs produced by the contemporary composers of Tin Pan Alley. Musical arrangements for western songs became more complex, and vocal styles were

Old Santa Fe. The year after that, Autry starred in *The Phantom Empire*, a bizarre science-fiction/western serial that was soon followed by his first full-length feature film, *Tumbling Tumbleweeds.* The latter film also featured Autry's long-time sidekick, Lester Alvin "Smiley" Burnette, an accordionist and songwriter. In other movies that followed Autry was joined by country groups such as the Light Crust Doughboys (named after their sponsor, Light Crust Flour), a western swing band whose original members included the forefathers of western swing, Bob Wills and Milton Brown. Autry went on to appear in more than one hundred musical westerns, firmly establishing the singing cowboy in the minds of moviegoers across the United States and all over the world.

In the late 1920s, before he became a movie star, Autry was known to radio listeners across the midwest as "Oklahoma's Yodeling Cowboy," appearing on Tulsa's KVOO ("the Voice of Oklahoma") with a performing style that closely resembled that of Jimmie Rodgers. By the early 1930s, he was a regular on *The National Barn Dance* on Chicago's WLS and had made a number of recordings for different labels, including Conqueror, a Sears label produced by the American Record Company (ARC). (WLS was also owned by Sears—its call letters stood for "World's Largest Store.") Autry's records were advertised in the Sears-Roebuck catalog, along with songbooks and guitars that bore his name. During this period of his career, even though he was known as a cowboy singer, Autry was first and foremost a hillbilly artist, and his first major hit, a collaboration with Jimmy Long entitled "That Silver Haired Daddy of Mine" recorded in 1935, was one of many hillbilly songs he released. Autry was a versatile vocalist, however; his classic theme song, "Back in the Saddle Again," written by Autry and Ray Whitley and released in 1939, seems smooth and polished in comparison to his early songs as well as to most of the western material recorded by the artists of the 1920s. Unquestionably one of the most popular cowboy singers of this century, Gene Autry set the standard for the singing cowboy; as Bill Malone states, he "created the stereotype of the heroic cowboy who was equally adept with a gun and guitar."

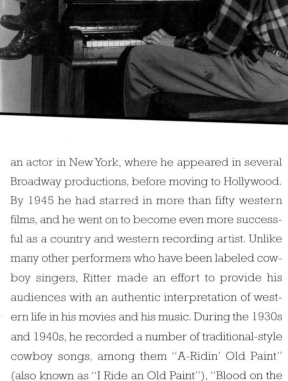

Above: *Cowboy singer/songwriter Ray Whitley was a steel worker before he became a popular entertainer.* **Right:** *Tex Ritter (sitting on the piano) is known for performing such songs as "Rye Whiskey" and "High Noon (Do Not Forsake Me)," which received an Academy Award when it was used in the Gary Cooper movie of the same name in 1952.*

Encouraged by Autry's success, movie studios and record labels began producing singing cowboys in droves. In 1936 Maurice Woodward "Tex" Ritter and Raymond Otis "Ray" Whitley both began their careers as cowboy singers in the movies. The son of a Texas farmer, Ritter was fascinated by cowboy music and folklore as a teenager, and he pursued this interest as a student at the University of Texas, where he encountered western scholars J. Frank Dobie and John Lomax. After considering a career in law, he decided to became an entertainer, and he performed on a Houston radio program, *The Cowboy and His Songs*, in the late 1920s. He was later featured in such radio shows as *The Lone Star Rangers*, *Cowboy Tom's Roundup*, *Death Valley Days*, and *WHN Barn Dance*. Ritter gained experience as

an actor in New York, where he appeared in several Broadway productions, before moving to Hollywood. By 1945 he had starred in more than fifty western films, and he went on to become even more successful as a country and western recording artist. Unlike many other performers who have been labeled cowboy singers, Ritter made an effort to provide his audiences with an authentic interpretation of western life in his movies and his music. During the 1930s and 1940s, he recorded a number of traditional-style cowboy songs, among them "A-Ridin' Old Paint" (also known as "I Ride an Old Paint"), "Blood on the Saddle" (about a bronco rider who was killed in a rodeo accident), and "Bad Brahma Bull."

Southern-born Ray Whitley, one of Ritter's better-known contemporaries, made a name for himself as a singer in New York in 1931, performing with a group on radio station WMCA under the title Ray Whitley and His Range Ramblers (later called the Bar-Six Cowboys). After being hired for a role in a Hopalong Cassidy feature, Whitley went on to portray singing cowboys on screen in a number of films.

Roy Rogers

King of the Cowboys

By the time Roy Rogers made his film debut, as a member of the popular western group the Sons of the Pioneers in *The Old Homestead* (Liberty Pictures, 1935), he and the other members of the band were already fairly well-known thanks to live performances, exposure on the radio, and a number of recordings. He and the Sons of the Pioneers had been working in the Los Angeles area for a couple of years when the opportunity to appear in the musical western arose. Little did Rogers (or Len Slye, as he was then known) guess that one day he would become one of the most respected and beloved of all the singing cowboys.

Rogers was born Leonard Franklin Slye in Cincinnati, Ohio, on November 5, 1911. As a young adult, Slye moved to the West Coast looking for work as a fruit-picker, taking on singing jobs whenever he could. Having found his way to Los Angeles, Rogers, singer Tim Spencer, and bass player/songwriter Bob Nolan formed a group

called the Pioneer Trio. During their first on-air appearance, the announcer gave their name as the Sons of the Pioneers and—although it irked the band members at first—the handle stuck. Soon the trio was joined by two brothers, talented guitarist Karl and fiddle player Hugh Farr. The Sons of the Pioneers had a terrific sound that was founded on the bedrock of solid songwriting and tight vocal harmonies. A particularly gifted songwriter, Nolan wrote many wonderful songs ("Cool Water" and "Tumbling Tumbleweeds") that evoked the romance of the Old West.

After *The Old Homestead*, the Sons of the Pioneers appeared in a number of musical westerns (many with singing cowboy Charles Starrett), broadening their fan base. Then in 1937, Slye left to audition for Republic Pictures, whose tempestuous Herbert Yates had over time managed to infuriate the studio's prize pony, Gene Autry, and was on the hunt for a backup star. Slye was given the name Dick Weston and was "tested" in a couple of pictures, including Autry's *The Old Barn Dance* (1937) and the Bob Livingston musical oater *Wild Horse Rodeo* (1937). The youthful, athletic-looking Weston was a hit. He was given the new name Roy Rogers and would soon be given a starring role. Citing numerous complaints about Yates' business practices, Autry walked out on Yates after filming for *The Old Barn Dance* was completed.

Joined by Autry's longtime sidekick, accordionist Smiley Burnette, Rogers appeared in *Under Western Stars* (1938), a movie that followed the fortunes of a cowboy leaving the Dust Bowl and traveling to Washington to appeal to the U.S. Congress for aid. The name Roy Rogers was mentioned throughout the film (a popular ploy when studios tried to launch a star); thus, when the movie and its handsome young cowpoke proved to be box-office smashes, Roy Rogers became a household name in no time. With the return of Autry a year or so later, Republic was blessed with two stars. When Autry enlisted in the armed

forces in 1942, Yates simply focused his energies on Rogers (who did not qualify for service). It was during this period that Yates reportedly began calling Rogers "King of the Cowboys."

In 1946 Rogers' first wife died, following the birth of Roy Rogers, Jr. On New Year's Eve, 1947, Rogers married the talented and beautiful Dale Evans, who had just appeared with him in the movie *The Cowboy and the Senorita*. Over the years Evans and Rogers became one of the most popular entertainment couples, appearing in numerous movies and on a television series that aired from 1951 to 1957. With Dale at his side, Rogers rode his remarkable horse, Trigger (called "The Smartest Horse in the Movies," the palomino had been ridden by Olivia de Havilland in *The Adventures of Robin Hood*) to stardom.

Also in the 1950s, Rogers began a solo recording career that would span the decades, continuing into the 1990s. Over the course of his life Rogers recorded solo and with many other performers, including the Sons of the Pioneers, Dale Evans (most of their collaborations were gospel-oriented), western swing bandleader Spade Cooley (*Skip To My Lou and Other Square Dances*, 1952), Roy Rogers, Jr. (*Many Happy Trails*, 1984), and several other notables. In 1974, "Hoppy, Gene, and Me" was a hit for the singer and in 1991, his most recent effort, *Tribute*, charted in the United States. The Roy Rogers Museum in Victorville, California, is a shrine to Rogers' distinguished career.

Roy Rogers (center) and the Sons of the Pioneers appeared together in several musical westerns during the 1940s, including **Utah** *(Republic Pictures), which also starred Dale Evans and Trigger, "The Smartest Horse in the Movies."*

In addition he became a successful songwriter and the leader of a western swing band. Other singing cowboys of the 1930s who made themselves heard on radio and in the movies included John Nicholas "Dick" Foran, Tex "The Lonely Cowboy" Fletcher, Smith Ballew, Bob Baker, Carl Stuart Hamblen, Bill Bender, Doie Hensley "Tex" Owens (an authentic cowboy who wrote the western song "Cattle Call," popularized by Eddy Arnold), and Wilf "Montana Slim" Carter.

Another western artist who should be mentioned here is Herb Jeffries, who had the distinction of being the first African American singing cowboy movie star, a career launched in 1937 with the movie *Harlem on the Prairie*. Jeffries went on to star in several all-black musical westerns during the late 1930s, including *Harlem Rides the Range* and *The Bronze Buckaroo*.

As the only singing cowboy who came close to rivaling the popularity of Gene Autry, Roy Rogers earned the title "King of the Cowboys" early in his career as a film star. In the early 1930s, Rogers performed music using his real name, Leonard Slye, as a member of a group called the Sons of the Pioneers. Responding to a call for singing western heroes from Republic Pictures, Slye appeared on a trial basis in two cowboy films under the name Dick Weston. In 1937 he signed a contract with Republic (Autry's studio was looking for a replacement for Autry, who had walked out in protest over the way he was being treated) on the strength of those two outings, taking the name Roy Rogers. He later recorded popular and western songs for Decca and RCA, and went on to star in his own television program, *The Roy Rogers Show*, for six years in the 1950s. The show ended with the theme song "Happy Trails," written by Roy's wife and costar Dale Evans, who was referred to as the "Queen of the West." In 1974 Rogers had a hit country record entitled "Hoppy, Gene and Me," recalling the glory days of B-movie westerns.

Although Rogers became famous as a solo performer, he made his most important contribution to western music as a member of the Sons of the Pioneers, an act that originally came together in California in 1933. Initially, Bob Nolan, Roy Rogers

Above: *The African American singing cowboy Herb Jeffries (far right) sang with Duke Ellington's band during the late 1930s and early 1940s.* **Right:** *Shown here in the movie* **Take Me Back to Oklahoma,** *western swing king Bob Wills got his start promoting Light Crust flour on the radio.*

(still Leonard Slye at the time), and Tim Spencer called themselves the Pioneer Trio, and they performed smooth three-part vocal arrangements accompanied by upright bass and guitar. In 1934 Hugh and Karl Farr, brothers who played fiddle and guitar, respectively, joined the group, which was dubbed the Sons of the Pioneers by a radio announcer who felt its members were too young to be called pioneers. They began appearing in movies in 1936, and despite a number of personnel changes continued to sing on screen until the late 1940s. The group's recording career lasted into the mid-1950s, producing such western favorites as "Cool Water" and "Tumbling Tumbleweeds."

During the height of their popularity, the Sons of the Pioneers sang and acted in films with such stars as Gene Autry, Roy Rogers, Bing Crosby, Eddie

Patsy Montana

The Cowboy's Sweetheart

The first female country music star and the first woman to sell one million records as a solo performer, Patsy Montana was born Ruby Blevins near Hot Springs, Arkansas, on October 30, 1912, the only daughter in a family with eleven children.

Fascinated with "cowboy music" (or, at least, what was being marketed as such) at an early age, Blevins taught herself to sing and yodel like her radio favorites (in particular Jimmie Rodgers). She later took up the violin as a student at the University of the West (now the University of California at Los Angeles).

The talented and aspiring Blevins formed an all-female singing group in the late 1920s, calling it the Montana Cowgirls. As part of singer Stuart Hamblen's musical revue, the trio appeared at small events and on radio shows, and it was with the Cowgirls that Blevins changed her name to Patsy Montana.

Gene Autry poses with Jane Storey (left) and Patsy Montana (right) in a promotional picture for **Colorado Sunset** *(1939).*

Montana achieved wider recognition in 1933 when she joined the Prairie Ramblers, a male quartet that appeared on big-time radio shows, including *The National Barn Dance* on Chicago's WLS. The singing cowboy craze was just beginning in those years, and the Prairie Ramblers remained a very popular act until the end of the 1940s. It was during her years with the Ramblers that Montana had her historic success with "I Want to Be a Cowboy's Sweetheart" (1935). She also appeared in a number of serial westerns with Gene Autry.

Montana followed "Cowboy's Sweetheart" with a number of similar, but less successful songs, including "Sweetheart of the Saddle" (1936), "There's a Ranch in the Sky" (1937), "Singing in the Saddle" (1939), and "Shy Little Ann from Cheyenne" (1940).

In the 1940s Montana continued to record, both with the Sons of the Pioneers and the Light Crust Doughboys. She had a hit with the World War II song "Goodnight, Soldier," and at the end of the decade relocated to Arkansas. In the 1950s she and her family moved to California and the Cowboy's Sweetheart went into temporary retirement.

In the 1960s Montana resumed her career and continued to record on small labels into the 1980s. Sadly, Montana died in 1996.

—P.B.

Albert, and John Wayne. Many of the singing cowboys who appeared in western films were backed by harmonizing vocal acts or western swing bands. Other groups who were seen in supporting musical roles on the silver screen include Foy Willing and the Riders of the Purple Sage and the ever popular Bob Wills and his Texas Playboys, who were featured with Tex Ritter in *Take Me Back to Oklahoma*. Many more western groups of the 1930s and 1940s, like the Swift Jewel Cowboys (sponsored by Swift and Company's Jewel Salad Oil), Bill Boyd's Cowboy Ramblers, Jimmie Revard and his Swing Oklahoma Playboys, the Bar-X Cowboys, Merl Lindsay and his Oklahoma Night Riders, the Blue Ridge Playboys, and Al Clauser and his Oklahoma Outlaws, were known for their performances at clubs and dance halls and on radio.

During the heyday of the singing cowboy era in the 1930s and 1940s, some western artists developed large followings through their performances on such border radio stations as XEPN in Piedras Negras, Mexico. Because these stations were located just across the Mexican border, they were not legally required to follow U.S. broadcasting restrictions and were able to operate extremely powerful transmitters that sent out signals reaching across North America and beyond. Performers such as Nolan "Cowboy Slim" Rinehart—who Ken Maynard said was "the greatest cowboy singer" he had ever heard—and Dallas Turner, Rinehart's protégé (who became popular in the 1940s), were known to hundreds of thousands of listeners all over the country. Referred to as the "King of Border Radio," Rinehart profited from mail-order sales of the cowboy songbooks he advertised over the airwaves. Although his music was recorded on sixteen-inch discs (known as radio transcriptions) that were played on every existing border station, Cowboy Slim died in a car accident in 1948 without ever making any commercial recordings. Turner, who appeared on various border stations under at least a dozen different names, including "Nevada Slim," "Tex Vernon," and "Yodeling Slim Dallas," has been called "an encyclopedia of cowboy popular culture" by historian Guy Logsdon. Turner has written more than a thousand country and western songs and made numerous recordings for independent western labels.

Although women often appeared in musical westerns, usually playing damsels in distress, romantic interests, or both, they generally were not allowed to sing. However, during the 1920s and 1930s, a few female country artists established themselves as performers of cowboy material. Billie Maxwell became the first woman to make recordings of western songs in 1929. One of the six tunes she recorded for Victor Records was a traditional cowboy song entitled "Billie Venero," a version of which had been published in Lomax's *Cowboy Songs and Other Frontier Ballads.* Six years later, Ruby Blevins, better known as cowgirl Patsy Montana, became the first female country singer to sell over a million records. Backed by a band of musicians called the Prairie Ramblers, she achieved her success with "I Want to Be a Cowboy's Sweetheart," a song she composed while touring with Gene Autry on "The WLS Round-Up." In addition to performing on border radio stations during the 1930s with Nolan Rinehart, Montana was the star of the ABC radio show *Wake Up and Smile* in the mid-1940s, and she appeared in one movie with Autry, *Colorado Sunset.*

The Girls of the Golden West—sisters Mildred Fern "Millie" and Dorothy Laverne "Dolly" Goad (they later changed their last name to Good)—were a popular duo who also performed with Autry on *The National Barn Dance.* Their flawless harmonies and precision yodeling helped them achieve success with songs like "Give Me a Straight Shootin' Cowboy" and "Two Cowgirls on the Lone Prairie." Like many other artists who called themselves cowboy or western singers, the Goad sisters claimed to be native westerners—giving Muleshoe, Texas, as their birthplace—when in fact they were not.

Other women singers formed duos with male vocalists or, like Patsy Montana, fronted western bands. These performers included Kitty Lee (who sang with her husband, "Powder River" Jack), Louise Massey and the Westerners (a family act known for the pop crossover hit "My Adobe Hacienda"), and the Maddox Brothers and Rose (who wore custom-

Cindy Walker
The Songstress

The daughter of a Texas cotton buyer, Cindy Walker became one of the most successful songwriters in country music history. On vacation with her father in Hollywood, Cindy met fellow Texan and father of western swing Bob Wills. Impressed with the young Walker's songwriting skills, Wills and the Texas Playboys recorded four of her songs on the OKeh label in July 1941.

This happenstance relationship with Wills, one of the most influential male stars of country music, led to commercially lucrative deals writing music for the thriving western film industry. All the songs in the eight films of Bob Wills were penned by Walker.

Walker's knack for meeting the musical needs of artists who were to cover the material made her skills invaluable. Eddy Arnold covered her traditionally flavored song "Take Me In Your Arms and Hold Me" in 1950 as well as country pop numbers such as "You Don't Know Me." Artists such as Ernest Tubb ("Warm Red Wine"), Jim Reeves ("This Is It," 1965, and "Distant Drums," 1966), and Hank Snow ("The Gold Rush Is Over," 1952) have Cindy Walker to thank for much of their commercial success.

With a career that spanned thirty years, Walker demonstrated an impressive ability to change with the ever-expanding definition of country music. Writing everything from motion picture cowboy songs

Cindy Walker's talent for writing songs that were suited for a particular singer's voice led her to compose such hits as Roy Orbison's "Dream Baby."

to rockabilly and bluegrass—and even drinking songs—Walker continued to write hits all the way through the 1960s. Cindy Walker was elected to the Songwriter's Hall of Fame of the Nashville Songwriter's Association in 1970.

—A.H.

made matching cowboy outfits). Jenny Lou Carson and Cindy Walker were lesser-known country performers and recording artists who later gained recognition as songwriters. Walker, who has been called "the greatest female country composer in history," wrote over fifty songs recorded by Bob Wills, including the western hit "Dusty Skies."

Dusty skies, I can't see nothin' in sight
Good old Dan, you'll have to guide me right
For if we lose our way, the cattle will stray
And we'll lose them all tonight.
—Cindy Walker

In the late 1940s California country singers like Sollie Paul "Tex" Williams had begun imitating the movie cowboys by wearing gaudy outfits designed by Nudie Cohen, better known as "Nudie the Tailor." While numerous country singers performed in western attire, very few of them recorded western material. As country music evolved during the postwar period, cowboy and western performers found themselves being replaced by the electrified sounds of honky tonk and rockabilly artists. A new crop of singing cowboys that included Johnny Bond, Edward "Eddie Dean" Glosup, Jimmy Wakely, Monte Hale, "Ken" Curtis Wayne Gates (who played Festus in television's *Gunsmoke*), and Rex Allen was appearing in musical westerns, but these stars' popularity was largely confined to the movie screen. Bond and Wakely came to California from Oklahoma after Gene Autry hired them as members of his *Melody Ranch Show* on CBS radio. Allen, who is generally considered to be the last of the Hollywood cowboy singers, competed in rodeos before joining the *National Barn Dance* program. He made nineteen westerns in the early 1950s before the singing cowboy trend ended.

In contrast to the heroic stereotype of the cowboy that was predominant in the 1930s, some country and western artists adopted a different type of cowboy persona—that of the renegade loner. Hiram "Hank" Williams pioneered this outlaw movement, wearing cowboy suits and performing with his Drifting Cowboys as early as 1937; he also made a

Spade Cooley (left) led a western swing orchestra featuring Tex Williams (right) as the lead singer. Williams left Cooley's band in 1946 to form his own group, and he had a #1 hit in 1947 with "Smoke, Smoke, Smoke That Cigarette."

number of recordings under the pseudonym Luke the Drifter. Many of the singing cowboys of movies and television served as role models for their younger fans, who adhered to the cowboy code of conduct established by Gene Autry. But artists like Williams, whose addiction to drugs and alcohol eventually led to his death, and Donnell Clyde "Spade" Cooley helped to destroy the myth of the clean-living cowboy. (Cooley, a popular performer who was known as the "King of Western Swing" in the late 1940s, murdered his wife in a drunken rampage in 1961.) Although children continued to enjoy watching Roy Rogers ride Trigger across the plains on television, by the early 1950s most country music fans had apparently lost interest in the singing cowboy.

As the era of the singing cowboys and the B-movie western came to a close in the 1950s, many country performers from the western United States were heading east to Tennessee. Nashville had begun to emerge as the capital of country music in the late 1940s, and it soon became a headquarters for most major country recording artists. By the mid-1950s the Nashville Sound, characterized by lush arrangements that included strings and syrupy background vocals, set the standard for country singers. Marty Robbins, who hosted a Phoenix television program called *Western Caravan* (and began recording for Columbia in 1951), established himself as a country artist with a number of pop crossover singles that featured this new style. However, as Bill Malone notes in *Country Music, U.S.A.*, "Robbins was a singing cowboy who had been born just a few years too late." Inspired by his boyhood idol, Gene Autry, Robbins recorded several western songs in 1959, including two original compositions: the #1 hit "El Paso" and its follow-up release, "Big Iron." He recorded several albums of "gunfighter ballads" that contained such traditional cowboy songs as "The Strawberry Roan" and "Little Joe, the Wrangler," along with more recent western tunes like "Cool Water."

Although cowboy music's popularity only lasted for about two decades, the influence of the singing cowboys can be seen in numerous recordings that were made many years later, such as Glen Campbell's 1975 hit "Rhinestone Cowboy," a 1978 duet by country outlaws Waylon Jennings and Willie Nelson entitled "Mamas, Don't Let Your Babies Grow Up to Be Cowboys," and "My Heroes Have Always Been Cowboys," which was recorded separately by both Jennings and Nelson. Other artists, such as Arizona balladeer Tom Russell, Canadian singer/songwriter Ian Tyson, and Texan Michael Martin Murphey, have helped to revive interest in authentic western music with their recordings of cowboy material. Toward the end of 1991, Russell released *Cowboy Real*, a powerful collection of acoustic western songs, including as "Roanie," the story of an old man who claimed to have been a cowboy:

Old Roanie wernt nothing but a drug-store
    vaquero
Who'd been tellin' his lies too damn long
Hummin' the tune to the "Strawberry Roan"
But forgettin' the words to the song
And now Roanie and the West are both gone.

As a result of the success of Murphey's 1990 album *Cowboy Songs*, Warner Brothers established Warner Western, a subsidiary label that has released recordings by Don Edwards, Herb Jeffries, Red Steagall, and the Sons of the San Joaquin, among others. In 1991, after producing more than twenty albums on his own label, cowboy singer and rodeo champion Chris LeDoux was signed by Capitol Records. LeDoux's substantial following became even greater after he recorded a duet with country superstar Garth Brooks called "Whatcha Gonna Do with a Cowboy." Although the heyday of the singing cowboy is long gone, the popularity of contemporary western performers and cowboy-themed country songs indicates that the legacy of cowboy music will continue to exist for many years to come.

Marty Robbins

The Man in the White Sport Coat

Marty Robbins was an eager purveyor of country pop, which swept Nashville in the late 1950s and 1960s. His work included cowboy ballads ("El Paso" and many other gunfighter songs), teen pop ("A White Sport Coat and a Pink Carnation"), and romantic, middle-of-the-road tunes ("My Woman, My Woman, My Wife"). He appeared in many movies, including *Ballad of a Gunfighter* (1963), and was one of the first country stars to perform in Las Vegas. He was also a skilled stock car driver and competed in some the biggest NASCAR events.

Born on September 26, 1925, in Glendale, Arizona, Robbins was the grandson of a barker with a traveling medicine show who performed and collected cowboy songs. Enthralled by such silver screen heroes as

Growing up in Arizona, versatile singer Marty Robbins fell in love with cowboy and western songs and helped perpetuate their influence on country music.

Gene Autry, Robbins recalled later that he would work all week picking cotton just to earn the price of admission to a Gene Autry movie.

Robbins joined the U.S. Navy at the age of nineteen and began playing guitar and writing songs in the course of his three-year tour, during which he was stationed mostly in the Pacific. When he returned to Arizona, he began sitting in with a local country band, working by day as a ditch-digger in Phoenix. He eventually formed his own band, which became popular enough to win him a radio show and a weekly Phoenix television show called *Western Caravan*. One of the guests on the radio show was singer "Little Jimmie" Dickens, who was later instrumental in helping Robbins land a recording contract with Columbia Records in Nashville. Robbins' first release, "I'll Go On Alone" (1953), topped the country charts for two weeks.

Robbins' smooth style and his promise as a hit maker won him a spot on the *Grand Ole Opry* in 1953. His "Singing the Blues" (1956) topped the charts, though for the remainder of the 1950s he recorded mostly teen-oriented pop songs, switching in the 1960s and 1970s to the pop ballads that made him famous.

A stock car enthusiast, Robbins was usually ranked among the top ten drivers on the NASCAR circuit, surviving a number of accidents along the way, including a spectacular 150-mile-per-hour (241.5kph) crash in 1972 at the Daytona 500. Robbins finally gave up stock car driving, evidently not wanting to push his luck.

Chronic heart problems led to Robbins' death in Nashville on December 8, 1982. His musical legacy includes nearly seventy albums, eighteen #1 pop and country hits (twelve of which he wrote), and two Grammy Awards for Best Country Vocal, Male.

—P.B.

Chapter Four

More Than a Cowboy's Sweetheart

Women in Country Music

by Judith Mahoney Pasternak

The winding and often uphill journey of women in country began before fore-mothers Sara and Maybelle Carter made their legendary Bristol recordings and stretches into the future, past such modern country women as Mary-Chapin Carpenter and k.d. lang. Spurred by vast changes in the lives of American women in general, women's roles in country music have grown exponentially as country has blossomed from a folk oddity into a full-grown, multibillion-dollar international industry. Yet the expansion of that role has always been delimited by the conservatism of the country audience and by the fear of that conservatism on the part of promoters and performers alike.

Two generations of the most influential family in country, "Mother" Maybelle Carter and daughters Helen (on accordion) and Anita (on stand-up bass), at the Grand Ole Opry in 1965. Maybelle's recordings from the 1920s continue to be covered today.

By and large, the country road has been traveled by white women despite the genre's roots in African American music. Though a handful of women of African American and Native American ancestry have stepped onto the path from time to time (one super-star brags of one-eighth Cherokee blood), the very short list of African American country stars is all male (as is the equally short list of Latino stars).

With that said, there has always been more space for working-class white women in country than in many other American music and entertain-ment genres. If in the beginning the image of women in country was one of home and hearth and apple pie and church on Sunday, the same image also incorporated the hard, gritty labor it took to produce those things. Now, with more women in country than ever and more songs by and about women than ever, the images of women—both in the songs and among the performers—are more varied than ever. Country—which has embraced good girls, honky-tonk girls, and cowgirls—has finally at least acknowledged real, live, flesh-and-blood women. In its songs—and in increasing numbers, among its singers—there have been proudly traditional women, proudly iconoclastic women, and recently one (only one) out-of-the-closet lesbian.

None of which is to say that women in country are liberated at last, any more than are women in mainstream cul-ture. The country establishment still promotes cer-tain ideas of what constitutes a proper woman, and if these ideas constrict her a little less than formerly, they don't come near to reaching "anything goes." It may even be that in some ways the combined effects

of the sexual and feminist "revolutions" have permit-ted new kinds of exploitation of women in country—as they have in the mainstream.

Still, the map of the country woman's journey is a fascinating one. It shows a road that has often run parallel to that of women on the main roads of the United States, while coming in each decade to cross-roads and detours peculiar to the country terrain.

Following the European settlement of the New World there was American country music for cen-turies, and women as well as men played it. Many of the singers and guitarists, the fiddlers and banjo players of the wild Appalachian hills and the Deep South were women, who sang and played in their homes and at barn dances and roof raisings. There were fewer women, however, among the itinerant musicians who played in traveling tent and medicine shows. "The road" was not considered a proper place for a lady, or for an honest country working girl, wife, or mother.

The invention of the phonograph late in the nine-teenth century led, inevitably, to the birth of the music industry at the turn of the twentieth. Within the first years of the new century, record companies were churning out popular music with a southern flavor. (Many such songs would be covered decades later by "hillbilly" performers.) Once the early sound engineers solved the technical problem of recording women's higher voices, it became possible for women to perform in the relative privacy of the stu-dio, and almost as soon as the companies put women on their rosters, the producers began to search out southern and western material for them to sing.

One popular style at the time was the audio equivalent of the then-prevalent blackface minstrel shows; white performers who performed in this style, unblushingly called "coon singers," recorded songs in bad imitations of African American dialect. The popular chanteuse May Irwin, for instance, had an early "coon" hit in 1907 with "The Bully Song," which later became a country standard. Meanwhile, African American women were singing the blues in black communities around the nation; nevertheless, the recording industry remained lily-white for most of the next decade, until record companies created the "race record" category for marketing music in African American communities.

By 1913 Columbia Records had a section in its catalog listing what were called "barn dance" songs; the label's biggest "barn dance" star was Ada Jones, who in the course of her career recorded more than two thousand cylinders and discs, with titles such as "Are You From Dixie?" and "Queen of the Ranch." In 1915 Alma Gluck made the first record by a woman to sell a million copies, "Carry Me Back to Old Virginny"; her "The Little Old Cabin in the Lane" also became a hillbilly classic.

Country music received an immeasurable boost with the spread of broadcasting in the 1920s. Desperate for cheap live entertainment, many radio stations outside the "sophisticated" Northeast began putting on programs they called barn dances, booking amateur traditional performers in addition to the stars of the new record industry.

The biggest such broadcaster was Chicago's WLS, which blanketed the region with *The National Barn Dance*, an immensely popular show that was started in 1924. In 1926 WSM in Nashville began broadcasting the barn dance program that in 1928 would be renamed *The Grand Ole Opry*. Midwestern radio stations were more willing to book women than were those in the more conservative South—*The National Barn Dance,* for example, had a woman star from the beginning, the sedate Grace Wilson, who remained with the show for its entire thirty-six-year run.

In 1927 many of the elements that have come to characterize the country music industry coalesced at the legendary Bristol sessions, which set the gender (and racial) pattern for the much of country's early years. Jimmie Rodgers sang wild, blues-influenced, innovative, yodeling songs; the Carter family—two women under the aegis of a man—sang more traditional melodies like "Keep on the Sunny Side," "Wildwood Flower," and their biggest hit, "Single Girl, Married Girl." (Nothing is entirely black or white, however, especially in U.S. popular music; Maybelle Carter's famous guitar lick also had blues roots.)

The young country music industry tried to distinguish its women from the dubious morals associated with the stars of ragtime, jazz, and the theater, presenting such performers as Grace Wilson (right) and Alma Gluck (below, with her children) as paragons of respectability.

released the records because the subject matter, love gone wrong, was so distasteful (particularly when sung by women). The records were rediscovered in 1979, but by then nothing was known about the singers, not even their names.

As the overriding aspect of U.S. life in the 1930s, the Great Depression necessarily influenced the burgeoning country music genre and the opportunities for women within it.

Facing the Depression's grim realities, the public had two choices: fight or flight, engagement or escapism. Political opposition and protest swelled to record proportions, while Hollywood conjured up a musical West that had never existed, driving the nation cowboy crazy. Women played roles in both political action and in the manufacture of celluoid fantasies, which together affected the ways that American women and women in country music perceived themselves and were perceived by others.

Country music was inadvertently moved further away from its folk roots in the 1930s when many folksingers were swept north and east into the largely Communist-led wave of union organizing and political protest against the system that had betrayed the American dream and impoverished so many. The balladeer Woody Guthrie came out of dust-smothered Oklahoma into folk music history; and out of Harlan County, Kentucky—"Bloody Harlan," scene of some of the nation's most violent labor struggles—

Above: Adelyne Hood's spunky songs belied her demure appearance. Above, right: Minnie Pearl was the most beloved comic of the Opry stage. She started out in the 1930s with ambitions to be an actor, but made such a hit with the Opry audience that she stayed for forty years. Her impact on country history goes deeper than her characteristic "Howdee!" greeting; her immense popularity ensured that people would be reminded of country's vaudeville roots for generations.

Less sedate than Grace Wilson was famed fiddler Adelyne Hood, partner—and lover—of country's first superstar, the operatically trained Vernon Dalhart. Hood cultivated a spunky image, epitomized by her 1929 hit "Calamity Jane." But for the time being, most country women were more restricted by propriety. When a group came along called the Blue Ridge Mountain Singers, who sang harmonies of near-angelic beauty, Columbia recorded ten of their songs—and then never came the singing union organizer "Aunt" Molly Jackson and her much younger half-sister, Sarah Ogan Gunning.

Jackson's father had been blinded in the Kentucky coal mines; a brother, a son, and her first husband had died in mining accidents. Jackson herself had served ten days in a Kentucky jail for organizing among the miners. Musical as well as fervent, the sisters had a gift for reworking traditional hymns and ballads into fiery labor anthems.

The weathered, pipe-smoking, middle-aged Jackson became a musical symbol of labor's uphill fight. She recorded "Kentucky Miner's Wife" for Columbia's country division in 1930, and in 1935 and 1939 recorded more than a hundred songs for the Library of Congress, which also recorded Gunning's traditional ballads and labor songs.

Although Gunning remained on the folk music circuit through the 1960s, the country music industry in the 1930s was becoming much more commercial (just as folk was becoming became downright anti-commercial—one of Gunning's Library of Congress recordings was of her own, frankly titled "I Hate the Capitalist System").

More to the taste of the barn-dance radio producers were women like the Tennessee moonshiner's daughter, the gum-snapping Lulu Belle (Myrtle Eleanor Cooper), who became the first woman superstar of WLS' *National Barn Dance*. In 1932 WLS discovered that studio audiences would pay to get into *Barn Dance* broadcasts; Lulu Belle debuted the same year. Tomboyish, almost rowdy, she and her partner Scotty (Scott Wiseman) became the "Sweethearts of Country Music" in radio and movies. (One of their hits was "I Wish I Was a Single Girl Again," a song with sentiments similar to those of the Carters' legendary "Single Girl, Married Girl.")

The decade also saw the first-known all-women's string band in country, the Coon Creek Girls, led by Lily Mae Ledford. The standards for women were changing with the era. In filmdom, frivolous flappers were out and broad-shouldered career women were in; the country version was cowgirl Patsy Montana (originally Rubye, née Ruby, Blevins).

The only daughter in a family of eleven on a farm in western Arkansas, Montana knew what she was singing about when she created a female counterpart of Hollywood's singing cowboy. In 1935, "I Want to Be a Cowboy's Sweetheart" became country's first million-selling record by a woman.

The song's message, however, was not quite what the title suggested; the cowboy whose sweetheart Montana claimed she wanted to be was in fact conspicuously absent from all but the title line of the song:

In the 1930s country began to capitalize on the popularity of its folk roots, as evidenced by the cover of this Lulu Belle and Scotty songbook (left) and this publicity photo (below) of the all-women string band, the Coon Creek Girls.

I want to be a cowboy's sweetheart,
I want to learn to rope and to ride,
I want to ride o'er the plains and the desert,
Out west of the Great Divide.
I want to pillow my head near the grazin'
    herd,
While the moon shines down from above,
I want to strum my guitar and yodelayhee-o,
Oh, that's the life that I love.

It wasn't a cowboy's sweetheart she wanted to be; it was a cowboy. It was not an image that would have passed muster earlier, no matter how camouflaged, but in the gritty 1930s, it sold. The song continued to sell forever after, in fact, and has been

Below: *Some of the big-band singers of the 1940s brought country roots and a down-home sensibility to their performances for U.S. troops fighting the Second World War, including "Nashville Nightingale" Dinah Shore (seen here, singing to soldiers in France).* **Right, top:** *Million-seller cowboy's sweetheart Patsy Montana was a pioneer in the music industry and on the silver screen, where she appeared as a cowgirl.* **Right, bottom:** *Real-life cowboy's sweetheart, movie star, singer, and successful country songwriter Dale Evans poses with a canine friend on the set of* **Lights of Old Santa Fe.**

covered at least once in every decade since. It was a hit all over again in the 1950s as sung by that genuine cowboy's sweetheart, the singer/songwriter Dale Evans.

One 1930s trend, however, never reached country music. In the jazz world and among some of the era's big bands, pop music was making at least sporadic attempts at racial integration. But country had one lone black performer, the Grand Ole Opry's harmonica player Deford Bailey. African American women who wanted pop music careers had to find them far from country music.

Just as the Depression had shaped the 1930s, World War II shaped the 1940s. Even before it began, the impending war ended the Depression, amplified new

American migratory patterns, and offered women enormous new career possibilities.

During the 1930s, many people across the United States had left their home towns and states in what was often a futile search for work; in the 1940s jobs materialized as the country mobilized for war. More Americans moved than ever before, spreading and deregionalizing the culture. Country music, too, went national.

Then, in 1942, the American Federation of Musicians began a several-year strike against the recording industry that had the unintended effect of thrusting vocalists—who were not allowed into the union—further into the forefront of U.S. pop music, an event that would cast a long shadow on the mainstream and, a decade later, on country and its women.

Among the pop stars brought forward by the combined influences of the war and the strike were several with country

backgrounds. Dinah Shore was the daughter of a Jewish businessman in Nashville. After a childhood battle with polio, her first singing appearances were on the *Grand Ole Opry*. She tried unsuccessfully to rid herself of her drawl, until it became clear that audiences loved it. By the end of the war, the "Nashville Nightingale" was among the most beloved of American big-band singers.

The California-born big-band singer Jo Stafford grew up listening to her southern-born mother sing songs from her native Tennessee. When Stafford tried to break into music in California in the 1930s, she wound up on *Hollywood Barn Dance*, a barn dance program broadcast over KNX. She was still young when the big bands faded away, and her career continued without them. Stafford probably covered more country hits than any other pop singer, including "I'm My Own Grandmaw" and Hank Williams' "Jambalaya."

New trends were developing within country as well, including an unprecedented acceptance of women as songwriters. Among the most successful was the versatile Cindy Walker, who started out writing for Bob Wills and His Texas Playboys and wound up writing for dozens of country and mainstream performers over the course of three decades. Her recording career didn't last as long, but included hits like "When My Blue Moon Turns to Gold Again." (She also flirted briefly with a movie career.)

A postwar curiosity was Dorothy Shay (Dorothy Nell Sims), who brought country to the cities as the "Park Avenue Hillbilly." Shay had also worked hard to get rid of a drawl that eventually turned out to be an asset. She found somewhat startling success singing country-style songs like "Feudin' and Fightin'" in northern clubs, dressed not like a hillbilly but like a movie star—or like the cabaret singer she was.

The nation still loved its cowboys, of course—or rather, Hollywood's cowboys. Texas-born Dale Evans (Frances Octavia Smith) became a star of radio and Hollywood as "That Gal from Texas" during and just after the war. Evans' success was hard-won; she had been married at fourteen and a mother at fifteen. In 1947 Roy Rogers became her third husband, but even

when she was better known as his wife than in her own right, she continued to write and record gospel songs like "The Bible Tells Me So." (She also wrote "Happy Trails to You," the theme song of Rogers and Evans' popular 1950s television show.)

Right: Singer "G.I. Joe" Jo Stafford, another popular entertainer who joined the war effort, made a new career covering such country hits as Hank Williams' "Jambalaya" after the big-band era faded. Below: When the Maddox Brothers and Rose—"the most colorful hillbilly band" in the United States—disbanded, sister Rose Maddox successfully switched to honky-tonk, charting country hits alone and with Buck Owens.

Rose Maddox (Rosea Arbana Brogdon) also began as a western-style singer, working with her brothers as The Maddox Brothers and Rose. The ensemble made a country hit in the late 1940s out of Woody Guthrie's sardonic song "Philadelphia Lawyer," but they eventually disbanded; when Maddox went on as a solo act, she became one of the first women to take up honky-tonk.

The end of the decade saw two country land-marks. The quiet debut of Kitty Wells (Muriel Deason) on the *Grand Ole Opry* in 1947 gave no indication that Wells was destined to become country's biggest woman star to date. And in 1949 big-band singer Margaret Whiting's cover of Floyd Tillman's "Slippin' Around" went to #1 on the pop charts, marking the first time a country crossover hit the top spot and moving honky-tonk further into mainstream awareness.

The 1950s were never as silent or dead as historians and decade-watchers then and since labeled the era. It's true that the government was in the hands of elderly men and men who aped the elderly; that the infant television industry was putting its money on the unreal visions of *Leave It to Beaver* and *Father Knows Best*; and that pundits and advisers in every field were putting equal expenditures of energy into purging the nation of "godless communism" and pushing women back into the kitchens from which the war had temporarily liberated them. Yet beyond the reach of the sitcom cameras, among working people around the nation and especially among African Americans and young white people, all hell was breaking loose. In hindsight, Elvis Presley and Rosa Parks characterized the decade at least as much as did presidents Dwight Eisenhower and Richard Nixon.

Elvis had female counterparts in the music industry. Indeed, it was in the 1950s that country women came into their own for the first time; if they did not yet reach equality with men, they achieved greater prominence in greater numbers and with greater autonomy than ever before.

Honky-tonk was booming as country's vigorous new subgenre, and perhaps the first sign of change to come was the demure Kitty Wells' answer to Hank Thompson's "Wild Side of Life."

A Nashville native, Wells had changed her name at the suggestion of her husband, Johnny Wright (who had chosen it from the song "Kitty Wells" by the Pickard Family). The Hank Thompson hit had described the way(s) that women lead men astray; "It Wasn't God Who Made Honky Tonk Angels" put the blame back on men. When it became

Above: *Under her ladylike exterior Kitty Wells concealed an independent soul, a winning combination that allowed her to (gently) rebut many of the stereotypes about women found in country music. An immensely talented singer and songwriter, Wells has over eighty charting country hits to her credit, almost fifty of which made it into the top ten. In recognition of her talents, Decca gave her the rare honor of a lifetime contract in 1959.* **Right:** *Big-band singer Margaret Whiting, better known for such ballads as "Moonlight in Vermont," became an unlikely honky-tonk pioneer when she brought Floyd Tillman's ode to philandering, "Slippin' Around," to the #1 spot on the pop charts.*

Brenda Lee

Little Miss Dynamite

Brenda Mae Tarpley (b. 1944) began her career in music at the age of five, winning a local talent contest in her hometown of Lithonia, Georgia. By the age of seven, Brenda was appearing regularly on the radio program *Starmakers' Revue* and as a guest on *TV Ranch*, both broadcast out of Atlanta.

Brenda saw her career take hold when country legend Red Foley asked her to perform on his show, the *Ozark Jubilee*. Foley's manager, Dub Albritten, began booking appearances for Foley and Tarpley as a duet, and the two appeared on every hit television show of the time. Steve Allen, Ed Sullivan, Red Skelton, Bob Hope, and Danny Thomas all helped introduce Brenda Lee to North America.

Signing with Decca Records that same year, 1956, Lee had her first country hit, "One Step at a Time." At the age most children are content to successfully make the transition to puberty, Brenda was the leading female singer of country music.

Songs like "Dynamite" (1957), "Sweet Nothin's" (1959), and "Rockin' Around the Christmas Tree" made Brenda Lee an "acceptable" female counterpart to Elvis in the United States. Most Americans at the time were convinced that she (in contrast to the dangerous Elvis Presley) was too young to mean anything by her shaking hips. Ballads such as "I'm Sorry" and "As Usual" led her back to standard (if somewhat pop-heavy) country, ensuring her permanent place in the history of the music she adored.

By 1969 forty-eight of her singles and fifteen of her albums had reached the popular charts. In the late 1950s and early 1960s, she was one of the leading popular singers in the United States and Europe. In the 1970s and 1980s, she appeared as a guest with several other country music notables in concerts and on recordings (including Kris Kristofferson on "Nobody Wins" and, with Loretta Lynn and Kitty Wells, on k.d. lang's *Shadowland*). In 1993

Brenda Lee, pictured here with the Casuals, shimmied her way to the top of the charts with her pubescent brand of Elvis-like gyrations.

Lee stormed across the United Kingdom in a sold-out concert tour that reaffirmed her reputation as a dynamic performer.

—A.H.

the first record by a woman to hit #1 on the country charts in 1952 (country charts were not yet being kept when Patsy Montana sang "I Want to be a Cowboy's Sweetheart"), it did more than make Wells a star; it also brought a woman's perspective to the fore.

Wells went on to become the "Queen of Country Music." She was home-loving and a little straitlaced—a country version of the stereotypical 1950s house-wife—but the space she made for women in country had more room than that model suggested. Indeed, after her breakthrough, many other women stars of the decade were less reserved.

Oklahoma-born Jean Shepard, for instance, who had already attained some prominence fronting the first all-female western swing band, became one of the first women honky-tonkers. By the time country tossed rockabilly into the explosive mix of rock and roll, there was some room for women even in that raucous genre.

It was limited room, though. The teenage star Brenda Lee, who had made her radio debut at the age of five, got away with rockabilly suggestive-ness in part because she seemed too young and innocent to know what she meant by shaking her hips. The prematurely "liberated" Wanda Jackson never did make it quite to the top of the *Billboard* charts, her frank sexuality ("Let's Have a Party") remaining just a little too much for country audi-ences. (They loved her in Japan, though, where her blistering "Fujiyama Mama," sung in Japanese, was a major hit.)

It was Patsy Cline (Virginia Patterson Henley) who, late in the decade, found the perfect proportion of authentic emotionalism for a country woman. Her passionate, wrenching singing evoked Hank Williams, and, as Hank's had, crossed over beyond country to the mainstream. She was the first country woman, in fact, to make the top ten and top twenty on the pop charts, a coup she achieved first in 1957, with "Walkin' After Midnight," and again in 1961 and 1962, with "I Fall to Pieces" and "Crazy," respectively. The parallel with Williams extended tragically to her early death in 1963 in a plane crash (which also

Contrasts in style: the frankly sexual Wanda Jackson (left), who pushed the rockabilly gender barrier touring with Hank Thompson and Elvis Presley, and the demure Patti Page (right), whose wistful blockbuster "Tennessee Waltz" (written by Redd Stewart and Pee Wee King) was the epitome of 1950s propriety.

killed Jean Shepard's husband, the up-and-coming-performer Hawkshaw Hawkins).

Cline's crossover hits stood out even in a decade marked by unprecedented interaction between country and the mainstream. Oklahoma-born Native American Kay Starr had begun her career as a country singer before she achieved pop stardom in the early 1950s. Pop singers kept covering Hank Williams' hits throughout the decade, both before and after his death. Jo Stafford virtually made her career covering country songs, and the Oklahoma-born Patti Page (Clara Ann Fowler) first made it to the top of the pop charts with her fabulously successful version of "Tennessee Waltz" in 1950.

But perhaps the most successful crossover artist was Skeeter Davis (Mary Frances Penick). Davis started out as half of a country duo, the Davis Sisters, in the early 1950s. Her partner was her close friend, Betty Jack Davis; they had a hit in 1953 with "I Forgot More Than You'll Ever Know." When Betty Jack was killed in an auto accident in 1953, Skeeter left music for several months before teaming up with Betty's sister Georgia for awhile. She came back as a solo pop singer sometime in 1955 or 1956 and has been working steadily ever since, going back and forth between pop and country with little trouble. Curiously, she is better known today in Europe and Asia, where she is known as one of America's most popular country singers.

By 1960 country was bigger, more commercial, and further from its rural southern roots than ever. But simmering up from the counterculture into in the mainstream, those roots—along with political activism—were undergoing a renaissance.

The civil rights movement that began among African Americans in the Deep South captured the imagination of the nation, especially its young people, (both black and white). Out of a new generation of activists came the movement against the expanding war in Vietnam and ultimately a broad and

Above: *Kay Starr (née Katherine Starks) went from country music to big-band jazz (performing with the ensembles of Bob Crosby and Charlie Barnet) to solo pop stardom, but her biggest hits—including "Bonaparte's Retreat" in 1950 and "Wheel of Fortune" in 1952—retained at least a hint of her Oklahoma origins.* **Left:** *The original Davis Sisters, high school friends Skeeter Davis (née Mary Pennick) and Betty Jack Davis, had already recorded a #1 country hit ("I Forgot More than You'll Ever Know," which also went to #18 on the pop chart) when Betty Jack was killed. When Skeeter resumed her career she first attempted a second incarnation of the Davis Sisters with Betty Jack's sister, Georgia (on the left), that lasted only briefly.*

Patsy Cline

Walking After Midnight

Patsy Cline's tragically short run as a top recording artist came at a time when Nashville was struggling to halt, or at least slow, the encroachment of rock and roll, which was beginning to cut significantly into radio time and record sales. Cline reigned with Kitty Wells at the top of the charts during a period of fundamental change in Nashville. While Wells stuck with a more traditional approach to country music, which, unfairly or not, eventually cost her the allegiance of radio programmers (though she remained popular with concert crowds), Cline got aboard the new country-pop bandwagon, reluctantly at first, and was just beginning to reap its rewards when she died in a plane crash in 1963.

Virginia Patterson Hensley was born on September 8, 1932, in Gore, Virginia. She was a lively youngster who soon became adept at tap dancing and playing the piano. Virginia (or Patsy, as she soon came to be called) was encouraged to sing by her mother, and the two often performed duets in church. Virginia's early exposure to music may have been the main inspiration for her run at a singing career, and as a teenager she landed a number of singing jobs, including a stint with a small-time country band called Bill Peer and His Melody Boys.

Patsy Hensley married Gerald Cline (about whom not much is known) in 1952 and divorced him five years later, but kept the name Cline professionally.

As a young woman, Cline made several treks to Nashville in efforts to advance her career. She even appeared on Roy Acuff's *WSM Dinner Bell* radio show, a broadcast that always featured conservative, traditional country talent. But Nashville was changing from a loose confederation of like-minded country artists and businessmen into a bottom line—oriented entertainment machine; performers like Cline who had grown up embracing the songs of country's pioneers were finding that record companies were less and less interested in recording that kind of material.

Mostly through perseverance, Cline landed a recording contract in 1955 with a shady California-based outfit called the 4 Star Sales Company. She was paid a single fee for each song she recorded and was prohibited from singing material other than songs provided for her by 4 Star. It was a dreary and not very productive association, probably because of the lackluster songs with which she was saddled. But she was making records, and even though they were mostly unspectacular, Cline had her chance to make a mark in the business.

Cline's fortunes changed when she began working with producer Owen Bradley, one of the architects of the Nashville Sound, which was then beginning to take shape. Bradley and such colleagues as Chet Atkins were hoping to bolster the fast-fading popularity of hillbilly music by toning down its twangier elements in favor of the more marketable pop sound. Patsy Cline was a reluctant contributor to the hybrid, but nevertheless recorded the bouncy "Walking After Midnight" in November 1956, under Bradley's guidance.

It was Cline's appearance on *Arthur Godfrey's Talent Scouts* television show several months later that alerted the nation to "Walking After Midnight." Her bluesy rendition that night thrilled the audience and they gave her a standing ovation. The record took off, hitting the #3 position on Billboard's country chart. It also rose to #17 on the pop charts.

Despite this success, Cline remained reluctant to break with her country roots. This was reflected in her stage show, which was traditional enough to win her an invitation in 1960 to join the Grand Ole Opry. But it wasn't until 1961, after the birth of a daughter conceived with her new husband,

Patsy Cline may well be to country what Bessie Smith is to the blues: a phenomenal talent with a larger-than-life personality. Cline's extraordinary intensity still inspires countless imitators decades after her untimely death.

Charles Dick, that Cline scored her next hit record—two hits in fact—the classic country weeper "I Fall To Pieces" and the pop hit "Crazy," written by Willie Nelson.

4 Star had by then shut down, one step ahead of the law, and Cline's new label was Decca Records. With a wealth of material suddenly available to her, hits followed hits. In 1962 there was "She's Got You" and "When I Get Through With You (You'll Love Me Too)." The following year she made the top ten with "Sweet Dreams (Of You)," probably her most characteristic number.

"Sweet Dreams" was released posthumously. On March 3, 1963, as she was returning to Nashville from a benefit performance in Kansas City, Cline and three friends were killed when the plane in which they were flying crashed in bad weather near Camden, Tennessee. Cline was thirty-one years old. She had been performing for more than twenty of those years, but recording for less than eight. Her relatively small collection of songs was potent enough to sustain her popularity through the 1970s, and more than a few of her recorded performances will always be thought of as country music classics.

Patsy Cline's influence on country music was vast. She and Kitty Wells were the first women to rise to the top of their profession on merit, easing acceptance for such women as Loretta Lynn, Tammy Wynette, and Dolly Parton, all of whom were on the way up in the early 1960s. Musically, much of the work done by Cline and Owen Bradley is as impressive and evocative today as it was more than thirty years ago. A recently released album of her greatest hits sold more than three million copies and was certified triple platinum in 1991. Cline's life was dramatized in the film *Sweet Dreams* (1985), starring Jessica Lange. Finally, she was honored by her colleagues in 1973 by being inducted into the Country Music Hall of Fame.

—P.B.

diverse movement for social change. And, as had their political forebears a generation earlier, the new activists took up their guitars and sang.

First on and around college campuses, then in urban coffeehouses across the North and East, activists followed two stars: a scruffy young singer-songwriter from Minnesota and an ethereal half-Mexican from Boston with an achingly pure soprano voice. At first Bob Dylan (Robert Zimmerman) and Joan Baez represented the two poles of the folk revival, with Dylan as the topical balladeer and Woody Guthrie's heir, and Baez as the neotraditionalist heir of the Carters. By the mid-1960s, however, styles and genres had received a vigorous shuffling; Dylan went electric, shocking the Newport Folk Festival in 1965, and Baez was singing "We Shall Overcome" and other anthems for the civil rights and antiwar movements.

The revival reached back to the early days of country and introduced a new generation of listeners to the Carters and their contemporaries; Maybelle Carter was still around to enjoy the new audiences, as was Sarah Ogan Gunning. Women, old and young, occupied a prominent position in the new folk music. The trio Peter, Paul and Mary, featuring the strong alto of Kentucky-born Mary Travers, had several pop-chart hits. The classically trained and multitalented Judy Collins attained folk stardom equal to Baez's. A long list of others achieved headliner status at least on the folk circuit, including many who defined themselves as much by their politics as by their music: elderly songwriter Malvina Reynolds, who wrote "What Have They Done to the Rain?" and "Little Boxes"; the militant Barbara Dane, who took for the title of her first album Sarah Ogan Gunning's "I Hate the Capitalist System"; and working-class advocate Hedy West.

Above: *Joan Baez and Bob Dylan were among the many luminaries of the 1960s folk revival who eventually made their way to Nashville. On tour after going electric in 1965, Dylan was backed up by the Band, which included several ex-members of the Hawks, a band started by rockabilly star Ronnie Hawkins.*

For all its country roots, folk remained the province of the young, the educated, the urban, and the left. (Like country, folk music was also almost entirely white, with a few exceptions including the Cree Indian Buffy Sainte-Marie and the powerful-voiced African American Odetta [Odetta Holmes Felious Gorden].) Throughout the decade, country music proper would largely reject the counterculture's values, as expressed by Merle Haggard in "Okie From Muskogee." Yet change was creeping in, especially in the work of country women.

Loretta Lynn (Loretta Webb), for instance, shaped a career out of pride in her country roots, country values, and one-eighth Cherokee ancestry.

Loretta Lynn

The Coal Miner's Daughter

Just when country music seemed through with telling the rural American story, Loretta Lynn (b. 1935), "The Coal Miner's Daughter," put the "country" back into the ever-changing definition of popular southern music.

Born in Butcher Hollow, Kentucky (a town so small that it is described in relation to another small town, Van Lear), Loretta lived a life typical of an impoverished Kentucky woman, marrying her first husband, Oliver V. "Mooney" Lynn at the age of thirteen. Moving her new family to Bellingham, Washington, Loretta began her career as a singer in honky tonks and on the radio.

Loretta Lynn's ultracountry persona may have made her pro-woman messages more palatable to even the most conservative audiences.

At twenty-five, Lynn cut her first single, "Honky Tonk Girl," which she ambitiously marketed to every radio station and music industry agent in her surrounding area. She was picked up by the Wilburn Brothers' talent agency, which immediately had her signed to Decca Records.

Thus began a series of television performances that exposed Lynn to the general public for the first time. Appearances on the Wilburn Brothers' own syndicated television show as well as an appearance on the *Grand Ole Opry* ensured her place in the heart of America.

It is Lynn's lyrics that have guaranteed her place as the 1960s' queen of country music. Her honest, thought-provoking words consistently cut to the heart of the subject at hand. Her hits from the 1960s, which include "Don't Come Home A' Drinkin' (With Lovin' On Your Mind)" and "Fist City," provide a woman's perspective on a male-dominated world.

With the help of her autobiography, *Coal Miner's Daughter*, written in 1970 (and made into a movie of the same name in 1980, starring Sissy Spacek as Lynn), Loretta Lynn became a legend in her own lifetime. Throughout the 1980s Lynn recorded with several artists, most often with Conway Twitty, and continues to record in the 1990s. At this writing, her most recent original album was *Honky Tonk Angels* (recorded with Dolly Parton and Tammy Wynette in 1993).

—A.H.

A coal miner's daughter from Butcher Hollow, Kentucky—pronounced "Butcher Holler"—who bore her first child at fourteen and fought her way to success between babies, Lynn turned out song after song celebrating Butcher Hollow in particular and country in general (as expressed in the line, "When you're lookin' at me, you're lookin' at country)." At the same time, she made an equal point of a kind of assertiveness that was new to country, an anti-masochism that insisted a woman could be feminine while demanding respect. "Don't Come Home A Drinkin' (With Lovin' on Your Mind)," she sang, and "Your Squaw Is on the Warpath"; and, to a potential rival, "You Ain't Woman Enough (to Take My Man)." No one objected to her feistiness; for most of the decade, Loretta was the unchallenged queen of country.

Dottie West (Dorothy Marsh) came to a similar self-assurance in the 1960s, midway through a career that had begun with a more conventional persona. Born in Tennessee and the oldest of ten children, Dottie was a rarity among country women: a singer/songwriter with a degree in music. She married guitarist Bill White while still very young and for a decade or so refused to sing anything that didn't fit her image as a contented housewife and mother. But when the marriage ended in 1966, West took stock of her life and came up with an entirely new style—in music and in her private life. Before an auto accident claimed her life in 1991, she had married a second and then a third husband, each of whom had been considerably more than ten years her junior.

Heartbreak heroine Tammy Wynette (Virginia Pugh), in contrast to West, has devoted most of her long career to what some critics see as a celebration of female masochism. Her 1968 anthem, "Stand By Your Man," was a restatement of one facet of country womanhood in the face of the decade's challenges to that vision—challenges that would become more insistent in the 1970s. (Wynette had only married twice when she wrote it, though she continued to sing it even through marriages three, four, and five.)

The 1960s saw another country milestone when an African American woman hit the country charts for the first time, with rhythm and blues singer Esther

Dottie West

The Country Sunshine Girl

By many country music historians' accounts, Dottie West (1932–1983) may well have been the first truly liberated woman of country. At first conforming to the accepted roles of women in country music, West did an about-face nearly halfway through her career. Her music, lyrics, and persona changed from the image of the happy housewife to the picture of a woman who desires and demands more from life.

Dorothy Marsh (Dottie's given name) grew up in a family of ten children who had been abandoned by their father by the time Dottie was fourteen. The majority of her and her siblings' time was spent helping their mother run a small neighborhood restaurant near their home. Upon graduating from high school, the young and beautiful Dorothy made her way to Tennessee Tech, following her dreams of becoming a musician. While studying here she met her first husband, Bill West, a steel guitar player. Both would soon become professional musicians in Nashville. Once in Nashville, the couple quickly became close friends with other aspiring songwriters. Dottie West was to be friends with Willie Nelson and Roger Miller —all at that time unsuccessful in their careers—for the rest of her life.

From the mid-1960s to the mid-1980s, Dottie had some sixty songs chart in United States, beginning with "Let Me Off at the Corner" in 1963 (the same year that a song she wrote, called "Is This Me," was a #3 country hit for Jim Reeves). The next year she broke the top ten in a duet with Reeves called "Love Is No Excuse." Also released that year was her song "Here Comes My Baby," which entered the top ten and the next year won her a Grammy for her efforts (making her the first female country singer to do so). In the 1970s and 1980s, she continued to have chart hits, including several duets with the likes of Jimmie Dean and Kenny Rogers, but by the 1990s troubles with money would coincide with a commercial drought.

The Wests had four children together, three of whom were boys—Morris, Kerry, and Dale. Their only daughter, Shelley West, has become a country star like her mother. The Wests' marriage failed after twenty years, leaving Dottie free to navigate an entirely new path for herself both professionally and personally.

Before the divorce, Dottie's self-image was based on her role as a mother and wife. The songs she sang were carefully chosen so as not to give any other impression. At one time, she refused to sing a Kris Kristofferson song because the lyrics were too sexy. Directly following the divorce, however, she recorded the racy "She Can't Get My Love Off the Bed." Something had definitely changed for West.

Although she had always been described as a positive thinker, happiness for Dottie was fleeting. It was as if, when joy was found, the euphoria of love and good luck would quickly disappear into the mundane routine of daily living. Her need for companionship led her to marry her drummer, twenty-nine-year-old Bryon Metcalf, a man fifteen years her junior. Within only a couple of years, however, the happiness had disappeared without notice again, leading to their sudden separation and divorce.

As if West's marriage to a man fifteen years younger wasn't enough to set Nashville on its ear, rumors began spreading after the second divorce that she was keeping a veritable stable of young men, mainly new country talent. In fact, Larry Gatlin was "discovered" by Dottie (apparently Gatlin was living at West's mansion).

At the age of fifty, Dottie West again remarried, this time to Alan Winters, age twenty-eight, who was West's sound engineer. Following their marriage, Alan, a farm boy from Pennsylvania, left the road to watch over Dottie's fifty-acre ranch and tend their extensive garden. With experience under her belt from the other two marriages,

Dottie West (above, in 1979) was still going strong at the age of fifty when a fatal car accident cut short her career and her search for lasting happiness.

Dottie thought it wise that the two of them not be on the road together.

Even caution, however, could not keep the sun from setting on Dottie West's happiness. Seven years after that marriage, in 1983, the two were divorced. The ranch Allen had tended was soon foreclosed and their valuables sold off to pay over two and a half million dollars in debts, the majority of which was owed to the IRS. On top of all this, Dottie had two car crashes within that same year. The first hospitalized her and the second killed her. On her way to the Grand Ole Opry, the car she was being driven in (by an elderly neighbor) careened off the ramp from Nashville's parkway to the Opry parking lot. After three operations to repair damaged organs (she was bleeding heavily), West's heart gave out.

The world will always remember Dottie West. "Here Comes My Baby" (her Grammy-winning single), "Every Time Two Fools Collide," and "What Are We Doing in Love?" are not just songs but permanent memories of the beautiful Dottie West.

—A.H.

Tammy Wynette

Heroine of Heartbreak

A beautician from Mississippi, Virginia Wynette Pugh earned her stardom through ambition, determination, and the help of Nashville producer Billy Sherrill. Her recorded material and her tumultuous personal life, which includes five marriages, numerous hospitalizations for depression, and a purported kidnapping, have brought her the moniker the "Heroine of Heartbreak."

Wynette was born on May 15, 1942, on her grandfather's cotton farm in Itawamba County, Mississippi, and was reared by her grandparents. Her father, a cotton farmer and guitarist, died when Virginia was eight months old, and her mother traveled to Birmingham, Alabama, to work in a defense plant—not uncommon work for women in the war years.

Married for the first time at seventeen, and divorced at twenty, Wynette worked as a hairdresser in Birmingham to support her three children, one of whom had spinal meningitis. Even as a girl Wynette had dreamed of a career as a country performer; as a young woman she made several pilgrimages to Nashville, none of which paid off until she met Billy Sherrill, who saw her potential and agreed to help try to launch her career.

One of the first things Sherrill suggested was that Virginia Pugh change her name to Tammy Wynette, a much more likely handle for a country star. More importantly, he provided Wynette with top-notch musical material, including her first hit, "Apartment No. 9," and the follow-up, "Your Good Girl's Gonna Go Bad," one of 1967's biggest sellers. The next year Wynette released "D-I-V-O-R-C-E" and "Stand By Your Man," the record that proved to be her high-water mark as a recording artist. In 1968 Wynette also married George Jones, one of country's biggest stars and a man with personal demons of his own. Their marriage, which was

rocky from the start, ended in 1975, though the pair continued to perform together and remained in demand at concerts for many years afterward.

The course of Tammy Wynette's career is something of a mystery to most people. The tabloid press has made much of her frequent hospitalizations and shock treatments for depression. The ransacking of her Nashville home and a reputed kidnap attempt were widely seen as a bid for publicity when her career was at a low ebb. Despite all this, Wynette continues to record and perform and still has countless loyal fans.

—P.B.

Slowing down as she hits middle age, Tammy Wynette has stood by George Richey—man number five—for roughly two decades.

Phillips' crossover hit, "Release Me" (1962). Phillips' success didn't exactly open the country floodgates; country's de facto segregation continued virtually unabated, although at the end of the decade, in 1969, Linda Martell made another piece of history by becoming the first African American woman ever to appear on the *Grand Ole Opry.*

Feminism hit country—and especially its women—like the proverbial ton of bricks. The "Stand By Your Man" ethic was on trial, and no one could ignore the questions being raised.

Loretta Lynn had been facing those questions in her own way all along and kept right on doing so, sometimes a little too frankly. Her "Fist City" (1968) took a hard look at domestic violence, and "The Pill" (1975) expressed a woman's gratitude for the freedom promised by easier birth control (albeit almost fifteen years after birth control pills had become widely available); some radio stations refused to air the latter song.

Tammy Wynette stood by her traditional values. At the beginning of the decade, she and then-husband George Jones were the reigning royalty of country. The marriage eventually fell victim to Jones' drinking problems, but nothing could induce Wynette to question her belief in the traditional model for women's happiness. "We're Gonna Hold On," she sang with Jones while they were still fighting to keep their marriage alive; as soon as their troubled union ended, she recorded "I Still Believe in Fairy Tales."

Wynette has always claimed that feminist critics misread her message and that she never meant a woman should accept whatever a man chooses to dole out. Like much of mainstream country, however, her work over a now-twenty-five-year career suggests a faith in the possibility of living happily ever after that is astonishing in its tenacity.

Dolly Parton took a judicious middle road through the challenges of the decade to become one of country's great all-time successes. As proudly blue-collar as Loretta Lynn—the Tennessee-born Parton was the first person in her family ever to finish high school—she created a public persona that exaggerates traditional femininity virtually to the point of parody. Yet under the bewigged, bosom-flaunting exterior beats a heart that, like Loretta's, accepts no clichés regarding women's roles. In songs like "Dumb Blonde" and "Just Because I'm a Woman," which attacked the sexual double standard, and "My Blue Ridge Mountain Boy," which looked sympathetically at prostitution, she assailed stereotypes and defended the despised.

It proved to be a winning combination. Dolly Parton is now not only one of the most respected and beloved of country stars, but also, as one of the richest people in U.S. show business, living proof that a woman can be feminine as all get-out and a successful businessperson at the same time.

Yet throughout the decade, at the fringes of country, the messages of feminism were creeping in more explicitly via the brief but vibrant phenomenon called women's music. It was not a genre or style of music, though the largest number of its performers and writers were in the folksinger/songwriter vein; rather, it was an infusion of a specifically feminist sensibility into many genres. Few of its performers ever made it to the big time, but one or two (like Holly Near and, later, the Canadian singer-songwriter Ferron) came close enough so that their respective genres felt the touch of that sensibility.

A minority of singer/songwriters in the field of women's music found themselves in country music. The openly lesbian lyrics of Casse Culver and Florida-born Willie Tyson restricted their audiences to women's music festivals and community radio listeners, but the country-rock trio the Deadly Nightshade—guitarists Anne Bowen and Helen Hook and bassist Pamela Brandt—managed to get some airplay outside that restricted world.

By a fluke of fate, however, the women's music performers who became best known beyond the movement's small audience were the two who formed the duo Hazel and Alice. Hazel Dickens and Alice Gerrard were folk/bluegrass singer/songwriters who put out a couple of records on Rounder Records, a small folk label. In 1975 Diana Ciminella, a young divorcee with two small daughters, moved to rural Berea, Kentucky, to sort out her life. In a local

Dolly Parton
Brilliant Blonde

Native Tennessean Dolly Parton (b. 1946) is at this writing estimated to be worth seventy million dollars and is one of the five most powerful women in show business. With the voice of an angel, the brains of a great business woman, and undeniably good looks, Parton has done more with a high school education than most any other person in the world. From abject poverty on Locust Ridge to her legendary status in Nashville, Parton has carved out a brilliant path for herself.

Being the granddaughter of a minister meant an early introduction to the traditional church music that is the backbone of country. Her talents were apparent at a very early age. When she was a child, her Knoxville uncles presented her to Tennesseans for the first time on their television program, *Farm and Home*. Parton knew from that moment she was meant to be in the spotlight.

Immediately after high school, Dolly Parton moved from her family's shack to Nashville. In her first week in Nashville she met her soon-to-be husband Carl I. Dean. Dean happened to be driving past the Wishy Washy Laundromat in downtown Nashville as Dolly stepped out of the laundromat for a soda. Being from the country, she waved innocently (she admits now that she was flirting, "but only a little") at the tall, dark young man, who immediately circled back to speak to her. Described by those who know him personally as kind and honest, Carl has been given a hard time by the press for almost the entirety of Dolly's career due to his determination to stay out of the limelight. With respect for each other, they have honored each other's needs—Carl remained a private citizen while Dolly conquered the world.

By twenty-one Parton had appeared regularly on Porter Wagoner's television series, and in the fol-

One of the greatest of the more recent generations of country's blue-collar sweethearts, Dolly Parton rose to unprecedented heights on the strength of her remarkable voice, songwriting ability, and innate business sense.

lowing year, 1968, she began recording with Monument Records. As a songwriter Dolly had her greatest successes with "Jolene" in 1973, "Coat of Many Colors" in 1971, and "9 to 5" in 1980. Nevertheless, throughout the 1980s Parton recorded important material that will always be associated with her, including such critically acclaimed numbers as "I Will Always Love You" and "Tennessee Homesick Blues." In 1987 her collaboration with Linda Rondstadt and Emmylou Harris, *Trio*, won a Grammy. In the 1990s Parton continues to record (the album *Eagle When She Flies* was released in 1991) and perform, adding all the while to the splendor of her Nashville entertainment shrine, Dollywood.

Whether singing spirituals, mountain ballads, or rock-influenced pop, Dolly Parton always brings her considerable talents to bear, making each song uniquely her own.

—A.H.

store, she bought a record called *Hazel and Alice*. It was a purchase that made a country legend: enchanted by the music, Diana bought a guitar and started singing with her eleven-year-old daughter Christina. In the 1980s, after changing their names to Naomi and Wynonna and using Diana's family name, Judd, they would become the most successful mother-and-daughter duo in country history; when life-threatening chronic hepatitis forced Naomi's early retirement in 1991, Wynonna went on to an equally successful solo career.

The 1970s was also the decade when a one-time Miss America and sometime country/pop singer named Anita Bryant achieved her greatest fame—not by singing, but by becoming the spokeswoman for Florida orange juice and against gay rights. The unlikely conjunction occurred when Florida was debating a gay civil rights bill, and the born-again Bryant couldn't stand the thought of having her adopted home state grant equal rights to homosexuals. Her campaign won her fifteen minutes of notoriety and provided a rallying cry for the growing gay movement.

Bryant aside, it was a decade marked by openness to change. It was even becoming marginally easier for African American women to have country hits. The rock/soul icon Tina Turner (Annie Mae Bullock) made a couple of country albums in the 1970s, and the Pointer Sisters (Ruth, Anita, Bonnie, and June) won the Best Country Performance, Duo or Group, Grammy in 1974 for their crossover hit, "Fairytale" (the irony of which was presumably unintentional).

Not much more than half a century after country had emerged as a distinct American genre—in the form of hillbilly music—it had all but reintegrated itself into the mainstream. There were no more hillbillies, and American pop music in general was becoming one giant, cross-country mega-industry. With the advent of MTV and other national music broadcast vehicles, the genres were merging or nearly merging in several aspects (except racially—it was some time before MTV aired a video starring an African American). Accordingly, country had

Naomi and Wynonna Judd reunited at Super Bowl XXVII in 1994, three years after ill-health forced Naomi's retirement.

become big business in the 1980s, and women were a major force in that business.

Perhaps an even more profound change lay not in where the new women in country were heading, but in where they were coming from. In a sharp break with the past, the country queens of the 1980s had started life literally in a different class from that of most of their forebears—namely, the middle class. Not since Dolly Parton has a woman climbed up from abject poverty to the top of country music, a shift that must, in turn, affect the content and nature of the music itself and even the ways these women are perceived and perceive themselves.

Some proportion of that phenomenon is due to post–World War II changes in U.S. social and economic structures. The socioeconomic stratum from which many of today's country stars arose didn't exist in the genre's early years; these performers are the baby-boomers of the postwar's newly prosperous blue-collar workers.

Tanya Tucker actually had her first hit in the 1970s, but she was only thirteen at the time. Her father, a Texas construction worker, had decided when she was nine that the family would fare better on her talent than on his and had brought her to Nashville; four years later, the song "Delta Dawn" established her as an even more precocious star than Brenda Lee.

One difference between Tucker's career and Lee's is that audiences no longer needed to be reassured of a teenaged girl's innocece. "Delta Dawn" was followed by such increasingly explicit songs as "Would You Lay With Me (in a Field of Stone)"; if Tucker's story is any example, the double standard to which Dolly Parton objected, which had governed the first several generations of country women, seemed to have died in the onslaught of the so-called sexual revolution of the 1960s. No rock and roller ever surpassed Tucker's headline-generating escapades, which included bouts with cocaine, a string of famous lovers (many twice her age), and two children born (as people continue to say) out of wedlock. Her onstage persona is as wild as the headlines she generates—and wows country audiences.

Reba McEntire's country career also started out in the 1970s but came to stunning fruition in the 1980s. Reba was born in Oklahoma into a family of rodeo champions. Her early musical inspiration was Patsy Cline and her first milieu among the country "outlaws." But though she had reasonably strong hits with Cline songs like "Sweet Dreams," her career didn't catch fire until she saw which way the wind was blowing and repackaged herself and her music. In the 1990s she is one of country's megastars, as well known for her lavish presentations as for a vocal intensity reminiscent of Cline's.

The Judds—sweet Naomi and sultry Wynonna—also came out of the new blue-collar world; Diana Judd's father was a gas-station owner in the small city of Ashland, Kentucky, who hoped his daughter would "do better" by getting an education. She got pregnant at seventeen instead, with the baby who turned out to be Wynonna; her early marriage to high-school boyfriend Michael Ciminella—and their subsequent early divorce—seemed to doom her father's dream for her. Her uphill battle from struggling single motherhood through striking success to near-tragic illness has been much chronicled, most recently in a lavish television miniseries.

More and more, in fact, country stars in the 1980s were emerging even further from country's poor white roots. Alabama country/folk pioneer Emmylou Harris was a Marine Corps brat, an officer's daughter who arrived in New York City's Greenwich Village in 1967 with folksinging ambitions, only to find out that folk's Greenwich Village heyday was past. Her voice, her spiritual presence, and her beauty ultimately found a home in country.

Right: Reba McEntire helped bring about a return to traditional country music values in the 1980s with such smash hits as "How Blue" and "Somebody Should Leave." **Below:** Tanya Tucker has surmounted many of the difficulties inherent to child stardom to forge a career as one of country's great performers.

And Texan "folkabilly" poet Nanci Griffith was even more white-collar in her origins than was Harris; her parents worked in publishing and real estate. Harris, Griffith, and their ilk have brought to country a new level of literacy and a connection with the world beyond the genre's traditional borders; Griffith is probably country's first novelist-star.

Increasingly, still another source for contemporary country artists is previous generations of country performers. While some second-generationers have lived in the shadow of a parent's fame, others, like Barbara Mandrell, have eclipsed their parents.

The daughter of a country music family, Mandrell was a member of her father's band, the Mandrells, as a child. It was that background that gave her such a

Emmylou Harris

Grievous Angel

With her beautiful southern voice, Emmylou Harris (b. 1947) has carved out an eclectic career in both country and urban folk music. By the time Emmylou found her way to the folk scene in Greenwich Village, New York City, in the late 1960s, it was quickly fading. Although she was able to record an album for Jubilee Records in 1969 called *Gliding Bird*, she soon realized she would have to move or face leaving the music business altogether. Moving to Washington, D.C., she began working at The Cellar Door Club, where she met singer-songwriter Gram Parsons. From 1971 until Parson's death in 1973, Emmylou recorded and toured with him. Their last album together, *Grievous Angel*, was critically acclaimed.

Reprise Records offered Harris a recording contract in 1974 and the following year she released *Pieces of the Sky*, a rock and country album that did not bring her much exposure. One song from the album was recorded later by the Louvin Brothers— "If I Could Only Win Your Love" reached the country top ten.

With the help of Elvis Presley's former band, Harris embarked on a successful European tour that led to the recording of her first Grammy-winning album, *Elite Hotel* (1976), which had two hit singles, "Sweet Dreams" and "One of These Days."

By the late 1970s, Emmylou's music was moving closer and closer to standard country and further away from the rock-roots tradition with which she had begun her career. Her album *Luxury Liner* (1977) included a hit single written by Jimmy Works, "Making Believe."

Harris also recorded country standards such as Loretta Lynn's "Blue Kentucky Girl," which was the title cut on Harris' 1979 album. On her *Quarter Moon In a Ten Cent Town* (1978), Harris covered Dolly Parton's composition "To Daddy," which shot to #3 on

The queen of country rock since the mid-1970s, Emmylou Harris can make any song her own, even an old show tune like "Diamonds Are a Girl's Best Friend."

the country chart. From 1976 to the present, Emmylou Harris has worked with just about everyone in country music, from Buck Owens ("That Lovin' Feeling Again") to Roy Orbison, Don Williams, and Dolly Parton and Linda Ronstadt (with whom Harris recorded the Grammy-winning album *Trio* in 1987. In 1995, she realeased the albumn *Wrecking Ball*.

In the 1980s and 1990s, Harris has released several albums, most of which met with considerable critical acclaim but failed to be commercially successful. Nonetheless, Emmylou Harris is rightly venerated as a major figure in country music history.

—A.H.

wide range of instrumental prowess—she is a talented and creative vocalist, banjo player, guitarist, and saxophone player. For a few years of her adolescence, she thought she wanted to get away from "the family business." Then she changed her mind, and the rest, as they say, is history.

Like McEntire, Mandrell first made her mark in country in the 1970s, but with a style more akin to that of the next decade: big, slick, and well packaged. In 1981 she became the first woman ever to be named Entertainer of the Year twice in a row by the Country Music Association. She was then sidelined by a serious car crash in 1984, but came back bigger than ever in 1986.

There was one rags-to-riches story in the 1980s that involved the country world tangentially, though white southern gospel singer Tammy Faye Bakker didn't exactly acquire her millions singing. Instead, it was the hellfire exhortations of her husband—Praise the Lord televangelist Jim Bakker—that brought the money rolling in, until he was caught with his hand in several cookie jars all at once and his empire and hers came crashing down around them.

The 1990s have proven to be different from the extravagant 1980s. Country has its own nationwide music channel (The Nashville Network) and video channel (Country Music Television), and a wide enough reach to embrace a host of subgenres ranging from country rock to bluegrass. It becomes harder and harder to pin down a style that defines, so to speak, mainstream country.

Country music is still almost entirely white, though. Nisha Jackson, a young African American social worker from Texas, won a Nashville Network talent contest in 1987. Her grand prize included an appearance on the *Grand Ole Opry* and a record release. Her powerful voice won wide acclaim and her record, *Alive and Well*, made it to the country charts, but record company executives said Nisha wasn't "country enough." "Try pop," they told her. Today she's still trying country, but she doesn't have high hopes.

Except in its continuing resistance to people of color, however, country as a whole continues to move ever further from its beginnings among working-class and poor whites. A surprising number of its younger stars were born into the genre. Rosanne Cash, for instance is the daughter of the Man in Black, Johnny Cash, and her stepsister Carlene Carter is the daughter of June Carter (herself a second-generation country star). Pam Tillis' father was the late Mel Tillis, and Shelly West's mother the late Dottie West. Others,

like the blues-influenced Mary-Chapin Carpenter, and the young bluegrass fiddler Alison Krauss, are coming from higher and higher up in the nation's social strata.

Whether there's a connection between country's changing demographics and its increasing tolerance of unconventional sexuality is a provocative question, and one for which the history books provide no easy answer. That tolerance, however, was almost tested to its limits (so far) in the 1990s by a new Canadian star, the cheerfully androgynous k.d. lang.

Lang was a Patsy Cline fan to start with, calling her band the reclines and singing Patsy's

Above: *Barbara Mandrell is one of the most versatile instrumentalists—male or female—in country music today.* **Left, top:** *One of the most intellectual of country stars, Texas folkabilly poet and novelist Nanci Griffith has a long list of acclaimed recordings to her credit. She has recorded with such notables as banjo whiz Béla Fleck (**Once in a Very Blue Moon**, 1985).* **Left, bottom:** *Third-generation country royalty, Carlene Carter is the daughter of June Carter, the granddaughter of Maybelle Carter, and the stepdaughter of Johnny Cash. As the story goes, she was taught to play the guitar at age ten by none other than Carl Perkins. Her latest album was* **Little Love Letters** *(1993).*

songs in a style as close to Patsy's as she could. But lang was far too creative to make a career out of imitation, and before long she had single-handedly created a new country genre that could be called country punk.

And lang is also a lesbian. She had never concealed the fact—her crewcut and wardrobe strongly suggested it, in fact—but she didn't admit it in public

Mary-Chapin Carpenter

Down at the Twist and Shout

What is the role of country music in a society that left the agrarian age more than one hundred years ago? Where are we headed, economically and personally, today? Mary-Chapin Carpenter (b. 1958) captures the essence of our time and place today through lyrics about ghost towns and gone-but-not-forgotten loves. In a society riddled with divorce and disenfranchisement, her music pays homage to the past, without resentment or indictment. Her music bears all the signs of a changing society, redefining the role of country music by speaking to the needs of women and men today.

Mary-Chapin Carpenter, whose music reveals a strong connection to "average" people, was not raised in an average family. Her mother, Bowie, worked at a private school while raising Mary-Chapin and her three sisters. Her father, Chapin, was an executive at *Life* magazine. These extraordinary, intelligent people were able to balance the comparatively luxurious life they led with the realities of the rest of the world, keeping Mary-Chapin and her sisters in touch with the struggles of the less fortunate. Through travel and a strong education, the Carpenter children gained a compassionate and informed view of the world.

In 1969 Chapin Carpenter was assigned to the Asian edition of *Life*, so the family left their home in Princeton, New Jersey, and moved to Japan. After two years abroad, Mary-Chapin and her family resettled in Washington, D.C. Back in the United States, Mary-Chapin attended the Taft Prep School in Connecticut. After graduation from Taft, she attended Brown University, where she received a Bachelor of Arts in American Civilization. By 1983 she had moved back to Washington, D.C., trying her hand at live performance while working during the day as an administrative assistant with a Washington-based philanthropic group. Carpenter's first few years back in D.C. were spent getting over shyness and general

With her cosmopolitan upbringing, Mary-Chapin Carpenter brought a refreshingly broad sensibility to contemporary country.

stage fright while friends and colleagues ambitiously promoted her songs to local radio stations.

Finally, in 1987, she signed with CBS Records and recorded her debut album, *Hometown Girl*, with friend and coproducer John Jennings in Jennings' basement. Although

Mary-Chapin was now signed with a major label, the next two years were profitless. She held on to her day job while touring when possible, always lugging equipment around in her car.

The star treatment from CBS Records did not begin until 1990, when Carpenter received a standing ovation at the 1990 CMA awards ceremony for her performance of "You Don't Know Me (I'm the Opening Act)." With this honor also came a bus and crew to move all the equipment around for her and the members of the band.

Mary-Chapin finally hit the top in 1991 with the release of her single "Down at the Twist and Shout," which deservedly brought her the prized Grammy award for best country vocal performance by a female. Her fourth album, *Come On Come On*, went platinum; songs like "I Feel Lucky" and "He Thinks He'll Keep Her" have made Mary-Chapin Carpenter and her music an institution. Carpenter's 1994 release, *Stones in the Road,* was a critical and commercial success, adding to her growing reputation as a major force in country music singing/songwriting.

A folk musician by nature, Carpenter has brought country music full circle. The term "country" has been used for the last eighty years to point out the difference between city and the rural folk. Now that folk music is again being accepted into the realm of country, the audience for country music is defying regional and educational boundaries.

—A.H.

until an interviewer for the national gay publication *The Advocate* asked her if she was in 1992. The jury is still out on whether or not it made a difference to country audiences, because k.d. fell in love with pop-torch singing almost immediately after the *Advocate* interview and walked away from country, at least for the time being.

A great deal has changed for country women since the Carters made their rickety way to Bristol. The 1995 Academy of Country Music Awards ceremony honored women in many categories, conferring the Country Pioneer award on Loretta Lynn and Country Entertainer of the Year award on then-forty-year-old Reba McEntire. An even more telling illustration of country women's increasing power and freedom, perhaps, was the fact that one of the three hosts of the ceremony was the two-time unwed mother Tanya Tucker, and that Naomi Judd won a stunning ovation by mentioning unmarried daughter Wynonna's new baby. Most important of all, however, is the fact that there are more women involved in the business and production ends of country than ever before.

But the awards ceremony also revealed some things that have not changed—yet. None of the women on stage had ever admitted publicly to having had an abortion. All were white; there are still no African American women country stars, though country music continues to borrow from African American music. That said, there is a major new star who is of Native American ancestry: Shania Twain, the Canadian-born singer who won the 1996 Grammy for best country album of the year (*The Woman in Me*). Born into severe poverty, Twain is descended from the Ojibway tribe.

Twain also offers a sharp contrast in style to her more demure country music forerunners, such as

Left: *A fresh breeze from the north, Canadian-born k.d. lang, one of Patsy Cline's biggest fans, smashed icons left and right during her short but spectacular country career.* **Below:** *After trying out several musical styles (jazz, rock, R&B, and pop), Pam Tillis accepted her roots and turned to country in the 1980s. In the early 1990s she began a string of top-five hits, including "Mi Vida Loca" (#1 in 1995).*

Cindy Walker and Kitty Wells. Like Tanya Tucker, the beautiful Twain is as well-known for her onstage wardrobe—notably a variety of lacy bodices and tight-fitting miniskirts—as she is for her considerable vocal accomplishments.

So country women, who once had to be as respectable as Maybelle Carter, can now be as wild as Tanya Tucker without necessarily risking their careers. And even if traveling the road toward liberation means having to endure the new kinds of challenges that accompany new levels of tolerance, women have become too powerful a force in country to let such things deter them from reaching the end of their journey.

Chapter Five

Bluegrass and Western Swing

Two Faces of Country

by Chris Seymour

A musician who's died and gone to heaven is getting a tour of the place, and her jaw drops every time she sees a dead hero. "Is that really Bessie Smith?" she asks her guide. "Is that actually Caruso?" Finally, she comes upon a white-haired man with sideburns and a huge Stetson hunched over a mandolin in front of the grandest mansion she's yet seen. "That can't be!" she exclaims. "Isn't he still...?" "No," replies her guide. "That's God—he just *thinks* he's Bill Monroe."

Above: *Seen here in 1925, bluegrass founder Bill Monroe (right) had a stormy musical partnership with his brother, Charlie (left), that started in their youth on their father's farm in Rosine, Kentucky.*
Right: *The Monroe Brothers' repertoire drew heavily on the white blues of country music's first superstar, Jimmie Rodgers (left, pictured with humorist Will Rogers).*

While mandolinist Bill Monroe doesn't pretend that he's all-knowing or all-powerful, he does claim credit as the creator of the sound that later became known as bluegrass (after the name of his band, the Blue Grass Boys). Likewise, Bob Wills, certainly the most popular western swing band leader ever, was inducted into the Country Music Hall of Fame as the inventor of the genre. Neither claim is completely off base, but neither is completely true.

Bluegrass and western swing are two branches that diverged from the star-singer course that country music had taken by the 1940s, and they are still alive and well today, if less lucrative entertainment product than mainstream country. Different as they sound from each other, western swing and bluegrass have a fair amount in common. Both styles are descended from the fiddle-dominated old-time string-band music played for square dances throughout the South from before the Revolutionary War through at least the 1920s, and the fiddle continues to play a leading role in each. Both are ensemble music, although, as in dixieland jazz, individuals take solos. Both have father figures (Wills for western swing and Monroe for bluegrass), and controversies abound regarding how much credit those figures should get for the creation of their respective genres. And, like the rest of country music—and American popular music in general—they both owe heavy debts to African American music.

American popular music has evolved as the result of a series of explosions of African and African American influences into European and European-American music. One of the earliest of these explosions was the nineteenth-century melding of African-descended rhythms and instrumentation (particularly the banjo) into the fiddle-dominated Scottish-Irish-English music that southern rural Americans danced to. Then, after the turn of the twentieth century, a second explosion, the blues—particularly its guitar and vocal styles—influenced country music. "Hillbilly" and "race"—the segregated recording categories OKeh's Ralph Peer (he switched to Victor later on) and other northern record company talent scouts used in the 1920s—

were arbitrary and inaccurate labels. There were black string bands playing square-dance music and white singers performing blues numbers they had learned from black entertainers. Jimmie Rodgers, the Blue Yodeler, was only the most famous example of the latter.

Indeed, a black man was one of the most important early influences on Bill Monroe. Arnold Schultz was a black virtuoso fiddler and guitarist who mined coal by day and played at local dances by night. Bill played backup at some of those dances in his teens, and Schultz's playing had a heavy impact on the young musician. Monroe's mother, born Malissa Vandiver, was a second major influence. She played fiddle, harmonica, and accordion and sang, inculcating a love for music in her son before she died when he was ten years old. Ironically, the bluegrass genre Monroe went on to found has been dominated by men, with women like fiddler/singer Alison Krauss only recently making headway in the scene, and is almost exclusively white—with some country fans seeking cultural refuge in bluegrass when black-rooted rock and roll began to penetrate country in the 1950s. But the fans who turned to bluegrass when artists like Marty Robbins, George Hamilton, and Johnny Cash electrified their instruments, were, in fact, listening to a relatively new musical form that also had strong black roots.

Bill's choice of instrument was dictated by his older brothers, Birch and Charlie, who wouldn't let him play guitar or fiddle but forced him instead to take up the mandolin (at the time almost exclusively used for backup). Bill was the youngest of six children, born on a farm in Ohio County near Rosine, in western Kentucky. He was shy and withdrawn and afflicted with poor eyesight. When his brothers handed him the mandolin it became the channel for all his frustrations. Although he dutifully played rhythm for the family's musical gatherings—and for Schultz and for his uncle, Pen Vandiver, a fiddler at local dances—he also began developing the mandolin as a lead instrument. Bill wanted to make the mandolin sing like his Uncle Pen's fiddle, but he also wanted to incorporate some of the blues sound he was hearing from Schultz and other black singers

Some white listeners, prejudiced against black music, sought solace in bluegrass when country stars like Johnny Cash went electric in the 1950s. They were unaware that bluegrass' black roots were as deep as rock and roll's.

and musicians who worked as laborers in the area. He also listened carefully to the outpourings of Jimmie Rodgers, who was then taking the southern airwaves by storm. In this fashion, Monroe developed a complex, driving, yet sensitive sound that revolutionized the way the instrument is played.

Bill went to live with Uncle Pen when his father died, but left home and joined his brothers in East Chicago in 1929. The Depression had hit the rural South long before the stock market crash, and his two brothers had gone north to look for work. Bill got a day job at the Sinclair oil refinery and worked there through the early 1930s, sometimes supporting his

brothers when they were out of work. Nights and weekends, Birch, Charlie, and Bill worked as a trio for dances and on area radio stations. Then they got hired as exhibition dancers with the touring unit of the WLS *National Barn Dance*, then the premier hillbilly music program. Through the contacts they made on tour came the opportunity in 1934 to say goodbye forever to the oil refinery: an offer to do a radio show in Shenandoah, Iowa. Birch wasn't ready to take the risk and stayed at Sinclair. So Charlie and Bill went on KFNF as a duet.

There were numerous brother duets performing hillbilly music at the time, but the Monroe Brothers' sound already had distinctive elements that would later be central to bluegrass. They sang in higher keys than their contemporaries, with Bill's tenor harmony producing the high, lonesome sound that would become the hallmark of classic bluegrass singers. Charlie's bass runs on the guitar and Bill's intricate, blues-inflected mandolin work were a striking accompaniment to the singing. And they played

faster than almost anybody else, giving their music extra punch. From 1934 to 1938 they moved from station to station in Omaha and then in the Carolinas.

Above: Bill Monroe and the Blue Grass Boys at WSM in 1940. Monroe (seated) eschewed the hillbilly image for his band (from left to right: fiddler Art Wooten, bassist Bill "Cousin Wilbur" Wesbrooks, and guitarist Clyde Moody), outfitting them instead in the riding breeches of the genteel Kentucky planter. Right: The jazzy fiddle sound of the onetime coal miner Kenny Baker, whom Monroe called the "best fiddler in bluegrass," helped define the music.

They were growing in popularity and drawing ever-larger crowds. Starting in 1936, they recorded sixty songs for Bluebird, Victor's hillbilly label. Then, in 1938, long-simmering tensions and rivalry came to a head. The Monroes quarreled and went their separate musical ways.

Charlie, who had been the leader of the duo, kept the recording contract and was initially more successful than his younger brother. Bill advertised in the newspapers for musicians to form a new band and eventually hired a young singer and guitar player, Cleo Davis, fiddler Art Wooten, and bass player/singer/comedian Amos Garen. Monroe parked his trailer in Greenville, North Carolina, behind a gas station, where he arranged to use a shed out back to rehearse his band, which he called the Blue Grass Boys, named for his home state. For a year and a half or so, they played on small radio stations and for small audiences while they developed their unique sound.

The addition of the bass was one innovation. Country musicians were just starting to use the instrument, already common in jazz, and it provided Monroe's band with the rhythmic grounding that allowed them to stay together while playing at breakneck speed. Christian songs were a big part of the hillbilly repertoire—Bill and Charlie had performed many of them—but the Blue Grass Boys took them one step further by adding the rich harmony of the black and white gospel quartets popular in the South in the 1920s and 1930s.

Spending their afternoons rehearsing in the garage, their evenings playing for small crowds at schoolhouses, and their mornings on the radio, the Blue Grass Boys developed into a cohesive unit. By

the fall of 1939, Monroe was ready to take them for a shot at the big time: the Grand Ole Opry.

The Blue Grass Boys wowed the Opry's Solemn Ol' Judge, George D. Hay, with a vastly speeded up version of Jimmie Rodgers' "Muleskinner Blues." Hay told Monroe, "If you ever leave the Opry, it'll be because you've fired yourself." Broadcast on WSM's 50,000 watts of clear-channel airwaves, the Opry exposed the band's evolving sound to a huge audience throughout eastern and central North America. When Davis, Wooten, and Garen each moved on, Monroe didn't have to advertise to find replacements; musicians were knocking his doors down.

Several of the fiddlers who played with the band in the next several years would help establish the bluegrass fiddle sound, which was jazzier as well as faster than traditional old-time dance fiddling. Howdy Forrester, who joined the band in early 1942, had lived in Texas from 1939 to 1941 and was influenced by the western swing style then burgeoning in the area. Forrester's successor, Chubby Wise, writer of the future bluegrass cliché "Orange Blossom Special," also had a swing background. So did

Flatt and Scruggs

Foggy Mountain Magicians

Guitarist Lester Flatt and banjo player Earl Scruggs were early disciples of Bill Monroe; they were also members of Monroe's Blue Grass Boys until 1948, when they split from Monroe's outfit to form the Foggy Mountain Boys. Because of their involvement with Monroe and their subsequent accomplishments, Flatt and Scruggs are among the founding fathers of bluegrass.

Lester Raymond Flatt was born on June 19, 1914, to a sharecropper family in Overton County, Tennessee. As a boy and as a young man he worked in Sparta, Tennessee, and Covington, Virginia. His love of the blues and his talents as a singer and guitar player later led to stints with a number of musical groups, including the Harmonizers in 1939 and the Happy Go Lucky Boys in 1941. Flatt spent 1943 and 1944 as the mandolin player and tenor vocalist with Charlie Monroe's Kentucky Pardners and then was recruited by Charlie's by-now-more-famous younger brother, Bill, to join the Blue Grass Boys in Nashville. By this time, Monroe had established himself at the Grand Ole Opry and was developing the music that become known as bluegrass.

Becoming a member of the Blue Grass Boys just after Lester Flatt, Earl Scruggs began to electrify Grand Ole Opry audiences with his virtuosic three-finger picking style. The banjo had traditionally been thought of as a comic instrument or a vaudeville prop because of its singular appearance and twangy sound. In the hands of Earl Scruggs, however, the instrument became a serious musical tool. Bill Monroe, who recognized brilliance when he saw it, often let the banjoist take lead parts.

Born on January 6, 1924, in Flint Hill, North Carolina, Earl Scruggs had a background much like Flatt's. Unlike Flatt, however, Scruggs was a prodigy: he had learned how to play the banjo before entering first grade. He came to love the blues as a child, and began plunking in the three-finger style common in his region of North Carolina. He

was a member of several bands as a young man, including the Carolina Wildcats and the Morris Brothers. He worked in textile mills in both North and South Carolina during World War II. Moving to Nashville in 1945, Scruggs played for a time on a WSM broadcast with "Lost" John Miller; when Miller quit the business, Scruggs was hired by Monroe and headed for the Opry stage.

Flatt and Scruggs stayed with Monroe for three years. In 1948 Scruggs left the Blue Grass Boys to carve out a career of his own, and Flatt accompanied him. Monroe considered their departure a betrayal, opening a wound that would never fully heal.

Scruggs cast the banjo in the lead role and began writing breakdowns for the instrument that imitated the swift, staccato fiddle style that had been popular in folk music for generations. They group began to be regularly featured on Virginia's WCYB radio station and began to record for Mercury Records. Their first instrumental release was "Foggy Mountain Breakdown," which has since become one of the most famous bluegrass compositions. By November 1950 they had moved to Columbia/CBS Records (where they stayed until the group split up), and in 1953 began appearing in a regular slot on WSM radio.

Touring almost constantly during the 1950s, the band became one of the premier bluegrass outfits in the United States by 1960. With their triumphant appearance at the 1960 Newport Folk Festival, the Foggy Mountain Boys were able to catch the folk revival wave that was sweeping the United States at that time and broaden its audience considerably. The band entered the cultural mainstream as authors of "The Ballad of Jed Clampett," the theme song for the television show *The Beverly Hillbillies*. Not long afterward, Flatt and Scruggs and the Foggy Mountain Boys became the first bluegrass combo to play Carnegie Hall.

In 1969 differences between the two musicians led to a breakup. Scruggs had begun tinkering with the sound

Banjo innovator Earl Scruggs and guitarist/singer Lester Flatt split with Monroe in 1948 and struck out on their own.

of bluegrass, which had remained virtually unchanged since 1948, adapting songs written by folk-rock writers as well as songs written by his three rock-oriented sons. Flatt disapproved, and the Foggy Mountain Boys broke up.

Scruggs went on to form the Earl Scruggs Review, incorporating drums, electric guitars, piano, and even synthesizer into the band's sound. Flatt formed the Nashville Grass, a pure bluegrass ensemble that released several successful albums.

Lester Flatt died of heart failure on May 11, 1979, in Nashville. He was visited in the hospital by Earl Scruggs—the two hadn't spoken to one another in ten years. Telling another visitor about it, Flatt said: "It came as quite a surprise and made me feel real good. We had a lot of good memories together."

—P.B.

consummate bluegrass fiddler Kenny Baker, who would join Monroe in the late 1950s through the early 1960s and again from 1968 through the mid-1980s.

In 1942 Monroe took a step that would prove fateful for the development of bluegrass: he hired his first banjo player, Dave "Stringbean" Akeman. Stringbean used the two-finger, clawhammer style. As was common for white banjo players of the era, he also did comedy skits in blackface with the group.

By popular demand, WSM's Artists' Service Department began sending the band out on the Opry's tent-show tours. By 1943 Monroe was able to start his own show, buying a nine-passenger Packard limousine with a roof rack (for the bass) and setting out with five trucks full of canvas and bleachers to barnstorm small towns around the South. The band often drummed up interest by fielding a baseball team to challenge local sluggers. Before wartime shellac shortages and a musicians union dispute stopped record-making for several years, the Blue Grass Boys recorded a number of sides for Bluebird, including their showstopper, "Muleskinner Blues."

Nineteen forty-five was a crucial year in the evolution of the music that nobody yet called bluegrass. First, guitarist and lead singer Lester Flatt joined the Blue Grass Boys. He wrote several songs with Monroe, added seamless vocal harmonies, and played guitar with the "Lester Flatt G-run" at the end of phrases that has come to define backup guitar in bluegrass. Flatt thought Stringbean's banjo slowed the band down and was dubious about the banjo's role in the music, so he was pleased when Akeman left the group. But the

Flatt and Scruggs and the Foggy Mountain Boys were the first bluegrass band to play at Carnegie Hall. A testament to the powerful influence of television, these talented musicians are probably best known for writing "The Ballad of Jed Clampett," the theme from **The Beverly Hillbillies.**

banjo player Monroe auditioned as Akeman's replacement changed Flatt's mind about the instrument.

Born on a farm near Flint Hill, in North Carolina, Earl Scruggs played the three-finger banjo style common in the area. The way he played it, however, was anything but common. North Carolina string band leaders like Charlie Poole and Snuffy Jenkins, probably influenced by black ragtime banjo pickers, had played the banjo "guitar style" in the 1920s, with thumb, forefinger, and middle finger. Scruggs took the technique to another level, picking out the melody and surrounding it with a shower of syncopated notes. And he was able to pick as fast as the Blue Grass Boys played.

Monroe hired Scruggs on the spot. The banjo wizard brought the house down at his first Opry performance, and the instrument became a defining element of bluegrass music forever.

The three years Monroe, Flatt, and Scruggs were together were golden. Flatt wrote songs such as "Will You Be Loving Another Man?" and the band went to town playing them, showcasing a new jazz-ensemble style that featured each instrument in a solo break. In the back seat of the limousine on the way to gigs, Monroe, Flatt, and Scruggs would work out arrangements of old songs from Bill's youth, like "Little Maggie," another bluegrass standard-to-be. That night, the band would dazzle audiences with the new material. Flatt, with his genial, casual stage presence, took on emcee duties for the group and Scruggs often soloed after every verse (audiences went wild over his banjo playing).

The band recorded twenty-eight songs for Columbia in 1946 and 1947, although only a few were released while the three were still together. One was Monroe's "Blue Moon of Kentucky," a waltz that Elvis Presley would later speed up and make into one of his early hits.

In 1948, exhausted by a grueling tour schedule, tired of taking orders from Monroe, and wanting to earn the serious money they could make as bandleaders rather than as employees, Flatt and Scruggs left the Blue Grass Boys. With Blue Grass Boys alumni fiddler Jimmy Shumate and bassist Cedric Rainwater, along with singer/guitarist Mac

Wiseman (who would later play with Monroe), Flatt and Scruggs founded the Foggy Mountain Boys. That spring they went on the air in Bristol, Virginia, over WCYB, which would become the country's premier bluegrass station. Already well known, they generated sacks of fan mail and requests for personal appearances, drawing hundreds to shows around the region.

They recorded for Mercury from 1948 to 1950, cutting classics like "Roll in My Sweet Baby's Arms" and "Foggy Mountain Breakdown," which Warren Beatty used as the theme for his 1967 film, *Bonnie and Clyde.*

Scruggs kept innovating on the banjo. In 1951 he started retuning his strings in mid-song to change keys and achieve a new sound. Probably to distinguish themselves from the Blue Grass Boys, Flatt and Scruggs never gave the mandolin much prominence: Curly Seckler sang superb tenor harmony, but, he recalls, just "held the mandolin," which was virtually inaudible. The Dobro, a Hawaiian-style guitar with a metal resonator, as played by Buck "Uncle Josh" Graves, was anything but inaudible. The first bluegrass Dobro player, Graves developed a highly syncopated style that resembled Scruggs' banjo style.

Monroe resented the departure of his right-hand man and his star banjo player, and he resented the consequent competition even more. For years he prevailed on WSM to keep Flatt and Scruggs' band from a regular slot on the Opry. But in 1955, over Bill's objections, the Foggy Mountain Boys won a coveted spot on the Opry roster.

During the previous ten years, bluegrass had become an established genre. Monroe wasn't flattered by the imitation, but the new sound had had such an impact that numerous country musicians had picked up their mandolins and banjos, hiked up their pitch and speed, and begun making music in the style of the Blue Grass Boys.

In 1947 the Clinch Mountain Boys, led by Carter Stanley and his brother, Ralph, released a version of the horse race song "Molly and Tenbrooks," arranged almost exactly as the Blue Grass Boys performed it. Ralph played three-finger banjo, and mandolinist Pee Wee Lambert sang a high Monroe-like

lead. The same year, former Opry performers the Bailey Brothers and the Happy Valley Boys, led by mandolinist Charlie Bailey and guitarist Danny Bailey, recorded "Rattlesnake Daddy Blues," which sounded quite similar to "Muleskinner Blues." Their instrumental "Happy Valley Special" showcased each band member, just as "Blue Grass Special" did for the Blue Grass Boys.

The Stanleys went on to carve out a niche as the most old-fashioned of the first generation of bands playing the music that fans and deejays began calling bluegrass sometime around 1950. Carter wrote many of the group's songs himself, penning religious and secular numbers that ached with loneliness, and Ralph's high nasal harmony stood out, becoming almost a

Left: *Brothers Ralph (left) and Carter Stanley earned Monroe's enmity by closely emulating the bluegrass legend's sound, but by doing so they helped cement the genre.* **Bottom:** *Like the Stanleys, the Bailey Brothers—Charlie (front, left) and Dan (front, right)—initially borrowed heavily from the Blue Grass Boys.* **Below:** *After Carter Stanley died in 1966, Ralph (center) continued playing with his band, the Clinch Mountain Boys.*

the rearranged tune. Other former Blue Grass Boys went on to front their own successful bands, including Mac Wiseman and Sonny Osborne, who played with Monroe at the age of fifteen and teamed up with his older brother, Bobby, in 1953 to form a band that became regulars on the Opry.

When rockabilly hit in the early 1950s, some bluegrass performers went electric, but others—in particular Flatt and Scruggs, Monroe, and the Stanleys—stuck with their

lead voice. When the Clinch Mountain Boys signed with Columbia in 1949, Monroe moved to Decca, refusing to stay with a label that recorded artists he regarded as copycats.

Don Reno, the banjoist who had replaced Scruggs in the Blue Grass Boys, left in 1949 to form the Tennessee Cutups with singer-guitarist Red Smiley. Reno was a musical innovator on the level of Scruggs and Monroe: he added jazzy sounds borrowed from the electric and steel guitars to his banjo playing, presaging the "progressive bluegrass" sound that developed in the early 1970s. Reno was also the first to play lead guitar with a flat pick, influencing flat-pick guitar hero Doc Watson. Reno was the cocreator of what is probably the best-known banjo tune ever, "Feuding Banjoes," which—rearranged and performed by Eric Weissberg as "Dueling Banjos"—was the theme from the 1971 film *Deliverance*. Reno and Arthur "Guitar Boogie" Smith had recorded the song in 1955, and subsequent to the film soundtrack's release won a lawsuit against Warner Brothers that established their authorship of

Above, left: *Partisans of banjo player Don Reno (pictured with his band, the Tennessee Buddies) credit him as much as Scruggs with creating the bluegrass banjo sound.* Above: *The Country Gentlemen were among the first bands to apply bluegrass instrumentation to pop songs.*

roots. These purist performers became favorites of the urban-based folk music revival, whose partisans demanded all-acoustic instrumentation. Appearing in large halls and folk festivals around the country in the late 1950s and 1960s, the bluegrass founders attracted a second generation of musicians to their sound. Bill Keith was one of these young adherents. Captivated by the bluegrass

music on tap at the Hillbilly Ranch (a club in Boston's notorious "combat zone") in the 1950s and 1960s, Keith helped form the Charles River Boys, one of the first northern bluegrass bands. He went beyond "Scruggs picking," developing the "chromatic" banjo style, in which he actually hit every note in the melody. He worked briefly with the Blue Grass Boys in 1963.

The Country Gentlemen are the most important of the second generation bands. Formed in 1957, they pioneered a sound between traditional bluegrass and the emerging "progressive" bluegrass sound. They gave the music a second (or third or fourth) infusion of jazz, and drew on everything from Bob Dylan to vintage country songs for repertoire. Anchoring what would develop into the strongest urban bluegrass scene in the country, in the Washington, D.C. area, the band's early lineup included singer/guitarist Charlie Waller, singer/mandolinist John Duffey, and banjo player Eddie Adcock. The Country Gentlemen were among the first bluegrass bands to build their repertoire by listening to classic 78rpm recordings of country singers, such as Molly O'Day's "Poor Ellen Smith."

The band has functioned like the Blue Grass Boys in incubating new talent, nurturing many of today's bluegrass lions. Adcock left in 1971 to found The Second Generation. Duffey left the same year to start the versatile and high-energy The Seldom Scene with Mike Auldridge, a hot Dobro player who had been heavily influenced by Uncle Josh Graves. Multi-instrumentalist Doyle Lawson played mandolin with the Country Gentlemen in the 1970s and now fronts Quicksilver, known even more for shining a cappella harmonies on gospel songs than for their undeniable instrumental virtuosity. Singer/mandolinist Ricky Skaggs, now a mainstream country star, worked with the Clinch Mountain Boys from 1970 to 1973 before joining the Country Gentlemen in 1974 and hooking up with banjo player J.D. Crowe's New South in 1975. New South also included innovative flat-picking guitarist Tony Rice and Dobro player Jerry Douglas.

Scruggs embraced the movement toward eclecticism in this period, but Flatt did not, and the pair split in 1969. Flatt founded the Nashville Grass, which he fronted until he died in 1979; Scruggs led the Earl Scruggs Revue, featuring his sons on electric instruments. Newgrass Revival, founded by singer/mandolinist Sam Bush in 1972, picked up on the electric trend Scruggs helped start. They were the first counterculture bluegrass band, sporting long hair (which earned them hassles from traditionalists) and incorporating long, free-form instrumentals a la modern jazz, Indian ragas, and Bay Area rock.

The "newgrass" movement launched instrumentalists like Newgrass Revival banjo wizard Béla Fleck and mandolin virtuoso David Grisman into new realms beyond bluegrass. But young traditionalists like Dudley Connell of the Johnson Mountain Boys, Ron Thomasson of the Dry Branch Fire Squad, and Lynn Morris of the Lynn Morris Band are reinvig-

Top: *Country Gentlemen mandolinist Cliff Waller kidded former Gent John Duffey (with guitar) about how long it was taking Duffey's new band to start performing: "What do you call yourselves, the Seldom Seen?" he asked. The name—changed to the Seldom Scene—stuck to this tight yet casual progressive band.* **Above:** *Earl Scruggs liked his sons' experiments with electric instruments and formed the Earl Scruggs Revue with them after he and Flatt split over musical differences in 1969.* **Left:** *Flatt (far right) kept his bluegrass pure with his band The Nashville Grass.*

orating the music's old roots. Heirs to Ralph and Carter Stanley, these bands are building their repertoires by mining old-time country music and writing new material in a traditional vein. The performers in these groups play their instruments well, even dazzlingly in some cases, but the instruments are always at the service of the songs, which they sing with feeling as well as technique.

Although it gets relatively little airplay on country music stations, bluegrass today is thriving, with avidly loyal fans thronging to the more than five hundred festivals around the United States and dozens more overseas. Looking back, Bill Monroe made up with his former bandmates years ago, accepting the role of bluegrass patriarch and regularly sharing festival stages with the likes of Ralph Stanley. Looking forward, Union Station, a bluegrass band fronted by Grammy Award–winning singer/fiddler Alison Krauss, was recently invited to join the Opry cast. The first bluegrass performers to become Opry regulars in decades, Union Station represents bluegrass' third generation; they grew up listening to second-generation bands like Doyle Lawson and Quicksilver and J.D. Crowe and the New South. With healthy doses of both tradition and innovation, the future of the music seems assured.

After the blues, the next African American musical eruption was jazz, coalescing in New Orleans around 1900 and becoming the base for much of mainstream American popular music by the 1920s. Bluegrass artists were emulating the jazz form when they took solos, but jazz had its most profound impact on country music through the creation in the 1930s of western swing, which pulled thousands onto dance floors throughout the West and Southwest in the pre– and post–World War II years. Western swing took from dixieland and big-band jazz an insistent dance beat, syncopation, blue notes, instrumentation (brass, string bass, electrified guitars), and an emphasis on improvisation and instrumental virtuosity.

Above: Bill Monroe (seen here performing at the Boston Garden in 1977) is still going strong at this writing, having put his eighty-fifth birthday behind him. Below: Banjo wizard Béla Fleck has moved from bluegrass to newgrass to an entirely new realm with his latest band, the Flecktones. Right: Many bluegrass fans pin their hopes for the future of the music on such young performers as fiddler/singer Alison Krauss, who won a Grammy in 1995.

If it hadn't been for a car crash on Highway 199 northwest of Fort Worth in April 1936, the story of western swing would have been a lot different. Singer Milton Brown, then the leader of Texas' most popular dance band, was killed in the accident, leaving the field to his friend, former bandmate, and rival bandleader, fiddler Bob Wills. Wills would go on to become the most successful western swing bandleader ever and leave an indelible mark on the way country music is played.

Brown met Wills not long after Wills had moved to Fort Worth from a farm in Hall County, west Texas, in 1929 looking for work (the same year Bill Monroe moved from Kentucky to Chicago for the same reason). Brown and Wills formed a band that went by several names, among them the Aladdin Laddies, and included Brown as lead singer, Wills on fiddle, and Herman Arnspiger on guitar. Wills, whose father and grandfathers were fiddlers (as were several aunts and uncles) grew up picking cotton with black workers. He brought to the group a large stock of old-time fiddle tunes and a love for the blues. Brown, who had lived in the city longer than Wills, had a hankering for up-to-date material; he used to learn the latest tunes at a friend's furniture store where records were also sold.

At the end of 1930, the band auditioned for W. Lee O'Daniel of the Burrus Mill and Elevator Company. O'Daniel committed the company to sponsoring the band on a small station, KFJZ, at 6 o'clock in the morning. Milton reworked a song by the Famous Hokum Boys, a black blues group featuring Big Bill Broonzy, as their theme song. The band, now called the Light Crust Doughboys and including Brown's brother Derwood on second guitar, went on the air promoting Burrus' Light Crust Flour.

The response was tremendous—mail poured into the station and flour sales shot up. O'Daniel started to get involved in the band, moving the show to a more powerful station at prime time—midday—and becoming the host of the show. O'Daniel wrote sentimental family songs for the band and inserted his poetry into the program. The band recorded a couple of songs for Victor in 1932 using the name Fort Worth Doughboys (they may have feared

With his band the Texas Playboys, Bob Wills (left) mixed frontier fiddling and uptown swing jazz to forge an irresistibly danceable music that came to be called western swing. Here he appears on the radio show **Rhythm Roundup.**

O'Daniel wouldn't approve of the risqué lyrics to "Nancy Jane," another Broonzy number they covered). The Doughboys played for hundreds on Saturday nights at the Crystal Springs dance hall outside of town. But dance halls didn't fit with the wholesome image O'Daniel wanted for Light Crust Flour, and in the beginning of 1932 he ordered the band to stop playing dances. Brown rebelled; he quit the band, taking along his brother, Derwood. He

recruited his own group, which he called Milton Brown and His Musical Brownies.

Brown wanted a more sophisticated sound, so he started by building a bigger rhythm section than the Doughboys had had: Ocie Stockard on tenor banjo, Wanna Coffman on bass, and Derwood on guitar. Later he would recruit piano player Fred "Papa" Calhoun, and fiddler Cecil Brower, both of whom could play hot, improvised jazz solos. Much of the Brownies' repertoire was popular "race music" (blues and jazz) of the day, such as "Easy Ridin' Papa" and W.C. Handy's "St. Louis Blues." (Their affinity for African American music did not stop the Brownies from recording at least one stereotype-laden minstrel song, "You're Bound to Look Like a Monkey When You're Old," for Decca in 1935.)

The Brownies' most innovative instrumentalist was steel guitarist Bob Dunn. He was probably the first country musician to record with an electrified

Tommy Duncan's silky singing helped make Wills' "New San Antonio Rose" an international hit in 1940; Duncan stayed with the Playboys for fifteen years, until Wills fired him for complaining about Wills' drunkenness.

guitar, a technique he reportedly learned from a black musician on the boardwalk at Coney Island, New York. When he auditioned for the band in the fall of 1934, he borrowed a National Steel guitar from Wanna Coffman, magnetized the strings, wedged a pickup under them, and started playing explosive solos that practically popped dancers' eyes out. The guitar playing of the hard-drinking Dunn has been compared to that of legendary European jazzman Django Reinhardt, who began recording three years after Dunn.

The band started playing dates all over Texas and recorded for Bluebird in 1934 and for Decca in 1935 and 1936. Before he crashed on the Jacksboro highway north of Fort Worth on April 13, 1936, Brown had been scheming to boost the band's popularity outside the state and really make it big. After Milton's death, Derwood tried to hold the band together, but two of its stars, Dunn and fiddler Cliff Bruner, formed their own, frequently overlapping, bands, the Vagabonds and the Texas Wanderers, respectively. Piano player Moon Mullican brought his rollicking barrelhouse style, patterned after that of black juke-joint players, to the Wanderers in 1937 and would later go on to play for the Houston-based Blue Ridge Playboys.

Meanwhile, Wills' own band, the Texas Playboys, was starting to take off in Tulsa, Oklahoma. The band had had a rough start: O'Daniel had fired Wills in 1933 for getting drunk and failing to show up for broadcasts one too many times. Several of the Doughboys had left with Bob, including singer Tommy Duncan, who stayed with Wills until 1948, and Wills' brother, Johnnie Lee, who played tenor banjo. Then O'Daniel muscled Wills off the air in Oklahoma City and slapped him with an ultimately unsuccessful lawsuit for billing the band as "formerly the Light Crust Doughboys."

But by 1935 the Playboys were packing halls six nights a week playing with more of a frontier tinge than the Brownies, provided by Wills and his family fiddle tunes. It was that sound that attracted the Brunswick Record Corporation's Art Satherly, an Englishman who loved American folk music. When Wills showed up in Dallas for a recording session in September, though, he had something else in mind than a few old-time hoedowns. He had hired Al

Stricklin, who played piano Papa Calhoun–style, and steel guitarist Leon McAuliffe, who was a strong musician, if not in Dunn's league. These additions were fine with Satherly, but he blanched at the use of horns (sax and trombone). He said mixing horns and strings would never sell—and he didn't like Wills' minstrel-style patter and shouts of enthusiasm, either. Asked to keep it down, Wills demanded of Satherly, "You hired Bob Wills didn't you? You want Bob Wills, you get Bob Wills, and I talk and sing and say what I want when I feel like it."

As it turned out, Wills' records outsold those of all other artists on Brunswick's Vocalion label in 1936, including jazz great Louis Armstrong, pianist Fats Waller, and singing cowboy Gene Autry. By 1940 Wills had built a fifteen-piece big band that swung with the best of them, playing music no one could hear without wanting to get up and dance. But he might not have achieved national prominence had it not been for a single song. "San Antonio Rose," which Wills recorded in 1938, was an instrumental he wrote, reworking his own "Spanish Two-Step," a mariachi-influenced number. The Irving Berlin Company offered to publish the tune—with lyrics. Wills didn't like the words the company came up with, so trumpeter Everett Stover and other Playboys helped him write new ones. The band recorded it in April 1940 as "New San Antonio Rose," with Tommy Duncan's smooth vocals and without the fiddle or steel guitar that marked a song as "hillbilly." The song was a crossover hit for the Playboys. The song also boosted the career of Bing Crosby, whose later recording of it was the crooner's second million-seller.

"San Antonio Rose" has been recorded by dozens of artists the world over and was even broadcast from space to an audience of millions in 1969 as sung by Apollo 12 astronauts Charles Conrad and Alan Bean. "New San Antonio Rose" also propelled Wills into the movies; he and a subset of the band appeared in *Take Me Back to Oklahoma*, a B western starring Tex Ritter, in 1940. This was the first of thirteen full-length westerns—and two musical shorts—featuring the Playboys from 1940 to 1946.

World War II interrupted Wills' musical and movie career. After the bombing of Pearl Harbor,

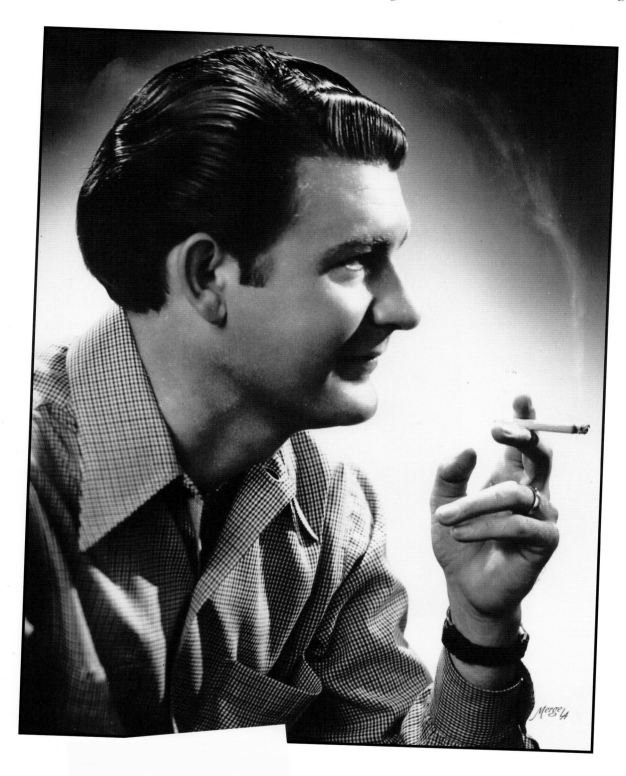

Bandleader Tex Williams was ahead of his time— and perhaps a little hypocritical—when he recorded "Smoke, Smoke, Smoke," a song about the hazards of tobacco for smokers and their friends.

for him at Camp Howze, near Gainesville, Texas. He was eventually discharged as physically unfit in July 1943 and moved with his fifth wife, Betty, to the San Fernando Valley in southern California, where he regrouped his band.

Southern California was primed for an explosion of western music, swollen as the region was with migrants from Oklahoma and Texas who were stationed in California or had moved there during the Depression or with the opening of wartime defense plants. Entrepreneur Foreman Phillips opened a huge new dance hall, the Venice Pier Ballroom, to cater to this crowd and hired Oklahoma fiddler Donnell Clyde "Spade" Cooley to lead a dance band there.

Cooley's band (which became a twenty-five-piece ensemble in 1950 with the addition of a string section) was slicker than the Playboys, and their solos were more orchestrated, less improvised. Cooley was joined by Illinois-born singer Sollie Paul "Tex" Williams, and the outfit drew record crowds—up to ten thousand—to Venice Pier, as did Wills' reorganized band. Cooley proclaimed himself "King of Western Swing," finally naming the sound that Brown and Wills had pioneered. Cooley's biggest hit, "Shame on You," recorded in Hollywood in 1944 for Columbia, was the first song he cut as a bandleader. A hard drinker with a violent streak, Cooley was tried for rape in 1945. He was acquitted of that charge but convicted of murdering his second wife, Ella Mae, in 1961. He died of a heart attack while on release from prison to do a benefit concert in 1969. Williams went on to front his own band, Western Caravan, in 1946 and recorded the ahead-of-its-time "Smoke, Smoke, Smoke" for Capitol in 1947, which detailed the difficulties of dealing with smokers.

Wills' band was smaller after the war, and musicians (especially horn players, who were then in short supply) cycled through the group rapidly. But singer Tommy Duncan and several other prewar Playboys had returned to the band, and Wills was still going strong, making movies and filling dance halls throughout the West. The band recorded sixteen-inch radio show transcription records for the Oakland, California, based Tiffany Company, which sold them to stations around the country.

one band member after another left for the armed services or defense work. Wills was initially deferred from service to finish a film project and then joined the war effort in December 1942, a few months shy of thirty-eight, the cutoff age. He caught flak for his fancy Cadillac and the sacks of fan mail that arrived

Spade Cooley

King of Western Swing

Donnell Clyde Cooley (1910–1969), known to his fans and friends as "Spade," was a seminal figure in the history of country music; he was also one of the few members of the country music community to be tried for and found guilty of murder.

Spade Cooley and His Orchestra, one of the most popular western swing bands on the West Coast during the early to mid-1940s, were best known for their stylish costumes and slick orchestrations. Thousands of fans regularly showed up for their beachside concerts.

Spade's first solo recordings were produced by Columbia in late 1944, and included the most popular song of his career, "Shame on You." The song became so popular with audiences that Bob Wills and His Texas Playboys, the most popular western swing band (and Spade's competitor), played and recorded it many times. Two films were made about Cooley in the wake of that song: *Spade Cooley, King of Western Swing* (produced by Warner Brothers) and *Spade Cooley and His Orchestra* (produced by Universal).

In 1945, at the height of his career, Spade was married for a second time (this time to a woman named Ella Mae). That year, he was accused of rape but was acquitted for lack of physical evidence.

After his contract with Columbia expired, Cooley and his clan moved to RCA Victor, where they recorded from 1947 to 1950. He then signed with Decca, where he stayed until 1955.

It was during this time that he began starring in his own television series. One of his last recordings for Decca was a song he had written (for a female voice) called "You Clobbered Me."

With his music and television career finished by 1958 (due to ebbing interest in him and in western swing in general), Cooley tried his hand at business. A large venture called Water Wonderland, which was to be a water-filled recreation park carved out of the Mojave Desert, was his last business undertaking as a free man.

Things fell apart rapidly for Cooley after he left the limelight. His marriage to Ella Mae had become intolerable because of his alcoholism as well as her constant bragging to acquaintances of an affair she was supposedly having with longtime Cooley confidant Roy Rogers.

On the night of April 3, 1961, Spade, strung out on pills and alcohol, began beating his wife. Then he forced their fourteen-year-old daughter to watch as he finished beating, and then burned, the unfortunate Ella Mae to death. Cooley's manager, a woman by the name of Bobbie Bennett, arrived at the house soon after and found Spade standing over the almost completely unrecognizable remains of Ella Mae.

Within the year, Spade was convicted of first-degree murder and spent the rest of his days in the Vacaville state prison, near Oakland, California. On November 23, 1969, just three months before he was to be paroled, Spade died of a heart attack.

—A.H.

Spade Cooley, who called himself the King of Western Swing, kept the huge Venice Pier ballroom in Santa Monica filled during the Second World War, when many dance halls were shutting down because gasoline rationing kept people close to home.

Wills also tried in these years to build up a dance circuit close to home, first in southern California and then in Sacramento, that would be big enough to support him and the band with less touring; he wanted to be able to drive home after each night's gig. But bad investments and questionable business decisions pushed him to keep making the kind of big money he could earn only on the road. Road trips in turn fueled his episodic heavy drinking, which was less of a problem when he was at home. He would sometimes fail to make performances, cutting the earnings of his band members and putting extra pressure on his veteran singer, Tommy Duncan, who had to face the fans and carry on with the show when Bob was blotto. Tensions built between the two, and finally Wills fired Duncan in September 1948 after hearing the singer sarcastically wonder aloud if his boss would show that night. Shortly afterward, fiddler Joe Holley, piano player Millard Kelso, and original Brownie Ocie Stockard left to join Tommy Duncan and His Western All Stars. Duncan's band was short-lived, lasting a little over two years.

Back east in Nashville, Hank Thompson (from Waco, Texas) was building a dual career as leader of the western swing band the Brazos Valley Boys and as a singer and writer of clever honky-tonk songs (he penned the super-hit "The Wild Side of Life," best known for its first line, "I didn't know God made honky-tonk angels," in 1951). And as the rock and roll revolution exploded, western swing's influence was felt there, too. Elvis had listened to Bob Wills as a boy, and Bill Haley had himself been a western swing musician, leading a band called the Saddlemen (which he later renamed the Comets). Some of Haley's early rock and roll songs show continued swing influence, including "Blue Comet Blues" and "Dim, Dim the Lights."

Saddled with debts from an ill-fated resort venture, Wills kept playing as his health deteriorated. He ended a relatively dry spell with a run at the Golden Nugget in Las Vegas in the late 1950s and early 1960s and began a two-year reunion with Duncan in 1960. He suffered his first heart attack in 1962 and a second in 1964, forcing him to give up his own band.

Bill Haley's band was called the Four Aces of Western Swing and later the Saddlemen before he remade himself as a rock and roller in the early 1950s and renamed the band the Comets.

But he still played dances, fronting for other bands, and recorded nearly one hundred tunes with session musicians from 1963 to 1969.

Interest in western swing had begun to wane in the late 1960s, but it was revived by Wills' induction into the Country Music Hall of Fame in 1968. Wills had never felt a part of country music and was surprised and overwhelmed by the honor. He had a crippling stroke in 1969 that partially paralyzed him and temporarily robbed him of his interest in music. He had recovered his interest in music by 1971, though he remained confined to a wheelchair. And at the end of 1973, Wills called together a bunch of former Playboys, including McAuliffe, Stricklin, and fiddler Johnny Gimble to record "For the Last Time," the coda to a recording career that had begun in 1929 and spanned more than 550 numbers. Merle Haggard, one of many country stars influenced by Wills, played fiddle on the recordings, and Wills himself led the first day's session from his wheelchair. That night, he had a stroke while sleeping and never regained consciousness. He died seventeen months later, on May 13, 1975.

music by grafting the popular sounds of hot jazz onto the same country dance music roots. The major irony is that both bluegrass and western swing owe such a great debt to African American music, yet there have been no prominent black western swing or bluegrass musicians and virtually no African Americans in either genre's audience.

Today, some western swing fans deride bluegrass—with its fast, high-pitched, percussive instrumentation—as "nervous music," while bluegrass artists tend to dislike swing's embrace of electricity. But a few musicians, such as banjoist Alan Carr and guitarist and mandolinist Joe Carr, are mixing the two. Formerly of the California-based bluegrass band Country Gazette, the pair is now teaching in the bluegrass music program at South Plains College in west Texas. During their time in the Lone Star State, the two bluegrass artists have acquired a love for swing music, and their latest album includes "Nancy Jane," the first song the Light Crust Doughboys recorded, as well as a couple of other numbers from the Bob Wills catalog; and even the bluegrass numbers on the album have the swingtime feel that fiddlers Howdy Forrester and Chubby Wise brought to the early editions of the Blue Grass Boys.

The Nashville establishment isn't overly fond of either genre, but with tens of thousands of devoted fans and scores of dedicated musicians who play their hearts out for the love of the music, bluegrass and western swing are clearly thriving branches on the venerable country tree.

Above: Asleep at the Wheel, led by guitarist Ray Benson (center), helped western swing find new audiences in the 1970s by fusing it with rock and roll. Below: The songs of country star George Strait reflect the influence of the western swing music he grew up with. He has recorded the Bob Wills standard "Right or Wrong."

Interest in the music continued to grow after the death of its most popular figure. In 1976 a Playboys reunion band played on the first *Austin City Limits* television program. Playboys alumni, along with vets like Hank Thompson, continue to play concerts, dances, and swing festivals in the Southwest. But western swing isn't a museum piece. Asleep at the Wheel, a rock-infused Western swing band led by Philadelphia-born guitarist Ray Benson, continues to bring western swing to younger rock listeners; there are third-generation bands playing the music in the Bay Area, Seattle, and the Southwest, including Fiddlers Two, featuring two brothers, Austin and Coleman Smith. The western swing amalgamation of old-time country music with blues and jazz has permeated much of mainstream country. Country star Ray Price, who was popular in the 1960s, used bluesy vocals and a heavily bowed fiddle, clearly showing his debt to Wills. More recently, George Strait released a swing album, *Right or Wrong* (1984), and proclaimed his conversion to the genre.

For genres that share roots in country dance music, blues and jazz, western swing and bluegrass

sound little alike, but that's hardly surprising. Bill Monroe and the other founders of bluegrass were looking back as much as forward, intentionally evoking the past. Even as they innovated, they were intensifying the old sounds of hillbilly dance music (rather than replacing them) and making many nostalgic references—to the old home place, the little white church, the aged parents, and so on. In contrast, Milton Brown, Bob Wills, and their followers were trying to create a modern

Merle Haggard

The Okie from California

Merle Haggard's enormous body of work is an impressive example of musical integrity, and his unwillingness to bend to the demands of commercialization has won him the allegiance of millions of fans and the admiration of his peers. In addition, his music is an important bridge between the roots of country music and the contemporary hybrids of country and rock. His unique expressiveness is personal, not commercially stylized. Listeners respond as much to his powerfully evocative singing as they do to his truthful lyrics. With his band, the Strangers, Merle Haggard continues to pump out his distinctive combination of swing, blues, and jazz that draws unerringly from the deep well of country's roots.

Born on April 6, 1937, in California, Haggard is the offspring of Depression-era "Okies" who blew West after quitting their farms in the Dust Bowl and settled in Oildale, near Bakersfield. His young life was troubled and included stints in juvenile homes and in the California State Prison at San Quentin (for burglary). He was in solitary confinement in San Quentin on his twenty-first birthday, an experience that was evidently painful enough to put an end to his youthful run of delinquency. Haggard recalled later that "I'm one guy...the prison system straightened out."

After he was released, Haggard returned to Bakersfield. In the early 1960s that city was called Nashville West because of its influential music scene that reveled in honky tonk and hard-edged country. Haggard began appearing as a backup guitarist at recording sessions and in bars in Bakersfield and Las Vegas. His association in 1962 with an enthusiastic Arkansan named Fuzzy Owen ultimately led to stardom.

Owen became Haggard's mentor and manager. In Owen's small studio Haggard recorded "Sing Me a Sad Song" and "All My Friends Are Gonna Be Strangers," both of which became hits. Their success led to offers from a

*Merle Haggard acknowleged his debt to western swing in 1970 when he recorded an album entitled A **Tribute to the Best Damn Fiddle Player in the World—Bob Wills.***

number of big record companies and Haggard signed with Capitol Records on the condition that he be allowed to continue his collaboration with Fuzzy Owen.

Haggard's success was meteoric: nearly every one of the songs he recorded for Capitol rose high on the charts, among them "I'm a Lonesome Fugitive" and "Today I Started Loving You Again." By 1968 he was one of country music's top stars and he had a fearsome blue-collar following, to whom he endeared himself completely with the songs "Okie From Muskogee" and the follow-up "The Fighting Side of Me."

Haggard was tagged as a spokesman for the nation's right wing, a role he never sought and did not want. Expectations that he would follow the two "fighting" songs with similarly patriotic numbers were frustrated when he instead returned to his main themes—the working man, the dashed lover, and the unfortunate prisoner. Haggard was prolific throughout the 1980s, releasing more than a dozen albums in that time (including *Poncho and Lefty*, with Willie Nelson, *Amber Waves of Grain*, *5:01 Blues*, and a handful of other others). The 1990s have seen both ups and downs for Haggard (he declared bankruptcy in 1993 and saw a five-volume tribute to him released on the Bear Family label in 1995), but he is as popular as ever with his fans and continues to tour.

—P.B.

Chapter Six

Let's Have a Party

Rockabilly

by William Spence

As is the case with most "original" American music—blues or jazz, for instance—rockabilly arose not in a sudden, overnight spurt, but gradually enough so that when it emerged as a recognizable strain of music it was difficult to say exactly how it had come to be. As with jazz, it was hard to say who had been the guiding light in rockabilly's development, although there were several people who no doubt saw themselves as its originators. And, finally, although rockabilly made possible the work of many future artists in country rock and is still being performed today—and since its birth has had practitioners in every generation—it had a golden era, the beginning and end of which coincided more or less with the beginning and end of the original Sun Records label and its associated recording studio, Sam's Memphis Recording Studio.

Left (from left to right): *Elvis Presley, Bill Black, Scotty Moore, and Sam Phillips were the founding fathers of the rockabilly sound. Black and Moore met playing for Doug Poindexter and His Starlite Wranglers, which recorded a Moore tune for Phillips at Sun. In 1954 Phillips introduced Black and Moore to Elvis, and a week later they all headed for the studio, where they recorded "That's All Right."* Below: *Sam Phillips' Sun Studio witnessed the birth of rockabilly and its prodigal son, Elvis Presley.* Bottom: *Carl Perkins (left) and Sam Phillips made rockabilly history with the Sun recording of "Blue Suede Shoes." Unfortunately, Perkins was unable to capitalize on the song's success.*

To say that Sam Phillips masterminded the sound or that Sun was the birthplace of rockabilly would be spurious; Phillips certainly guided several of the first rockabilly performers toward stardom, but this unique blend of American folk musics was already emerging around the South when he started capturing it in the studio. And while Sun Studio will always be legendary because of its association with Elvis Presley (whose first commercial recording was Sun Records No. 209, "That's All Right," a rockabilly number b/w his borderline-R&B version of the country ballad "Blue Moon of Kentucky"), scatter-shot entrepreneur Phillips' small complex of facilities was simply the main (though by no means sole) incubator where the rockabilly sound flourished for a brief while in the 1950s and early 1960s. Finally, as its name suggests, rockabilly is a combination of "hillbilly music" and rock and roll (or more accurately, rhythm and blues); therefore, the very concatenation itself indicates that a healthy number of collabora-

tors—however much they may have been unaware of it at the time—participated in furthering the evolution of the rockabilly sound.

From the music of the Appalachians and Ozarks, rockabilly inherited the European folk and sacred influences that had traveled across the Atlantic Ocean with the earliest settlers of the regions. Many of these elements, from the twangy guitar work to the folky vocal styling, unmistakably identify rockabilly as a variety of country music. In this regard, rockabilly is the stepchild of the traditional country music of such formative "hillbilly" legends as Gid Tanner and His Skillet Lickers, Uncle Dave Macon, the Carter Family, and Roy Acuff and His Crazy Tennesseans, to name a few. (Acuff may in fact have contributed a little something extra to rockabilly: sexually suggestive—and in some cases even explicit—lyrical content. As the frontman of Roy Acuff and the Bang Boys, Opry darling Acuff began his career as a singer of bawdy ditties.)

The truly defining aspects of rockabilly, however, are its up-tempo backbeat and bluesy progressions, both of which are derived from the music's blues parentage. The R&B and jump blues that Carl Perkins, Eddie Cochran, Gene Vincent, and other rockabilly greats may have listened to as they grew up aside, it was the energetically inclusive spirit of such pioneers as the Delmore Brothers, Jimmie Rodgers, and Bob Wills that foreshadowed rockabilly's unique flavor. Both Rodgers and Wills were curious and open-minded enough to incorporate in their music many of the dynamic sounds that they heard being played around them: in Rodgers' case vaudeville, operettas, and the blues he was exposed to in his tenure on the railroad, which took him across the southern United States, from one coast to the other; and in Wills' case, the heady mixture of polka, jazz, and the blues that he was exposed to growing up in Texas, a melting pot for several different strains of music from Central Europe, Mexico, Mississippi, and New Orleans, among others.

This is not to say that rockabilly was an evolving, complex, or progressive music; on the contrary, it was static, locked into a stylistic mold that was simplistic, if anything. Instead, rockabilly reflected the efforts of such performers as the Delmores, Rodgers, and Wills not in its instrumental wizardry or progressive musicality, but because it popularized an ear-catching blend of black and white music. (It should be noted that many "hillbilly" performers were heavily influenced by African American music, from gospel to blues to jazz—indeed, the rise of

Above: *The charismatic Roy Acuff was one of the first hillbilly superstars and as such contributed to the rural influence that gave rockabilly its unmistakable country twang.* **Left:** *Rabon (left) and Alton Delmore began their career playing ragtime guitar on the* **Grand Ole Opry** *in the early 1930s. By the 1940s they were touring and recording widely. Among the songs the pair wrote and recorded were the raucous "Hillbilly Boogie" and "Blues Stay Away from Me," both of which revealed their debt to the blues and pointed the way to the rockabilly of the 1950s.*

the recording industry in the 1920s had led to a wide dissemination of "race" music, which was eagerly studied by white musicians across the United States.) One performer who epitomized this blend and was a transitional rockabilly figure was Sidney "Hardrock" Gunter. Born in Atlanta, Gunter recorded a number of country boogie woogie tunes and rockabilly numbers (including "Gonna Dance All Night," recorded at Sun).

Thrown in with this relatively simple mixture of influences were a couple of elements that helped define rockabilly once and for all. One element was the use of a slapping bass technique (personified by Bill Black, the bassist who rode with guitarist Scotty Moore and Elvis to rock and roll stardom at RCA) that contributed to the music's herky-jerk energy. Second was the invention of the echo effect, a recording innovation that, according to popular history, was developed simultaneously and independently by Sam Phillips and Chicago impresario Leonard Chess (to whom Phillips had leased the first fruits of his recording efforts, mostly blues and R&B numbers, thereby enabling Sun Records to survive). The echo was used widely by Phillips in many Sun rockabilly recordings and was frequently criticized as a gloss that the savvy producer used to mask the vocal, instrumental, and lyrical deficiencies of the music. While this may be true, it hardly seems worth disputing; like rock and roll (which, ultimately, rockabilly may most closely resemble), rockabilly was about energy and presence, not technical ability or poetry. (In fact, the country rock of today, which has its roots in rockabilly, has taken ability more seriously, particularly with the likes of Charlie Daniels.)

Above (left to right): *Scotty Moore, Elvis, and Bill Black toured together for a few years, from Elvis' Sun period to his early involvement with RCA. Due to Colonel Tom Parker's aggressive style of management, the pay scale was considerably lopsided in favor of Elvis, a disparity that led the guitarist and bassist to leave the band in 1957. The sound of Elvis changed forever after the departure of Black and Moore; never again would the King benefit from the raw energy that Black and Moore brought to the table.* **Right:** *With the addition of D.J. Fontana, Elvis' band developed a unique sound that was at once polished and spontaneous.*

Just as the blues had been condemned by many people from many walks of life as Satan's music, rockabilly likewise scandalized audiences everywhere. Rockabilly was particularly frightening to conservative (read: "white middle class") music consumers because not only did it sound suspiciously like the music African Americans were playing and listening to, but its heroes were hip-wiggling, cousin-marrying, hard-drinking young men (and a handful of women) who sang in barely disguised (or utterly incomprehensible, depending on your point of view) ways about sex and other topics that were thought to be best left undiscussed, much less disseminated through the popular media.

This eschewal by the conservative public hardly mattered, of course, because the target audience of the outpourings of Elvis Presley, Carl Perkins, Jerry Lee Lewis, and the others was not after all the adults of mid-twentieth-century Middle America, but their children. The 1950s were a time of relative prosperity and contentment for the middle classes, still riding the wave of productivity that had been sparked by World War II. Accordingly, the children of the middle classes had money in their pockets. And, not surprisingly, these kids had distinctively different tastes from the previous generation; more to the point, they were defining themselves in sharp contradistinction to the values held by their parents. Rockabilly, much like its younger kissin' cousin, rock and roll, was the leather-jacketed, duck-tailed expression of this rebellion.

The embodiment of this youth uprising, its most prominent revolutionary, was Elvis Presley. He walked into Phillips' studios to record a 45 (the Ink Spots' "My Happiness" b/w "That's When Your Heartaches Begin") as a birthday gift for his mother, Gladys, in what turned out to be the first step toward musical deification. The producer of the gift record drew Phillips' attention to the youngster, and Phillips, who had been looking for a white performer who sang like a black man, was delighted. After cultivating Elvis' talent for almost a year, Phillips put together a backing band consisting of Bill Black and Scotty Moore and recorded a series of now-legendary records that bridged the gulf between rock and roll and country.

Charlie Daniels

— Fiddle Demon —

Charlie Daniels has been a member of various no-name bar bands and has put in time as a songwriter and session player in Nashville, but his main pursuit and claim to fame has been as leader of the fiery and iconoclastic Charlie Daniels Band, whose bluegrass-to-boogie repertoire has been a favorite of arena concert crowds for more than twenty years.

Daniels was born in 1937 in Wilmington, North Carolina. Unlike many children who go on to careers in music, Daniels had no personal experience with singing or playing until he bought a guitar at the age of fifteen and taught himself to play by listening to Elvis Presley rockabilly tunes and to WLAC, a black radio station. At seventeen, Daniels became enthralled by the bluegrass music of Bill Monroe. He was inspired to take up the fiddle and decided to make music his career.

Daniels paid his dues in a band called the Jaguars, performing mostly in bars and honky tonks throughout the South. A chance meeting with Nashville producer Bob Johnston in Fort Worth, Texas, led to the recording of one of Daniels' tunes, "It Hurts Me," onto the flip side of an Elvis Presley single. It also led to Daniels' first album, produced by Johnston, which was a flop. Undaunted and convinced that Daniels had star potential, Johnston used his clout in Nashville to arrange some session work for the burly fiddler and guitarist.

Never an enthusiastic session player, Daniels nevertheless plugged away between 1966 and 1971, contributing to a number of groundbreaking albums, including Bob Dylan's *Nashville Skyline*. He was useful in Nashville for his command of many styles, from

Fiddle whiz Charlie Daniels is seen here at his Grand Ole Opry debut in 1976. In spirit he owes much to the pioneering country rock work of Elvis and other rockabilly greats.

jazz to rock to bluegrass, but Daniels recollects that he was not very happy about playing "the usual Nashville thing." In 1971 he quit working as a session player and almost immediately formed the Charlie Daniels Band, hitting the road for what would become a regular touring schedule of as many as 250 shows a year.

Daniels' songs are mostly simple anthems centering on pride and can-do determination. Songs such as "In America" and "The South's Gonna Do It" honor the strength and nobility of working-class America. If his lyrics are light, however, his sentiments concerning patriotism and the American people are rock solid—and his musical accomplishments are impressive. It's not unusual in the course of a Charlie Daniels Band concert to be swept through a full range of contemporary styles—from pure country and rollicking bluegrass to full-bore, hard-driving rock.

Awarded a Grammy in 1980 for "The Devil Went Down to Georgia," Charlie Daniels continues to tour to enthusiastic audiences across the United States. He is also the host of Volunteer Jam, an annual concert event that turns Nashville on its ear each summer.

—P.B.

Although Elvis would continue to return to country music throughout his career, and according to some estimates ultimately recorded more than sixty certifiable country records over the years, it was during his brief stint as a Sun musician that Elvis was more or less a country performer. He toured regional dairy shows, performed on KWKH's *Louisiana Hayride* and the *Grand Ole Opry* radio shows, and became known throughout the South and Southwest as "The Hillbilly Cat" and "The King of Western Bop."

Both of these epithets, in addition to one of his Sun recordings from this period, "Milkcow Blues Boogie," illustrate some of the abovementioned rockabilly substrata: hillbilly music, western swing (and, therefore, jazz), and boogie-woogie blues (note especially the Delmore Brothers' 1945 country jumper "Hillbilly Boogie" and Nashville pianist Cecil Gant's 1950 romp "We're Gonna Rock").

Contrary to popular belief, rockabilly did not end with Elvis' 1956 departure from Sun Records for RCA Records (which inaugurated his titanic career as a popular entertainment phenomenon). While Presley was perhaps the first rockabilly star, he was by no means the last—or even the most representative (after all, Elvis' career survived until the late 1970s while the careers of many of his rockabilly colleagues had already come to an end by the early 1960s). Instead, Elvis was a shiver that ran down the spine of the nation and brought other self-styled musical outsiders in from the cold. In fact, the rockabilly greats who were inspired by those early Elvis recordings were the ones who truly set the music in stone, bringing their single-minded enthusiasm and raw energy to the genre.

Among the first to heed the siren's call was a young Tennessee musician by the name of Carl Perkins. Upon hearing Elvis' music for the first time, on the radio, Perkins and his brothers Jay and Clayton packed their belongings (including their instruments) and headed for Memphis to offer their talents up on the Sun Records shrine, arriving there in November 1954. In February 1955 a skeptical Phillips re-leased two cuts from the Perkins brothers' first session (back in late 1954), both of which were country tunes that failed to make any

Above: *If there were a Mount Rushmore of rockabilly the stone would be carved in the image of these four legendary Sun performers (from left to right): Jerry Lee Lewis, Carl Perkins, Elvis Presley, and Johnny Cash. These four men assembled at the Sun facilities in December 1956 and recorded a number of songs that wouldn't be released in their entirety until 1990, under the title* **Elvis Presley: The Million Dollar Quartet.** **Right:** *Carl Perkins was a great songwriter but a less-than-commanding presence on stage. By 1958, when this picture was taken, Perkins had left Sun for Columbia.*

impression in the market whatsoever. In August, two more Perkins tracks were released, one of which, "Gone! Gone! Gone!," was rockabilly through and through; once again, however, the cuts went nowhere. Then, having sold Elvis Presley's contract—the most valuable entertainment contract in the world—to RCA Records in November 1955, Phillips decided to focus on making Perkins a star. The result was "Blue Suede Shoes" (inspired by then-Sun Records artist Johnny Cash, who had suggested a number based around the phrase, "don't step on my blue suede shoes"). Written and performed by Perkins, the song entered the *Billboard* charts on February 18, 1956, and went on to become the first country record to chart simultaneously on the country (#1), pop (#2), and R&B charts (#2).

Due to a number of factors—he wasn't a dashing greaser like Presley, he wasn't a fireball like Lewis, or a devil-may-care like Vincent—Perkins never achieved the stardom or commercial success his talents might have suggested. As it turned out, Perkins wasn't even able to promote the dazzling "Blue Suede Shoes": an untimely car accident sidelined him and his brothers just as the tune was scaling the charts. And in the end, the song would be forever be associated with Elvis, whose remake eclipsed Perkins' version commercially. Nevertheless, the rockabilly material that Carl Perkins recorded for Sun (especially "Honey Don't," "Everybody's Trying To Be My Baby," and "Matchbox," all of which were later covered by the Beatles) is legendary. Just the same, by 1958 Perkins had left for Columbia Records and Phillips was already focusing on his most promising up-and-coming performer—the "Killer" himself, Jerry Lee Lewis.

Perhaps more than any of his rockabilly compatriots, Jerry Lee Lewis lived the rockabilly ideal, acting out against a number of societal conventions. Like his rockabilly contemporaries, Lewis adopted the aesthetic of youth revolt, dressing like a cross between a suburban dandy and a street punk and wearing his mass of curly fair hair in the characteristic 1950s pompadour. More importantly, Lewis was a demolitions expert who focused

Pictured here arm in arm are the two wildest of the rockabilly wildmen: Columbia Records star Gene Vincent (left) and the Killer, Jerry Lee Lewis, of Sun Records.

his incredible energies on dismantling pianos and audiences across the United States. His raw energy and searing, arrogant vocals made him a hugely popular performer; unfortunately, those wild, exuberantly youthful energies would also prove a hindrance to his career (especially abroad) and a danger to his life.

The Louisiana-born Lewis grew up in a devoutly religious household and as a result was immersed in music of several varieties from the very beginning of his life. He was performing as a pianist while in his teens, and at the age of nineteen secured a spot on the *Louisiana Hayride*. Like everyone else in the South—and particularly musicians—Lewis heard and was shaken by the Elvis Sun recordings. Following Perkins' example, Lewis packed up his things and headed for Memphis to find Sam Phillips' Sun enclave.

Following an audition with Phillips' assistant Jack Clement, Lewis came to the attention of Phillips himself and soon was on his way to becoming a star. Beginning with a modestly successful recording of Ray Price's "Crazy Arms," Lewis began to get a feel for the potential of his talents. At the end of a subsequent recording session (during which Lewis was attempting to record a follow-up to "Crazy Arms"), Clement told Lewis to go ahead and play whatever he wanted. Accordingly, Lewis and company launched into "Whole Lot of Shakin' Going On," which would go on to sell a million copies and sky-

Jerry Lee Lewis

The Killer

Even the most notorious of country outlaws bow to the ruthless behavior of "The Killer." Waylon Jennings once said of Jerry Lee Lewis (b. 1935), "Just don't get too close to him and you won't get hurt." It's hard to believe that Lewis at one time aspired to become a preacher like his first cousin Jimmy Swaggart. But the Bible college that he attended kicked him out for his interpretation of the hymn "My God Is Real."

At the age of nine, Lewis learned to play his first song, "Silent Night." His first professional gig came only five years later—just months before his first marriage.

By the following year, he had begun playing regularly at the Blue Cat Night Club in Natchez, Louisiana, and was getting airtime every Saturday for his own twenty-minute radio program on the WNAT radio station in the same town.

Lewis' big break came in 1956, however, when he sought out impresario Sam Phillips, owner of the legendary Sun Records in Memphis. The company, which had only a couple of years earlier brought Elvis Presley to national attention, signed Lewis. In the next two years, Jerry Lee gave Sun its two greatest hits: "Whole Lot of Shakin' Going On" and "Great Balls of Fire."

By 1958 Jerry Lee was giving the King of Rock and Roll a run for his money. Elvis, who was to leave the United States to serve his country in a two-year stint in the U.S. Army, wasn't sure his career could survive and was worried that Jerry Lee Lewis would replace him. Fortunately for the King, Jerry Lee was his own worst enemy.

The day that Lewis and his entourage landed in England for a tour of twenty-seven concerts, they were met by what seemed to be the entire British media. Word had spread that Jerry Lee had not only married a thirteen-year-old but that the girl was his cousin. The first and last questions of the press conference concerned his

marriage. Lewis tried to clear things up: "Myra and I are legally married. It was my second marriage that wasn't legal. I was a bigamist when I was sixteen. I was fourteen when I was first married. That lasted a year; then I met Jane. One day she said she was goin' to have my baby. I was real worried. Her father threatened me, and her brothers where hunting [me] with hide whips. So I married her just a week before my divorce from Dorothy. It was a shotgun wedding."

Lewis' concert tour was immediately canceled, and by the time Elvis returned from the service, nobody, not Carl Perkins or Johnny Cash had been able to take the King's throne. And Lewis, because of the bad publicity, was down for the count.

The June 9, 1958, issue of *Billboard* magazine ran a full-page ad taken out by Lewis' management trying to dispel the cloud that loomed over his career. The ad, entitled "An Open Letter to the Industry from Jerry Lee Lewis," explained that his exploits had been highly exaggerated. But to no avail: the man who had six months earlier been elected by random polling in Kansas City as "the real King of Rock and Roll" could no longer get his records played. His performance fee dropped from fifteen hundred to five hundred dollars a night.

Lewis has in his lifetime been accused of a multitude of transgressions, including shooting one of his bass players, killing one (or two) of his six wives, and threatening Elvis' life because the King wouldn't believe the prophecy in the book of Revelations that stated that the end of the world is

The explosive Jerry Lee Lewis leaps into the stratosphere, hair on end, at a performance at the Cafe de Paris in New York on June 10, 1958. The Killer revealed at the show that he had remarried Myra in order to "satisfy the people in the U.S. and England" that everything was aboveboard and legal.

near. ("I'll show you the end of the world is drawin' nigh!" he is reported to have bellowed outside the gates of the Graceland estate.) But in the face of these many trials and tribulations, the Killer has proven to be a survivor: at this writing he continues to perform, drawing regular crowds, and record (most recently *Young Blood*, 1995).

—A.H.

rocket to #1 on both the R&B and country-and-western charts; it even lingered on the pop charts for more than seven months. The song transformed Jerry Lee Lewis into a celebrity in a matter of weeks beginning in June 1957. And while "Whole Lot of Shakin'" would eventually go down in history as a rock and roll cut, it is nonetheless part of the rockabilly canon (particularly in its sexually suggestive lyrics and up-tempo backbeat, in this case propelled by the piano).

Lewis seemed unstoppable, recording a string of critical and commercial hits (covers of Otis Blackwell's "Great Balls of Fire" and "Breathless," for instance), crossing the United States back and forth, appearing on mainstream television programs (including even squeaky-clean Dick Clark's *American Bandstand*), and in general playing the daylights out of the piano everywhere he went. But the freneticism and recklessness of Lewis' personality were about to catch up with him.

In mid-1958 Lewis married his cousin, thirteen-year-old Myra Brown; almost immediately, the scandal surrounding this, his third marriage, caused the opportunities that had kept him perpetually on the

move the year before to dry up. His planned invasion of Europe, starting in London—where his music was adored—was aborted soon after his arrival at Heathrow. The Killer was expertly crucified by the press and, although British audiences didn't seem to

Left: Sidney "Hardrock" Gunter, born on September 18, 1918, in Birmingham, Alabama, pioneered the rockabilly sound with his country boogie style—first at Decca and later at Sun. **Below:** *Texas native Roy Orbison (second from left) started out playing country with the Wink Westerners while still in high school; in 1954 he changed the name of the band to the Teen Kings (surrounding Orbison) and recorded "Ooby Dooby," which he rerecorded as "Oobie Doobie." The second version hit the #59 spot on the pop charts and proved to be Orbison's only rockabilly hit as a performer (as a writer, Orbison had better luck, including the tribute to his wife, "Claudette," which was a hit for the Everly Brothers). Orbison bought his contract back from Sam Phillips in the late fifties and signed with Monument.*

care particularly whether or not he was guilty of incest, effectively forced out of the United Kingdom and into exile in his own country. Ironically, it was Lewis' id-driven exuberance—the same that had brought him to Memphis and made him a star—that skewered his promising future. But Lewis was also lucky, in a way: unlike many of his contemporaries the Killer survives to this day, continuing to put on "the greatest live show on earth," although the chaos that has always surrounded him continues to challenge his remarkable stamina (at this writing he is in trouble with the IRS and married to his sixth wife).

The rockabilly roster did not end with Lewis, however. Roy Orbison—before leaving for rock and roll ambassadordom—had recorded "Oobie Doobie" (1956) under the auspices of Sam Phillips and company, and Johnny Cash—before going on to become one of the most widely known and generally adored country artists of all time—had recorded a couple of rockabilly numbers there, including "Cry, Cry, Cry" and "I Walk the Line." And more to the point, there were others outside the Sun Records fold who had heard the call of the wild, as voiced by the King of the musical jungle, Elvis.

Following the release of Elvis' Sun recordings, which transformed the face of popular music in so

many ways, A&R executives everywhere were scrambling to jump on the rockabilly bandwagon. Not surprisingly, equally enthusiastic young hipsters, wanting to try on some blue suede shoes themselves, were cropping up around the United States. Among these aspiring young men were Ronnie Hawkins (who recorded for Roulette), Dale Hawkins (no relation, who recorded for Checker), and two others who not only would record seminal tracks but also would embody the rockabilly ideal with their lifestyles and abortive careers: Gene Vincent (who recorded for Capitol Records) and Eddie Cochran (a Liberty Records artist).

Virginian Gene Vincent was a prototypical rockabilly performer, a roustabout whose rambunc-

Top: *Ronnie Hawkins of Huntsville, Arkansas, was one of the most colorful of the rockabilly stars; his acrobatic onstage antics earned him the nickname Mr. Dynamo. He and drummer Levon Helms' Levon and the Hawks were later picked up by Bob Dylan as the Band.* **Above:** *Ronnie Hawkins (left) and Carl Perkins strengthen their bones in preparation for a little onstage mayhem.* **Left:** *Louisiana singer and guitarist Dale Hawkins had a couple of rockabilly hits on the Chess-subsidiary Checker label, including "Suzie Q," which charted in 1957 and was later recorded by many artists, including the Everly Brothers and the Rolling Stones.*

tiousness led to a motorcycle accident in 1955 (while he was in the U.S. Navy) that permanently disabled his left leg and planted the seed for chronic depression. In 1956 Vincent's "Be-Bop-A-Lula," which he had recorded promotionally the year before for deejay Tex Davis, was rerecorded for Capitol Records' Nashville studio. In a matter of weeks, the single was all over the charts and Vincent was the rebel celebrity du jour. Besides Vincent's taut vocals, the song featured back-up work by some of the finest Nashville musicians, the Blue Caps (whose lead guitarist, Cliff Gallup, left an indelible mark on the history of popular music with "Be-Bop-A-Lula" and subsequent songs). In 1957 and 1958 Vincent recorded a handful of raunchy singles that charted at a variety of spots: "Race with the Devil" (#96 on the pop charts, 1956), "Dance to the Bop" (#43 on the pop charts, 1957), and "Lotta Lovin" (#7 on the R&B and #14 on the pop charts, 1957). Despite this initial success, however, Vincent's career floundered by the tail end of the 1950s due to a combination of poor business advice, his crippled left leg and its attendant problems, and tough competition on the charts—especially from the dashing and limber hip-swiveler Elvis Presley.

Contemporary to Vincent was Minnesota native Eddie Cochran, a country-cum-rockabilly guitarist and singer who recorded only one certified hit, "Summertime Blues," during his extremely brief career. Nonetheless, Cochran will be remembered forever on the strength of that song (and just a handful of others, including the equally electrifying "C'mon Everybody") for his ability to capture perfectly the mindset of the mid-twentieth-century teenager. Also, unlike many rockabilly heroes (except Perkins, who was a skilled guitarist himself) Cochran was accomplished on his instrument. Of course, it also didn't hurt that, unlike Vincent and Perkins, Cochran was a handsome kid (in fact, his looks recalled two of the teen idols of the day—Jimmie Dean to some people and Elvis Presley to others).

In a manner that seems in retrospect to be typical of rockabilly's prodigal sons, the careers of Cochran and Vincent came simultaneously to a

Above: *Seen here in a scene from* **The Girl Can't Help It** *are Gene Vincent (center, with guitar) and His Blue Caps. Vincent's hiccupy vocal stylings reflected rockabilly's back-country roots.* **Right:** *Despite his crippled left leg, Vincent was a captivating performer who swaggered with the best of them.*

tragic end—in a taxi accident in Wiltshire, England. Both performers were participating in a rockabilly tour in the United Kingdom (where rockabilly was very hot, and in fact inspired the sensation known as skiffle) in 1960, when the taxi carrying them and songwriter Sharon Sheely blew a tire and veered off the road, killing Cochran and injuring the other two

Right: *Guitar whiz kid Eddie Cochran (left) began his career at the age of sixteen as part of a country music duo known as the Cochran Brothers, with Hank Cochran (right, no relation). One of the duo's early hits was a tribute to Hank Williams and Jimmie Rodgers, "Two Blue Singin' Stars."* **Below:** *Cochran high kicks it during a characteristically energetic performance. Although Cochran was a capable guitarist, it took his performance of "Twenty Flight Rock" in* **The Girl Can't Help It** *to boost the good-looking rockabilly player's career.*

passengers severely. This event seems to have worsened Vincent's earlier injury and launched him on a downward spiral through alcoholism and depression that led to his early death (he was thirty-six at the time) in 1971.

Perhaps the only rockabilly star to survive the second half of the twentieth century with both career and life intact is the most atypical of them all, the indomitable Wanda Jackson. Besides being healthy and having a thriving career (especially in Europe) at this writing, Wanda was one of the few female stars—including the young Brenda Lee, Lorrie Collins of the Collins Kids, and Janis Martin, billed by RCA as "the female Elvis"— in a genre otherwise overloaded with slouch-shouldered boys who lived fast and died very young.

The hot and sassy Jackson was raised in the heartland of honky-tonk and country music, following a classic pattern of location and relocation: born in Oklahoma, she moved with her family to Bakersfield, California, when she was four years old; then, when Wanda was twelve years old, she and her family moved back to Oklahoma. By the time she

Left: *Wanda Jackson (left) was convinced by Elvis, whom she briefly dated, to perform rockabilly. Although she had a few rockabilly hits, Jackson later returned to recording country and gospel.* **Below:** *Capitol Records was home to some of the most influential stars of country in the 1940s and 1950s (including Wanda Jackson). Seen here are (from left) accordionist Pee Wee King, who had played with Gene Autry and went on to top the country and pop charts in the 1950s; bandleader, guitarist, and singer Red Foley, whose innumerable accomplishments included playing the straight man for Minnie Pearl; singer Tennessee Ernie Ford, a multitalented performer whose 1950 recording "Shotgun Boogie" is a country boogie classic; pianist Jimmy Wakely, a huge recording and film star in the 1940s whose recording of Floyd Tillman's "Slipping Around" went to #1 on the country and pop charts; and bandleader and guitarist Hank Thompson, who recorded many hits and is credited with (among other things) discovering Wanda Jackson and bucking Opry tradition by bringing a snare drum to the stage.*

was a teen, Jackson was getting some notice as a singer, winning a local talent contest, which soon led to radio work. Thanks to the miracle of radio, Jackson's singing caught the ear of Hank Thompson, who invited her to tour with his band. Then at the age of seventeen, Jackson was signed to a contract with Decca Records and made a series of country recordings that were commercially successful. And finally, just as with so many of her contemporaries, Jackson was touched by the far-reaching influence of Elvis Presley.

In 1955 Elvis was touring with the Red Foley band, and on a swing through Oklahoma he met Wanda Jackson. Presley's recommendation to the attractive and talented young singer was to ride the wave of rock and roll and see where it took her. Accordingly, when she signed with Capitol Records in 1956, she began recording decidedly raunchier, more rhythmically driving numbers. Her singles from this period usually included a honky-tonk number on one side and a rockabilly number on the flip side. These gems, which were largely overlooked at the time (probably because most people felt that the sug-

gestive content and searing rhythms of such songs were sexy when performed by a man but intimidating when performed by a woman), included the wild up-tempo number "Fujiyama Mama," the delicious Elvis-inflected "Honey Bop," and her signature release (a song that Elvis had recorded earlier, indicating his impact on her career), "Let's Have a Party."

On "Let's Have a Party," the release of which Capitol inexplicably delayed a few years, until 1960, Jackson was backed expertly by Buck Owens and Vernon Sandinsky on guitar, Skeets McDonald on bass, Joe Brawley on drums, and Merrill Moore (or Big Al Downing) on piano. This was the only of Jackson's rockabilly numbers to hit the U.S. pop charts, which is too bad because she produced a string of great tunes that went for the most part unrecognized. Indeed, of all her rockabilly contemporaries (except Elvis and maybe Cochran), Jackson was the most accomplished vocally: she had great control, perfected a tenor vibrato below her natural range that allowed her to swagger with bravado, and used a wild gravely technique (note especially "Fujiyama Mama") that was instantly identifiable. Perhaps most unique about this wild child of rockabilly, though, is that her recording and performing careers have never slackened.

Wanda Jackson

Fujiyama Mama

Although Wanda Jackson (b. 1937) rarely made the top ten, she consistently placed in the top twenty on the pop and country charts for fifteen years, and her raucous, sexual, rockabilly persona paved the way for future generations of women of rock and roll.

Born in Maud, Oklahoma, October 29, 1937, Wanda began to be interested in music at the age of six, when her father taught her to play the guitar. By the age of nine she was playing piano and at twelve was performing daily fifteen-minute (soon to be half-hour) radio spots at KLPR in Oklahoma City, near her hometown. She quickly became the most popular radio personality in the region.

Hank Thompson invited her to sing with his band, the Brazos Valley Boys, in 1954, and together they began to pump out hits like "You Cain't Have My Love," a duet with Billy Gray and Jackson that reached #8 on the country charts. With a contract soon following from Decca Records, Wanda began touring in 1955 as a solo act.

Unfortunately, the world of music in general was not ready for the sexual revolution. Even Elvis, appearing on *The Ed Sullivan Show*, could not be shown from the waist down. A woman with a healthy appetite for life was not about to cross the threshold of liberation just yet. At the Grand Ole Opry, Wanda was asked to cover her bare shoulders (even noodle straps at this time were considered too sexy for public viewing). Wanda's career suffered not from a lack of interest but from the denial of the spectacle that garnered her attention.

Jackson's success was soon measured outside the United States; she became one of the first country stars to achieve international stardom. With her screeching rendition of "Fujiyama Mama," Wanda became an overnight sensation in Japan; in Germany, with a song called "Santo Domingo," Wanda finally gained acknowledgment of her astounding ability.

The beautiful and talented Wanda Jackson (left and above) had only one charting country hit when performing rockabilly material at Capitol, "I Gotta Know."

As a songwriter, she also found success with Buck Owens' rendition of her "Kicking Our Hearts Around" and with her own recording of "Right or Wrong," which was released in 1961 (other stars would score hits with this song, perhaps most notably George Strait). With her husband, Wendell Goodman, as manager during the 1960s, Jackson became the star of her own television series, *Music Village*.

By the late 1960s Jackson had returned to a more conservative country format. In the 1970s, finally tired of the limitations put on her by Capitol Records, Jackson returned to the music of her childhood, gospel, recording with MYRRH and Word Records. Now with the Swedish label Tab Records, Wanda is able to record all the types of music she likes—without limitations (she even recorded a return to her raucous roots with the album *Rock 'N' Roll Away Your Blues* in 1984).

—A.H.

Many people seem to view the year 1960 as the last in rockabilly's enormously influential but brief heyday. In 1960 Phillips moved Sun Records to new and larger premises. Ironically, the improved production capabilities of the new studio, which was symbolic of Phillips' success, drained the music of its basic, defining elements: specifically, the new range of effects that could be used (as opposed to just the bathtub echo, now gone forever) sapped the music's integrity by shifting the focus from raw energy to production values. Orbison and Cash had moved on by this point, Lewis had self-destructed a couple of years earlier, and the careers of other, lesser Sun rockabilly performers (such as Warren Smith and Sonny Burgess) had stalled. Finally, Phillips was beginning to focus more intently on some of his other, non-music-related business interests (the Holiday Inn chain of hotels, for instance).

Nineteen-sixty was also the year of the accident that killed Cochran and ended Vincent's career. Elvis returned from his army duty overseas in 1960 to assume the mantle of the King of Entertainment, recording tunes that were far from his raucous R&B and country roots, and acting in a slew of half-baked movies that capitalized solely on the strength of his popularity. And finally, new sounds, especially soul and a more experimental incarnation of rock and roll, were beginning to emerge from the South and around the country.

The truth of the matter, though, is that rockabilly never really disappeared. On the contrary, it has been with us all along, performed and recorded by those who grew up loving it—such as the indomitable Ray "Caterpillar" Campi, the vastly influential Charlie Feathers (a Mississippian and a contemporary of Elvis, for whom Feathers cowrote a couple of important tunes), the Johnny Burnette Trio (contemporaries of Elvis who were extraordinarily talented but sought commercial success in vain), and Sleepy LaBeef (the sole artist on the Sun label when Phillips sold it in July 1969)—and those who came to it after it had ceased, at least in the institutionalized sense, to be—including Ricky Nelson ,a talented performer and songwriter from New Jersey who never got his due), the

Stray Cats (a group from Long Island that achieved popularity in the rockabilly resurgence in the early 1980s), and the Cramps (a "punkabilly" group from Ohio whose early recordings were produced by Alex Chilton at the reincarnated Sun Records studio). And as new generations discover the raw power that fuels it, rockabilly will continue to play a role in the evolution not only of country but of many other strains of American music.

Clockwise from top left: *The Johnny Burnette Trio (from left to right, Johnny and Dorsey Burnette and Paul Burlison), whose "Train Kept A Rollin'" is a rockabilly classic; droopy-lidded Arkansan Sleepy LaBeef, who has kept the rockabilly faith for decades; Charlie Feathers (standing, center), a prolific performer who along with Sidney "Hardrock" Gunter was a pioneering rockabilly artist with Sun; and Ray Campi, a rockabilly hero who has never been given due credit as a major proponent of the sound.*

Chapter Seven

The Fightin' Side

―――

Honky-Tonk

by David Nelson

The title alone of Joe Maphis' "Dim Lights, Thick Smoke and Loud, Loud Music" sets the honky-tonk atmosphere: a crowded, smoke-filled roadhouse lit by neon beer signs; empty bottles of Falstaff, Schlitz, and Pearl on the tables; a jukebox in the corner fueling the fire with songs about drinking, cheating, and fighting. Honky-tonk country is both a celebration of the culture of the barrooms where the music has always found its most receptive audience and a document of the pitfalls of the honky-tonk life: alcoholism, heartbreak, broken homes, and time spent in jail. Honky-tonk country (like its African American forebear, the blues) offers some of the most good-timin' party songs ever recorded, but also the most brutally honest expressions of pain in American music.

Emmett Miller was an early (white) proponent of the blues, helping to bring the African American influence to country music that would figure so heavily in the honky-tonk player's style. The recordings he made in the 1920s—including "Anytime," "Lovesick Blues," and "Right or Wrong"—were later reprised subsequent artists (Eddy Arnold, Hank Williams, and Bob Wills, respectively).

jobs in urban areas (including unfamiliar northern and western cities). The transition was painful and lonely; not surprisingly, many of these displaced southerners found solace at the local beer joint in the form of a bottle, a favorite song on the jukebox, and the companionship of fellow sufferers rather than in the more traditional comforts of home and church.

The rise of honky-tonk music can be traced to bars that sprang up in Texas, Louisiana, and Oklahoma during the oil-field boom of the 1930s. Thirsty, lusty oil workers—often far from home and family—needed to let off steam on payday, and road-houses offering liquor, prostitutes, and dance music soon sprang up to accommodate them. Appropriately, the first known usage of the term honky-tonk in song came from Al Dexter, who ran just such a bar on the outskirts of Longview, Texas, in the early 1930s. Dexter set the tone for the genre with "Honky-Tonk Blues" and his early celebration of "Wine, Women and Song" and barroom violence. "Pistol Packin' Mama," Dexter's biggest hit, was based on the true story of a gun-toting wife's vengeance on her cheating husband and his lover: in good east Texas fashion the woman kicks out the windshield of her husband's car and chases his lover through a barbed-wire fence.

Honky-tonk's lyrical roots lie in the blues and the blues-based songs of country and western pioneer Jimmie Rodgers and such white blues interpreters as Emmett Miller ("Lovesick Blues"). Musically, however, honky-tonk is the direct offshoot of western swing, the jazz and boogie-woogie influenced evolution of southern string-band music that became popular in the dancehalls and bars of the Southwest in the 1930s. In order to be heard in the crowded, noisy dancehalls, western swing pioneers Bob Wills and Milton Brown added innovations to the fiddle-based music: Brown's band, the Musical Brownies, pioneered the use of an electric steel guitar, played by Bob Dunn, in 1934; Wills' Texas Playboys were the first to use a drummer, Smokey Dacus. In the hands of Wills, in particular, western swing evolved into a highly orchestrated big-band style that valued musicianship over lyrics. Honky-tonk went the other way, emphasizing the singers

Honky-tonk bars began appearing around the South and Southwest in the 1930s, a direct result of the invention of the jukebox in the late 1920s and the repeal of Prohibition in 1933, but also a symbol of changing ways of life for lower-class whites. The hardships of the Depression years and the increasing mechanization of agriculture forced many southerners out of their traditional, stable farming communities into transient labor camps or monotonous factory and lyrical substance over instrumental virtuosity. But honky-tonk retained the free-spirited flair of western swing, and the fiddles, electric steel, and driving beat that had been introduced in western swing defined the classic honky-tonk sound.

Honky-tonk and western swing continued to exchange influences, part of a healthy give-and-take long in existence in the South and Southwest among various musical styles, including black blues and jazz; white string bands; Mexican-American *conjunto* and *norteño*; polkas and waltzes from Texas' Czech, German, and Polish communities; and cajun and creole sounds from southern Louisiana and east Texas. Cajun fiddler Harry Choates (''Jole Blon''), a Louisiana native who grew up in Port Arthur, Texas, popularized the honky-tonk style in French-speaking Acadiana while also bringing cajun sounds into

Above: *Guitarist and bandleader Ted Daffan (center, surrounded by His Texans) got early musical experience and exposure to the seeds of honky-tonk playing alongside Floyd Tillman and Moon Mullican in the Blue Ridge Playboys. Daffan was among the first performers to amplify his instrument.*
Left: *Pictured here in 1933 at the Crystal Springs Dancing & Swimming Club, Texas (from left): two members of the Cunningham family, proprietors of the club; vocalist and bandleader Milton Brown; guitarist Durwood Brown; fiddler Jesse Ashlock; banjoist Ocie Stockard; and bassist Wanna Coffman. Western swing and honky-tonk were to gain a lot from each other over the years; the Hawaiian guitar work of Brownie Bob Dunn was a precursor to the electric steel associated with much honky-tonk.*

the Texas honky-tonk circuit. Choates was also one of the first honky-tonk stars to die as a result of the lifestyle associated with the music. A notorious drinker, Choates died in an Austin jail at the age of twenty-eight, apparently the victim of alcohol poisoning (although rumors spread that he had been beaten to death by a jailer). Honky-tonk would per-

sist as an important element in cajun music and western swing, especially as practiced by more obscure artists like Vin Bruce and Hoyle Nix & His West Texas Cowboys, who became institutions at particular dancehalls or on small-town circuits.

Leon "Pappy" Selph was an early western swing bandleader whose popularity never extended far

from his base in the Houston area. But out of Selph's band, the Blue Ridge Playboys, came three early honky-tonk innovators: Ted Daffan, Moon Mullican, and Floyd Tillman. Guitarist Daffan—a native of Beauregard Parish, Louisiana, who was raised in Houston—was an electronics nut who made homemade amplifiers and pick-ups in the early days of the electrification of the music. Even more importantly, he was a songwriter on the forefront of establishing some of honky-tonk's enduring themes.

Daffan's compositions "Worried Mind," "Headin' Down The Wrong High-way," and "Born To Lose" epitomized the down side of honky-tonk life—the alienation and confusion brought on by the Depression and the migration away from rural life, and the spiritual hangover suffered by a good-timin' and two-timin' honky-tonk man raised on the tenets of fundamentalist religion. Daffan also recorded "Truck Driver's Blues" in 1939, the first recorded example of what became a popular sub-genre of honky-tonk.

Aubrey "Moon" Mullican —a native of Corrigan, Texas—brought the black barrelhouse blues piano style of the Texas lumber and turpentine work camps into the honky-tonk tradition. Getting his start as a teenager playing in Houston brothels, Mullican played with a hard-driving style intended to "make the bottles bounce on the tables." Floyd Tillman—an Oklahoman who grew up in Post, Texas—wrote the honky-tonk standard "It Makes No Difference Now" (later a hit for Jimmie Davis, Bob Wills, and others) and was the first to realistically present the theme of cheating (destined to become one of honky-tonk's most popular subjects) with "Slippin' Around" in 1949. In keeping with the emotional tug-of-war at the heart of honky-tonk, Tillman followed up his hit with the remorseful "I'll Never Slip Around Again."

Above: *Legendary honky-tonk pianist Moon Mullican (who was weaned on the blues) earned his nickname after he left home to play the piano in Houston cathouses and honky-tonks, a job that kept him up nights and in bed all day.* **Right, top:** *Ernest Tubb, whose early years were spent closely studying the work of Jimmie Rodgers, emerged with his own distinctive style in the 1940s following a tonsillectomy that put an end to his yodeling. By the mid-1940s he was fronting his own band, the Texas Troubadours, and laying the groundwork for the honky-tonk style.* **Right, bottom:** *Floyd Tillman was widely admired for his guitar licks (both Merle Haggard and Willie Nelson claim to have been influenced by him) and recognized for his growling vocal delivery, but it is as a songwriter that he will always be remembered.*

The first real honky-tonk star, however, was Ernest Tubb (1914–1984), the Texas Troubadour. Born in Crisp, Texas, Tubb was influenced by Jimmie Rodgers but developed a style that became the embodiment of the honky-tonk sound: loping rhythms propelled by drums, electric steel, and "take-off" guitar (meaning the guitarist took solos in addition to playing rhythm), anchored by Tubb's warm, flat, ragged-but-right Texas drawl. Tubb had his first major hit for Decca in 1941 with "Walking The Floor Over You," and by the end of 1942 he was making appearances on the Grand Ole Opry. "E.T." (as he was known to his legions of loyal fans) hosted the popular *Midnight Jamboree* radio program (which followed the *Opry*) and toured widely until his death, always keeping his sound faithful to the honky-tonk style. Tubb's son Justin later continued the family tradition with his version of the good-ol'-boy anthem "Rednecks, White Socks, and Blue Ribbon Beer."

Ernest Tubb's success helped pave the way for honky-tonk's heyday, which lasted from the mid-1940s until the advent of rock and roll as popular music in the mid-1950s. During this time, the hard honky-tonk style ruled mainstream country and western, and its predominant themes were explicitly and extensively mined. One of the stars of the decade was West Monroe, Louisiana, native Webb Pierce, whose 1953 hit "There Stands the Glass" was the first popular country single to openly advocate alcohol as a remedy for pain, heartbreak, fear, and stress. The song's glorification of beer drinking caused it to be banned from some radio stations, but made it a lasting favorite on honky-tonk jukeboxes. Pierce also played the cheating game with "Back Street Affair," prompting the response song "Paying for That Back Street Affair," by Kitty Wells. Known for

*One of the original members of the **Louisiana Hayride** roster, Webb Pierce went on to become one of the most popular country songwriters and performers of all time, particularly of honky-tonk. His taste for ostentatious displays of wealth led him to purchase this custom-decorated Pontiac. (Johnny Cash immortalized Pierce's extravagances in the song "Let There Be Country.")*

his warbling tenor and his extravagant costumes and accessories (for instance, the guitar-shaped swimming pool at his Nashville home and his Pontiac customized with rhinestones, silver dollars,

and a six-gun gearshift lever), Pierce was also responsible, through his recordings, for popularizing the pedal steel guitar (played by Bud Isaacs) in mainstream country.

Singer Hank Thompson (born in Waco, Texas, in 1925) charted twenty-one times from 1949 to 1958, most notably in 1952 with "The Wild Side of Life," an ode to barroom ladies. This song also prompted a reply from Kitty Wells, the immortal "It Wasn't God Who Made Honky Tonk Angels." Thompson's musical style offered a return to the jazzier elements of western swing, but lyrically he often mined the newly opened depths of honky-tonk realism, especially with drinking songs like "A Six Pack to Go," "Hangover Tavern," and "On Tap, in the Can, or in the Bottle."

Kitty Wells

Honky-Tonk Angel

Kitty Wells, the first female superstar in the notoriously male-dominated country-music business, would be the first to reject the title "feminist." She has told interviewers that "women are supposed to be the weaker sex, and men are supposed to take care of them," and she was thrilled when former Tennessee governor Frank Clement described her as "an outstanding wife and mother, in keeping with the finest traditions of Southern womanhood." Nonetheless, throughout her career as a solo performer and in appearances with her husband, Johnny Wright, Wells was the first performer to regularly bring a woman's point of view to country music.

Despite such rare exceptions as Patsy Montana, women in the early days of country music were familiar mostly as members of singing groups, or they appeared as featured "girl singers" to support male stars. When Kitty Wells began her career in 1936, she was a girl singer backing up her husband over Nashville radio station WSIX. Wells continued in that role when Wright teamed up in 1939 with singer Jack Anglin to form the popular act they called Johnny and Jack. As time went by, Kitty landed her own recording contracts and released a succession of hit records, often promoting them with solo appearances. Her presence onstage as a main draw was a significant step in clearing the way for the acceptance of future female country stars, from Patsy Cline to Loretta Lynn to k.d. lang.

Kitty Wells was born Muriel Deason in Nashville on August 30, 1919, into a staunchly traditional family. When she was seventeen, Muriel married Johnny Wright, who came up with the stage name for Muriel, taking the handle from the folk song "Sweet Kitty Wells."

Wells hit her stride between 1949 and 1960, starting with a string of "answer songs" that put a woman's slant on hit songs by male artists. Her debut, "It Wasn't God Who Made Honky Tonk Angels" (1952), was a response to Hank Thompson's "The Wild Side of Life," which opens with the line "I didn't know God made honky tonk angels" and goes on to describe the loose morals of women who hang out in honky tonks. In her song, Wells argues that men are also to blame if a woman strays. "It Wasn't God Who Made Honky Tonk Angels" zoomed to the #1 position on the *Billboard* country chart, which was created in 1944. Wells was the first woman ever to perch there. It was during that period that she and Johnny and Jack were invited to appear on the *Grand Ole Opry*.

After a few more successful answer songs, Wells began recording purely original songs. She built a sublime body of work, mostly tearjerkers, in her distinctive, low-key, and sparse honky tonk style. Between 1952 and 1965, she racked up thirty-five top ten hits with such songs as "Release Me," "I Can't Stop Loving You," "Cheatin's a Sin," and "Makin' Believe." Her thick, pure-country style fell out of favor with radio stations in the 1960s, though not before she issued two of her best-loved songs, "Heartbreak USA" and "Will Your Lawyer Talk to God."

Kitty Wells was inducted into the Country Music Hall of Fame in 1976, and she was presented with a Lifetime Achievement Award in 1991 by the National Academy of Recording Arts and Sciences, the organization that presents the Grammys.

—P.B.

Kitty Wells grew up on music, singing in the church choir and learning to play the guitar at the age of fifteen. Like Jimmie Rodgers, Wells' father was a railroad brakeman who played the guitar.

A third giant of honky-tonk's glory days was William Orville "Lefty" Frizzell. Born in Corsicana, Texas, into an oil-field family, Frizzell grew up idolizing Jimmie Rodgers and had early, first-hand experience with the honky-tonk life. As country music historian Bill C. Malone writes in *Country Music U.S.A.*: "A honky-tonk in Big Spring, Texas—the Ace of Clubs—inspired [Frizzell's] most famous song, 'If You Got the Money,' while an overnight stay in a county jail in West Texas inspired his first recording, 'I Love You a Thousand Ways.'" Frizzell's emotional singing style endeared him to country fans and influenced many of the honky-tonk heroes who followed him, including George Jones and Merle Haggard.

The most influential star of late 1940s and early 1950s honky-tonk, however, was Hank Williams. Born and raised in southern Alabama, Williams was influenced by a local bluesman, Rufus "Teetot" Payne, and came of age playing a Butler County bootleg joint called Thigpen's Log Cabin. His songs and his short and tragic career are a poignant portrait of the dichotomy between the "wild side of life" and the Protestant fundamentalist upbringing of many honky-tonk singers. Williams' rowdy ways and heavy drinking were well publicized; his "Honky-Tonkin'" (along with Lefty Frizzell's "If You've Got The Money") remains a popular theme song for carefree bar-hopping party hounds; and his death, at the age of twenty-nine, was the result of a fatal mixture of booze and drugs. Williams' repertoire, however, reflected the struggle between the honky-tonk life and the church. One of his most powerful numbers, "Lost Highway," is drenched in the guilt, shame, and resignation brought on by a life of drinking, cheating, and gambling.

The emergence of rock and roll in the mid-1950s as the dominant force in American popular music signaled the end of honky-tonk's heyday—weeping fiddles and twangy pedal steel were suddenly too "hillbilly" for mainstream country music and too old-fashioned for the younger generation swept away by the likes of Elvis Presley and Buddy Holly. Honky-tonk continued to have a receptive audience in the working-class taverns, however, and a number of emerging artists kept hard

Lefty Frizzell
Honky-Tonk Hero

Lefty Frizzell (1928–1975), who was a musically innovative and personally troubled man, is acknowledged by many of country music's major stars as a prime influence on their careers. His wrenching, expressive singing style, in which notes and syllables are tortured and stretched, is the foundation for much of the distinctive vocalizing in country music. Performers such as George Jones, Merle Haggard, Randy Travis, and Clint Black all acknowledge Frizzell as their vocal ideal.

Frizzell himself was a disciple of the "Blue Yodeler," Jimmie Rodgers, whose records left a vivid impression on him. Frizzell also cited honky-tonk pioneer Ernest Tubb as a major inspiration—and it was in the realm of honky-tonk that Frizzell left his mark.

Born in Corsicana, Texas, on March 31, 1928, William Orville Frizzell was the son of an oil rigger who moved around a lot. A country music fan, his father encouraged the boy to take up the guitar and often sang along with the Jimmie Rodgers and Ernest Tubb tunes the boy learned to play. Frizzell's talent was such that he was able to find work as a solo entertainer even before he was a teenager; before he was old enough to legally drink alcohol, Frizzell was performing in bars and nightclubs, earning the nickname "Lefty" because of his effective left hook.

Nashville soon got wind of the charismatic young country singer, and Columbia Records released Lefty's "If You've Got the Money, I've Got the Time" in 1950. It was an immediate hit, rising to #1 on the country chart. The flip side, "I Love You a Thousand Times," went to the top of the chart the following year. Frizzell was so popular with crowds during the early 1950s that they sometimes mobbed him, and even tore his clothes—a preview of the mania that would surround Elvis Presley three or four years

later. Frizzell had a string of hits in 1951: "I Want to Be With You Always," "Always Late," and "Mom and Dad's Waltz." But problems with alcohol, which hounded him throughout his life, led Frizzell into a period of artistic inactivity that did not end until he released "Long Black Veil" in 1959.

Frizzell's unreliability, which was mostly due to alcohol abuse, caused Columbia Records to drop him in 1972. ABC Records picked him up almost immediately, but Frizzell died of complications resulting from a stroke in 1975. His career had been checkered, but the songs he recorded and his unique singing style were a revelation to his peers and to many country musicians who followed. Lefty Frizzell was inducted into the Country Music Hall of Fame in 1982.

—P.B.

Although he was an Opry member for a brief stint in 1952, Lefty Frizzell was an outsider from the mainstream country establishment all his life. He was enormously popular nonetheless, particularly in the 1950s, during which he recorded a string of top-charting country hits.

Hank Williams

The Drifting Cowboy

Although Hiram "Hank" Williams (1923–1953) was shunned by the Nashville establishment early in his career, he remains one of the most popular and influential country stars of all time.

Born to Lon and Lilly Williams of Mount Olive, Alabama, Williams showed a talent for music at an early age. Hank, employed by the age of ten as a shoe-shine boy and peanut vendor, found enough time to learn the guitar from a local bluesman named Rufe Payne (known as Tee-Tot). By the age of eleven, Williams had learned enough to begin writing his first songs. The following year, the precocious Williams won first prize for his tune "WPA Blues" in a local songwriting competition.

Soon after, Williams formed his first band, Hank Williams and the Drifting Cowboys, which played hoedowns and square dances and starred on their own radio program in Montgomery, Alabama, at radio station WSFA.

After the breakup of the band, Williams became a drifting cowboy himself, and made his way to Texas, where he tried his hand at the rodeo. After he fell off a wild horse, however, his dream of cowpunching ended. The spill left him with severe back problems that plagued him for the rest of his relatively brief life.

Hank was soon tired of the circuit, and near the end of World War II he went to work at the shipyards in Mobile, Alabama. After tiring of that job, Hank swore that he would commit himself full-time to a career in music. He again formed his Drifting Cowboys, this time with his wife, "Miss Audrey," singing backup, and worked steadily throughout the Southeast. During these years, Williams acquired his reputation as a great showman—and as a drunk.

At the age of twenty-three, Williams got his first audition with the *Grand Ole Opry*. Unfortunately, his reputation preceded him. As could be expected from the "family radio hour," the *Opry* did not ask Williams to be a regular guest on the program.

It was on this trip to Nashville, however, that Hank had his first stroke of luck. Fred Rose, cofounder and president of the Acuff-Rose publishing company, signed him to a writer's contract, which ensured that his songs, if not sung by Williams himself, would at least be recorded and promoted by someone else. Because Rose did not have to rely on Williams to show up on time (or sober) for public engagements, Rose didn't have the reservations about hiring Hank

Like Lefty Frizzell, Hank Williams didn't last too long on the **Grand Ole Opry** *(the difference being that Lefty quit and Hank was kicked out). Here, the legend performs on the Opry stage as "Popalong" Hank Williams (with the Popcorn Poppers) in a promotional spot for Pops-Rite Popcorn.*

that had prevented the young musician from finding a spot on the *Opry*.

Although Rose believed in Hank's talent, he could not change the negative perception that dogged the young singer-songwriter in Music City. But when a New York–based company named Sterling Records inquired about new "hill-billy" talent, Rose quickly recommended Hank the Drifter. Sterling paid for a series of recording sessions at Nashville's WSM Studios. These sessions went so well that Fred Rose decided to search for a better contract with a larger label for Williams.

The newly formed MGM label—the brainchild of Frank Walker, former president of RCA Victor and Columbia—quickly snatched Hank from the Sterling label and launched the troubled young man's international career. By 1949 Williams had become one of the most popular entertainers in American music. After the overwhelming success of "Lovesick Blues," even the Grand Old Opry decided they must have misjudged him and asked Williams to make an appearance on their show. His performance of "Lovesick Blues" on the Opry stage resulted in six encores, after which the Opry decided to make him a "permanent" member of their esteemed company.

By 1952, however, Williams' years of drinking and taking drugs began to take their toll. That year, Audrey left him, taking their son, Randall Hank, and half of Hank's personal assets with her. The Grand Ole Opry also could not tolerate his growing substance abuse and revoked his membership.

Although he quickly remarried (to a beautiful singer named Billie Jean Jones), his life and career were on a terminal downhill spiral. On the first day of 1953, twenty-nine year old Hank Williams died from an overdose of pills and alcohol in the back seat of a sky-blue Cadillac on his way to a performance. His last hit song, which was released posthumously, was eerily entitled "I'll Never Get Out Of This World Alive."

In his brief lifetime, Hank wrote more than 120 superbly crafted songs, of which more than thirty were chart-topping country hits. Sadly, all the awards that Hank was to receive came after his lonely death. Along with Jimmie Rodgers and Fred Rose, Williams was one of the first people to be inducted into the Country Music Hall of Fame in 1961. The Country Music Association gave him its Pioneer Award in 1973 and another posthumous award, for vocal collaboration (accomplished through the wonder of modern-day recording technology) with Hank Jr. on "There's a Tear In My Beer," in 1989. The song also earned father and son a Grammy in 1990. Hank's song "Your Cheatin' Heart" was given another Grammy in 1983, and in 1987 Hank Sr. earned the Lifetime Achievement Award from the Country Music Association.

The Drifting Cowboy's bronze likeness now overlooks the city park in his second hometown, Montgomery, Alabama.

—A.H.

Hank was immensely popular with audiences, even if bookers tended to fear his irregularities. In the early 1950s, the music of Williams and his pal Frizzell was everywhere; in the words of Merle Haggard's "The Way It Was In '51," "Hank and Lefty crowded every jukebox."

country fans satisfied while establishing themselves as country music stars.

Several of the new stars came from a country music breeding ground that had been established on the West Coast, where such artists as Bob Wills, Hank Thompson, and Lefty Frizzell had moved in the late 1940s and early 1950s. A more swinging West Coast honky-tonk sound had developed, typified by the western swing–slanted style of Thompson and Merle Travis (whose "Divorce Me C.O.D." took breaking up in stride) and the raucous hillbilly/honky-tonk/primitive-rock-and-roll fusion of the Maddox Brothers and Rose.

Above: Hank Thompson was a great songwriter and performer in the honky-tonk style (with such hits as "[I've Got A] Humpty Dumpty Heart," "The Wild Side of Life," and "Honky Tonk Girl"), but he was also an accomplished tinkerer: he contributed further to the popularity of his band by enhancing the sound and lighting of his live performances with his engineering know-how. **Right:** Born in a converted boxcar, Merle Haggard was a honky-tonk hero whose sensibilities were forged by hard times throughout his life. He provided for his family (wife Leona Hobbs and four children) with hard labor and a touch of armed robbery; imprisoned in San Quentin in 1957, Haggard was able to catch Johnny Cash's 1958 concert there.

In Bakersfield—an oil and cotton town largely populated by southern migrants and farmworkers—a more hardcore honky-tonk sound ruled. The underrated honky-tonk singers Tommy Collins ("High On a Hilltop") and Wynn Stewart ("Wishful Thinking") worked out of Bakersfield in the late 1950s and early 1960s, paving the way for two superstars of honky-tonk who would soon emerge from the area: Buck Owens and Merle Haggard.

Alvis Edgar "Buck" Owens was born in Sherman, Texas, and raised in Arizona. He moved to Bakersfield in 1951 and began gigging and working as a session musician (he played on many of Tommy Collins' recordings), before launching his own recording career for Capitol in the mid-1950s. While he is perhaps best known today for popping up out of the corn field with a red, white, and blue guitar on *Hee Haw*, Owens had a slew of hard-country hits during the 1960s, including "Together Again," "Excuse Me (I Think I've Got a Heartache)," and "Act Naturally."

Merle Haggard, who started off playing bass for Wynn Stewart and was encouraged by Tommy Collins, has always specialized in darker, more personal material than Owens, a trait that has earned "the poet of the workin' man" his position as one of the great songwriters in country music history, as well as one of the all-time jukebox heroes. Haggard was born just outside of Bakersfield to Oklahoma migrant workers living in a converted boxcar. His troubled youth, which included a stint in San Quentin Prison, is reflected in such classics as "Hungry Eyes," "Mama Tried," "Workin' Man Blues," "Branded Man," "I'm a Lonesome Fugitive," and "Sing Me Back Home." Haggard also mined the ups and downs of drinking on such poignant numbers as "Swinging Doors," "The Bottle Let Me Down," and "I Threw Away The Rose" (a gut-wrenching tale of a life wrecked by alcoholism). His well-known political statements of the late 1960s—"Okie From Muskogee" and "The Fightin' Side Of Me"—found favor in many a working-class tavern, cementing the image of the honky-tonk as a bastion of reactionary conservatism.

In Texas, as in California, honky-tonk was flourishing at the roots during the late 1950s and through

the 1960s. Oddly, Ray Price (b. 1926)—who later produced some of the most saccharine of Nashville country pop and gospel—was a honky-tonk hero of the period. The Perryville, Texas, native (a protégé of Hank Williams) recorded classic sides during honky-tonk's early 1950s heyday but first hit it big with the shuffle "Crazy Arms" in 1956. A pioneer of high-tenor harmony in honky-tonk, Price was also an innovator in bringing a strong western swing element into his Hank Williams–influenced sound, through the triple fiddle–led drive of his Cherokee Cowboys.

The most enduring living embodiment of the honky-tonk life (and its classic dichotomy with fundamentalist values) also came out of the east Texas dancehall circuit during the 1950s. Born in Saratoga, Texas, George Jones learned to sing in a hard-shell Baptist church and grew up witnessing both the Christian teachings of his mother and the ramblings of his alcoholic father, for whom the bottle was a constant source of shame and strife. Jones eventually followed in his father's path but, like Hank Williams, recorded gospel music along with honky-tonk during his hell-raising, whiskey-soaked career (tempered in recent years by Jones' recovery from alcoholism and drug abuse). Like Williams, Jones seemed to be constantly tormented by the conflict between the hard moral tenets of Protestant fundamentalism and the corruptibility of the flesh. In his biography of Jones, Bob Allen

Ray Price's Cherokee Cowboys at different times featured several country stars, including Willie Nelson, Roger Miller, and Johnny Paycheck. Price also helped introduce to the public the songwriting talents of Kris Kristofferson with a recording of the song "For the Good Times," which became a million-seller.

recounts a telling incident where Jones, influenced by a radio preacher, threw his whiskey and cigarettes out the car window, only to stop a few miles up the road with the intention of going back to look for them.

Left: The small and wiry George Jones looked like a U.S. Marine with his bullet head and severe haircut, but was as rowdy a honky-tonk performer as ever there was. Below: Mississippian Moe Bandy patterned his style on the work of Hank Williams and George Jones, and later became friends with Lefty Frizzell. A former bronco buster, Bandy performed for years before finally making it big in the 1970s with such hits as "Don't Anyone Make Love at Home Anymore" and "Bandy the Rodeo Clown."

("The Race Is On") and sad weepers ("He Stopped Loving Her Today," "Good Year For The Roses").

Jones' duets with then-wife Tammy Wynette ("Golden Ring," "We're Gonna Hold On") also found favor with the honky-tonk crowd. While Kitty Wells' responses to honky-tonk cheating songs helped to establish her as the Queen of Country Music, country's preeminent women artists have never been as closely linked to the honky-tonk tradition as their male counterparts, who are by nature better able to relate to the male-dominated atmosphere of the barroom, especially when the material glorifies manly drinking bouts, good-ol'-boy camaraderie, or reckless infidelity.

Tammy Wynette—whose honky-tonk-flavored solo material includes the biting "D-I-V-O-R-C-E" and the defiant "Your Good Girl's Gonna Go Bad"—and Loretta Lynn have been the most successful female artists to mine honky-tonk themes. Lynn, in particular, has performed and written outstanding material that is as hard-hitting and true to life as the best of Jones and Haggard. Born into a coal-field family in Butcher Hollow, Kentucky, Lynn affirmed her roots with her first successful hit, 1960's "I'm a Honky Tonk Girl." During the 1960s and 1970s, Lynn hit home with the hard-country crowd with a refreshing female perspective on familiar honky-tonk themes. Lynn stands up to a husband's chronic drinking ("Don't Come Home A Drinkin' [With Lovin' On Your Mind])"), fights off the competition for her man ("Fist City," "You Ain't Woman

Jones' personal torments have always been implicit in his singing and his material, making for some of the most heartfelt and tortured honky-tonk music ever recorded. His drinking songs, in particular, cover the joys and sorrows of the bottle with the intimacy of hard firsthand experience. Over the years, Jones has scored with enthusiastic endorsements of moonshine liquor ("White Lightnin'") and hangover remedies ("C.C. Waterback"), sympathetic expressions of why alcoholics drink ("Wino the Clown," "If Drinking Don't Kill Me [Her Memory Will]"), and a humorous account of a futile struggle to go cold turkey ("Bone Dry"), as well as laments about the effects of alcohol on the body ("I've Aged Twenty Years in Five") and the soul ("A Drunk Can't Be a Man," "Wine-Colored Roses"). Jones has also moved the honky-tonk audience time and time again with songs about heartache, both uptempo numbers

Enough [To Take My Man]''), and rules her household (''Your Squaw Is On the Warpath'').

The 1970s were a time of extremes in American popular culture—epitomized by disco, bell-bottoms, and double-knits—as well as in honky-tonk music. In the songs of artists like Moe Bandy, Gary Stewart, Johnny Paycheck, and Vernon Oxford, honky-tonk's themes soared to exaggerated and humorous heights and plummeted to occasionally frightening depths. Bandy and Paycheck, in particular, specialized in songs that glorified binge-drinking. Such material had been around for a while (Rocky Hill Ford's ''Beer Drinkin' Blues'' and Claude King's ''51 Beers'' being prime examples), but Bandy and Paycheck institutionalized the binge as a response to heartbreak (Bandy's ''The Champ'' and Paycheck's ''15 Beers''). Paycheck actually advocated drunk driving—a natural, but usually unspoken facet of the honky-tonk lifestyle—as a remedy for the blues (''Drinkin' and Drivin'''). Similarly, in the truck-driver genre, where little white pills and pots of coffee had been the normal quiet excesses, Dave Dudley went so far as to feel no remorse for wrecking his rig after chugging down twelve beers on the way to meet his lover (''Two Six-Packs Away'').

While George Jones and Merle Haggard were known for songs about drinking (and for their personal battles with the bottle), alcohol was not a part of either man's public persona. In the 1970s, however, Moe Bandy (later with his good-ol'-boy running buddy Joe Stampley) was actively marketed by Columbia Records with the hard-drinking crowd in mind. For a while Bandy was featured with a cold one in his hand on the cover of nearly every record he put out. The all-time classic is his 1976 LP *Here I Am Drunk Again*, the front cover of which features Bandy curled up inside a mug of beer. On the back cover, Moe sits at a table in a honky-tonk, pouring his sixth can of Pearl Light into a glass, the other five cans piled up in front of him. The cover of the album *Just Good Ol' Boys* features Moe and Joe leaning against an old primer-coated Cadillac with a fishing boat hooked on the back. They sport cold ones in their hands, baseball caps on their heads, beards on their faces, and cowboy boots on their feet. The image

Johnny Paycheck
Lovin' Machine

By the time Johnny Paycheck (b. 1941) had recorded and popularized "Take This Job and Shove It" in 1972, he was referring to himself as "on a comeback." Born Donald Lytle on May 31, 1941, in Greenfield, Ohio, Johnny Paycheck has come and gone from the limelight many times in his forty-year career in the music business.

Donald Lytle first decided upon the stage name Donnie Young. His tarnished reputation under that name (he spent time in jail for writing bad checks and for hitting an officer when he was in the U.S. Navy) worked against him, however, so he started all over again with a new name: Johnny Paycheck. (The original Johnny Paycheck had been a prize fighter knocked out by Joe Louis in the first round of a heavyweight bought. Apparently, Lytle figured out that Johnny Paycheck the first was no longer in need of his name.)

From the age of fourteen on, Johnny was on the road and in the recording studio with his band. He received his first recording contract in the 1950s, but it was not until the late 1960s, with the release of "The Lovin' Machine" and "Mr. Lovemaker," that he achieved much commercial success.

As a songwriter, Paycheck has also had success. His song "Apartment No. 9" was covered by Tammy Wynette. He is also an accomplished guitarist, and has played for George Jones, Ray Price, and many others.

Having quit school at the age of fourteen, Paycheck wound up completing his high school education while in prison. In 1988, after a barroom shootout, Paycheck was sentenced to nine and a half years in an Ohio correctional facility. The proceeds from the album that was released at the time of his incarceration, *Outlaw at the Cross*, went to children who suffered from AIDS. Two years after leaving prison (he

won an early release in 1991), Paycheck began building his own theater in country music's city of lights, Branson, Missouri.

Paycheck received both a Grammy and the career achievement award for "Take This Job and Shove It." Finally, like Waylon Jennings, Paycheck became a national spokesman for an organization that promotes the high school equivalency examination.

—A.H.

Along with Merle Haggard and David Allan Coe, Johnny Paycheck was among the honky-tonk stars whose rowdy ways landed them in prison.

Above: *Arkansan Vernon Oxford made a name for himself in the 1970s with a number of songs that extolled the honky-tonk lifestyle (including "Redneck!" and "Redneck Roots"), but has since become born again and now uses his songs as cautionary examples.* **Right, top:** *Although Hank Williams, Jr., was carefully groomed by his mother, he turned out to have a healthy supply of Hank Sr.'s blood in his veins, as evidenced by his struggles with substance abuse and his catalog of rough-and-ready songs.* **Right, below:** *David Allan Coe spent the majority of his youth in and out of reform schools and prison—experience that he was able to draw on while penning a slew of honky-tonk hits in the 1970s and 1980s (including "Longhaired Redneck," "Jack Daniels If You Please," and "Now I Lay Me Down To Cheat").*

struck a chord, and the "Moe and Joe" songs are still favorites on honky-tonk jukeboxes.

Barroom violence—especially when induced by alcohol—was also glorified in song to an unprecedented extent during the 1970s. Vernon Oxford's "A Good Old Fashioned Saturday Night Honky-Tonk Barroom Brawl," which describes fistfighting, flying beer bottles, and crying women as "a good time had by all," portrays the barroom brawl as an acceptable weekly ritual, a release of pent-up working-class tension, and a source of entertainment for the crowd. Johnny Paycheck—who later went to prison for killing a man in a barroom shooting in Ohio—scored a hit with "Colorado Kool-Aid," a tale of Coors-fueled mayhem in which a bar patron cuts off another man's ear with a switchblade.

Although songs like "Colorado Kool-Aid" and "Just Good Ol' Boys" bordered on novelty, Paycheck and Bandy also produced a lot of stellar, heartfelt honky-tonk material throughout the 1970s. In fact, hardcore, traditional honky-tonk songwriting and performances flourished during the decade, from the likes of veterans Jones, Haggard, and Lynn and from such outstanding newcomers as Gary Stewart (who specialized in tormented drinking and cheating songs like "Back Slider's Wine," and "She's Actin' Single [I'm Drinkin' Doubles]") and Red Steagall (who brought back the spirit of western swing with "Lone Star Beer and Bob Wills Music" and captured the honky-tonk mood with "Neons and Nylons"). Artists working out of the newly developing outlaw and country-rock scenes (Waylon Jennings, Willie Nelson, David Allan Coe, Gram Parsons, and Hank Williams, Jr.,for instance) also offered well-done reinterpretations of honky-tonk songs and themes. Coe's

"Take This Job and Shove It" (written for Johnny Paycheck) became a workingman's anthem on par with the best of Merle Haggard's output, while Coe's own version of "You Never Even Called Me By My Name" (written by Steve Goodman) remains a barroom sing-a-long anthem that effectively manages to both celebrate and parody honky-tonk's prevailing themes. Hank Williams, Jr., also made the barroom soundtrack, living up to his father's legacy with songs endorsing a diet of pills and 90-proof ("Whiskey Bent and Hell Bound," "Family Tradition"), while also intensifying the reactionary political stance that Merle Haggard had adopted during the 1960s ("A Country Boy Can Survive").

As the 1980s dawned, mainstream America turned conservative, and the hell-raising good-ol'-boy image was replaced by a trend toward wholesomeness, nostalgia, and clean-cut cowboys in white hats. Even Moe Bandy, the man who had once sung that "two cans of breakfast won't do me no harm," espoused "family values," toured with the George Bush for President campaign, and opened up a place in Branson, Missouri, a theme park dedicated to diluting and glossing over country and western's hardscrabble, honky-tonk roots. In general, increased public concern over drunk driving, substance abuse, and AIDS dampened enthusiasm for traditional drinking and cheating songs and caused an upsurge in idealistic country songs about rural life, commitment to marriage and family, and "the good old days." Increasingly, the jukebox at the county-line roadhouse gave way to formalized line-dancing at the suburban "boot-scootin' boogie" bar.

Fortunately for fans of hard country, however, some new artists have continued to produce top-notch honky-tonk material during the 1980s and 1990s. Among them are John Anderson ("Wild & Blue"), David Ball ("Thinkin' Problem"), Mark Chesnutt ("Brother Jukebox"), Earl Thomas Conley ("You Must Not Be Drinkin' Enough"), Vern Gosdin ("Set 'Em Up Joe"), Becky Hobbs ("Jones on the Jukebox"), Alan Jackson ("Here in the Real World"),

George Strait (who is among the many indebted to the superb vocal stylings of Lefty Frizzell) is one of the many contemporary performers who has demonstrated that the honky-tonk spirit is still alive, despite the forces of conservatism that swept the United States in the 1980s.

Doug Stone ("I'd Be Better Off [In a Pine Box]"), George Strait ("The Honky-Tonk Downstairs"), and Randy Travis ("There'll Always Be a Honky-Tonk Somewhere"). Revivalists like Dwight Yoakam (a Nudie-suited, non-drinking, vegetarian originally hell-bent on bringing back the classic Bakersfield sound of Buck Owens) and Junior Brown (an Ernest Tubb worshiper who dresses like a Sunday school teacher, plays a homemade guitar-steel combo called a "guit-steel," and writes and sings pure honky-tonk songs) have taken the genre in exciting directions. And, sadly, the death of promising honky-tonk singer Keith Whitley of an alcohol overdose at the age of thirty-four was a reminder of the enduring power and painful consequences of the honky-tonk lifestyle.

While the term "honky-tonk" naturally brings to mind Hank Williams, George Jones, Merle Haggard, and the genre's other stars, the music has always lent itself equally to performers outside of the limelight. These men and women haven't experienced the spotlights of success either because they can't entice music industry representation or because they refuse to. Just a few examples include Marvin Rainwater (who coined the immortal line "I'm gonna build me a bar in the back of my car/and drive myself to drink"); songwriters Sanger D. "Whitey" Shafer ("If I Say I Love You Consider Me Drunk"), Dallas Frazier ("Honky Tonk Amnesia"), and Paul Craft ("Hank Williams, You Wrote My Life"); and Vernon Oxford, who in addition to his novelty numbers "Redneck" and "A Good Old Fashioned Saturday Night Honky Tonk Barroom Brawl," recorded several brilliant, soon-to-be-forgotten honky-tonk albums for Rounder Records in the 1970s, leading writer John Pugh to pose the question in *Country Music* magazine: "Is Vernon Oxford really too country for country?"

As *Country Music* magazine editor Michael Bane eloquently writes, the honky-tonk bar is a "working class pit-stop between today and tomorrow; a buffer zone between exhaustion and despair...the American dream shrunken to beer, broads, and a bunch of loud music." The county-line roadhouses and dancehalls with "honky-tonk hardwood floors" that nurtured the music are not as prevalent as they once were, but honky-tonk keeps a receptive audience that appreciates music that meets life head-on, facing up to its struggles and sorrows with courage, humor, and grit (as well as guilt, self-pity, and despair), and celebrating its pleasures with hard-won relish and exuberant excess. Honky-tonk is not pretty: the lifestyle described by its lyrics are as real as semen stains on cheap motel sheets, a severed ear on a barroom floor, a folder of divorce papers, or a loved one with a drinking problem vomiting in the bathroom. But honky-tonk also expresses the possibility for redemption from such depths by acknowledging life's trials, recommending the healing companionship of friends and lovers, and, perhaps above all, advocating occasional visits to "Barstool Mountain," where the view of a tall cold one in a dimly lit bar with a jukebox playing loud in the background offers its own measure of peace.

Chapter Eight

The Wild Side of Life

Scandals in Country Music

by Judith Mahoney Pasternak

From early on in its history, country music and scandal have gone together like—well, like marriage and D-I-V-O-R-C-E.

At first glance this seems strange, for the world of country is notoriously conservative, its headwaters pooling at the center of the very heartland over which the family values banner waves most triumphantly. "We don't smoke marijuana in Muskogee," sang Merle Haggard in "Okie from Muskogee," with Muskogee, Oklahoma, representing the idealized town "where even squares can have a ball." Or as one-man woman Loretta Lynn—still with "Doolittle" Lynn, whom she married when she was thirteen—put it, "When you're lookin' at me, you're lookin' at country."

Hank—already ravaged by pain and alcohol and looking far older than his twenty-six years—is pictured here with his family in 1949: first wife Audrey Guy Sheppard, Audrey's daughter, and Hank Williams, Jr.

Yet no matter how enthusiastically country songs by the dozen celebrate the virtues of home, hearth, and the American heritage, country audiences have been consistently tolerant of scandal in the lives of those who sing the songs. Within limits, the fans have loved their idols all the more for the idols' headline-making weaknesses. On the record, it's when you look at folks who marry a lot, drink even more, and pop all the pills there are that you're lookin' at country music.

The contradiction is only on the surface. More than any other American music genre except the blues, country is rooted in the real lives of the working people who listen to it. It's an audience that has known hard times and cherishes music that reflects those hard times; for all its pieties, country music has always had another face, one that looked head-on at (many of) the harsher facts of life. (One aspect of U.S. life to which this does not apply, perhaps—speaking of the blues—is segregation. Country music, despite its deep musical ties to black American music in general and blues in particular, has a predominantly white audience and an almost all-white roster of performers.)

Of course, the moral standards of the nation at large have changed since the beginning of the country music recording business in the 1920s. Country is a form of show business, and celebrities of all sorts—

including country performers, and especially women in country—have far more latitude now than they once did. Yet even in 1927, when the dirt-poor but respectable Carter Family left Maces Springs, Virginia, and drove over the mountains to Bristol to record for Victor A&R man Ralph Peer, there were currents of riot swirling just under the placid surface of the music.

"Keep on the sunny side, always on the sunny side," urged the Carters. But in the wild oil fields of east Texas, hard-driving, hard-drinking oil-riggers who drank after work in the blood-bucket bars called honky-tonks wanted to hear about the wild side, not the sunny side. They wanted songs about cigarettes, whiskey, and wild, wild women; the men—and they were virtually all men—who sang in the honky-tonks supplied that demand.

Through the Depression and the war years that followed it, the record industry boomed. When the honky-tonks became juke joints after the war, a new subgenre of country—honky-tonk—grafted the wild side to the sunny side. The graft took; instead of rejecting the new subject matter, audiences everywhere drank it up.

The personification of honky-tonk was Hank Williams, who clawed his way from dire southern poverty to stardom in the late 1940s, his brilliant, raw talent eclipsed only by the monumental self-destructiveness that took his life but never dented his popularity.

When "Move It On Over" became a hit in 1947, Williams was twenty-three years old. As little, frail Hiram Williams, he had started singing for pennies in the streets of Greenville, Alabama, when he was twelve. He learned the rudiments of music under the tutelage of an older black street singer named Rufus Payne. With and without Payne, he drifted into local black bars and juke joints to listen to the blues and assimilate some of its elements into his own brand of honky-tonk.

Williams may have started drinking to excess almost as early—partly by inclination, partly driven by the severe pain he endured all his life from an undiagnosed spinal disorder. (His first visit to a doctor occurred when he was already a star.) By 1947 his body was already ravaged.

By then, Williams' marriage to would-be country singer Audrey Mae Sheppard Guy Williams was in deep trouble as well. Only three years before they had been so ardent that they had wed before her divorce from a previous husband was finalized (although since Alabama recognized common-law marriage, Williams and she had become legal spouses). Now the relationship was rapidly eroding under the pressure of Hank's wild binges and the all-too-frequent physical brutality that accompanied them. Audrey divorced him in May 1948.

Once apart, however, Audrey and Hank still longed for each other; their only son, Hank Williams, Jr., was born a year to the day after the divorce decree. Soon after Hank Jr.'s birth, Audrey had the divorce annulled.

Over the next three years an unbroken string of hits—"Lovesick Blues," "Cold, Cold Heart," "Jambalaya," "Your Cheatin' Heart"—propelled Hank to the pinnacle of country and beyond. He won a Grand Ole Opry contract; covers of his songs went to the top of the pop charts. Money was pouring in—and pouring out.

Williams' condition was deteriorating just as rapidly as his funds were running out. Then he met a convicted felon who called himself Dr. Toby Marshall, who had no medical qualifications except the ability to write prescriptions that would pass muster at a drugstore. Marshall prescribed—and Hank took—amphetamines and every available downer, including Seconal, chloral hydrate, and morphine. He kept drinking as well. Soon, paranoid fantasies began fueling the rampages that more and more often involved firearms and resulted in arrests and enforced visits to dry-out clinics.

Audiences still loved him—when he was able to perform. Early in 1952, in Richmond, Virginia, he drew boos and hisses when, reeling, he mangled the words to his own songs. The next day, a *Times-Dispatch* reviewer put the embarrassing details regarding the incident down in black and white. Hank was so angry that he opened his second-night performance with "Mind Your Own Business" and dedicated it to the too-honest journalist. The audience stood up and cheered.

But the people who had to live and work with Williams couldn't afford to be so tolerant, and 1952 was the year everybody fired him. The Grand Ole Opry canceled his contract, promoters were less and less willing to book him, and Audrey divorced him for the second and last time.

When Hank married Billie Jean Jones that October (as with his marriage to Audrey, it occurred before his bride's divorce was finalized),

Hank Williams had only a few months to live when he married Billie Jean Jones. Here, the wedding couple poses at a party in New Orleans on October 19, 1952.

he could hardly stand up for the ceremony. According to one biographer, Billie Jean discovered on their wedding night that her husband was by now all but incapable of consummating the marriage—and incontinent as well.

In fact, Williams couldn't do much of anything, but he was still Hank Williams. He got a couple of bookings: New Year's Eve in Charleston, West Virginia, and New Year's Day in Canton, Ohio. On December 30 he flew out of Montgomery, heading for Charleston, but was grounded by bad weather in Knoxville. He called his mother in Montgomery and asked her to send a driver for him.

By the time the driver, seventeen-year-old Charles Carr, arrived the next day, it was obvious that Hank wasn't going to be able to perform that night. Finally, Carr set out for Canton instead, in the hope that the sodden singer could be whipped into shape by the next day.

They never made it to Canton. Carr was pulled over for speeding in New Blaine, Tennessee; the cop who peered into the car said the man in the back seat looked dead. No, Carr said, it was Hank Williams, and he was just tired.

But in the early hours of January 1, 1953, in Oak Hill, West Virginia, Carr pulled into a gas station to check on Hank. He was stone cold.

No one knows just where or when Williams died, or how long Carr knowingly carted around the singer's corpse before he decided what to do with it, or indeed whether Hank was already dead when Carr put him in the car in Knoxville. His date of death is generally given as January 1, 1953, but it may well have been December 31, 1952.

A coroner's cursory examination concluded that Hank had died of heart failure. Twenty thousand peo-

Hank Williams, Jr.

Mr. Monday Night

Randall Hank Williams (b. 1949) was born in Shreveport, Louisiana, to the famous country music couple Hank and Audrey Williams, but his success as a songwriter/performer was due only in part to his birthright. Hank Williams, Jr., is a multitalented performer with a recording history that is now more than twice as long as that of his father. He is proficient on the guitar, banjo, piano, fiddle, steel and bass guitars, drums, and harmonica. He is also a prolific songwriter and the recipient of more than twenty major music awards.

Although things ended tumultuously between his mother and father, Hank Jr. was nonetheless groomed by Audrey Williams to follow in his father's footsteps. His professional career as a singer began at he age of eight when he performed songs that his father had made famous. At the age of fourteen, Hank Jr. was hired to score the soundtrack to the movie *Your Cheatin' Heart*, the biography of his father, which starred George Hamilton. The most interesting song of the film, "Standing in the Shadows," told the world that being the son of a famous singer was not easy. Hank Jr.'s nickname probably did not help: before his death, Hank Sr. had taken to calling his son "Bocephus," after the dummy of ventriloquist Red Brasfield, who appeared regularly on the *Grand Ole Opry*.

At the age of twenty-one, some twenty charting singles later, Hank Jr. had his first #1 song, "All For the Love of Sunshine." Within two years came another hit, "Eleven Roses." Neither of these successes, however, got him out from under his father's shadow in his hometown of Nashville, so Hank Jr. left Music City for Alabama.

Before beginning a year-long tour in 1975, Williams took a hiking trip through the mountains of Montana, which almost proved fatal. A 150-foot (46m) fall left him with a broken skull that required countless reconstructive operations.

After the release in 1979 of the album *Family Tradition*, Williams had a string of gold and platinum albums. By 1982 he had nine albums simultaneously on *Billboard*'s charts. The rest of the 1980s proved just as successful for him with hits like "A Country Boy Can Survive," "All My Rowdy Friends (Have Settled Down)," "All My Rowdy Friends (Are Coming Over Tonight)," "Born to Boogie," and "This Ain't Dallas." The 1990s saw him score with the hit "Don't Give Us A Reason"; Williams donated all royalties from the song to the American Red Cross. In 1991 he received an Emmy, television's highest honor, for the theme song to Monday Night Football.

With more than sixty albums under his belt, Hank Williams, Jr., like his father, is one of the most successful country artists of all time. The rowdy prodigal son continues to perform to this day, drawing sellout crowds on a regular basis.

—A.H.

"Bocephus"—Hank Williams, Jr.—grew up to be a star and hell-raiser in his own right.

ple attended his funeral in Montgomery on January 4; they called it Montgomery's saddest day since the Civil War.

And the Hank Williams scandals had only just begun. His two wives, Audrey and Billie Jean, fought each other for years for the right to be called his widow, and Audrey, Billie Jean, and Lillie Skipper Williams Stone, Hank's mother, waged a battle over his estate. (Though little was left of his earnings, his royalties would be worth millions.) Lillie died in 1955, Audrey in 1975; the lawsuits continued, with Hank Jr., by then in his twenties, replacing Audrey as the main claimant. (Hank Jr. would make his own small contribution to the annals of scandal in country music in 1988, when he sang his hit "If the South Woulda Won" at the Country Music Association [CMA] awards ceremony. It was the night he received the CMA's Entertainer of the Year award; *Billboard*'s Edward Morris resigned from the CMA in protest, later saying, "I did not want to be part of an organization that endorsed that kind of redneckery.")

In 1985 a fourth party joined the fight when then thirty-two-year-old Jett Williams filed suit in both New York and Alabama courts for a share in the estate, claiming that she was Hank's last child, the fruit of a 1952 relationship with one Bobbie Jett. A New York court validated her claim in 1989.

The royalties are still coming in; many of Hank's recordings remain available, and his songs continue to be covered—as does his life. Hank Williams remains not only a beloved and revered country icon, but an archetype of the male country singer, a mold into which many of the men of country have poured themselves in the decades since Hank's tragic death at the age of twenty-nine. (Williams' lifestyle was not considered an appropriate model for women in country, however; it was years before record companies, for instance, would dream of recording or promoting any woman half as wild as Williams.)

Like Williams—and without even his excuse of spinal agony—a startling proportion of country's brightest stars have drunk themselves into oblivion, awakened themselves with amphetamines, and then resedated themselves with downers of one kind or another. (In the cocaine-happy 1980s, many added coke to their recreational medicine cabinet, although almost to a man they have steered clear of heroin, the bane of rock and roll.) Like Williams, too, many have died young of accumulated excess, though few as shockingly early as he did.

While Hank was the reigning king of the hillbillies, in 1950 and 1951, a slightly younger contemporary, the troubled Lefty Frizzell, was turning out blockbuster honky-tonk hits like "If You've Got the Money, I've Got the Time." Then booze brought his career to a near halt, with occasional hits punctuating years of idleness, until his death—from a long life of alcohol abuse—at the age of forty-seven. There were many others, too. Gene Vincent, for instance, the rockabilly singer whose "Be-Bop-a-Lula" was a crossover country hit in 1956, died drunk at thirty-six.

Perhaps the most spectacular dissolution, however, was that of Elvis Presley. The King of Rock and Roll was only an occasional comet in the country sky, but always a bright one. Unlike Williams and the other lost souls of country, Elvis hated drink and rarely or never touched alcohol.

Instead, the King just took pills. But the pills did the trick: Elvis, too, died ravaged and much too young in 1977.

The list of country's alcohol and drug fatalities might be considerably longer if the full truth were known about all the small-plane crashes that have killed country performers, but plane crashes often destroy the evidence of their causes. Drugs were definitely implicated, however, in the 1985 disaster that took the life of sometime country star Rick Nelson and several members of his band.

Yet even the most thorough-going and extreme dissipation isn't always fatal to its country practitioners. Country seems to have a much lower fatality rate from alcohol and drug abuse than does rock and roll, for instance, and the country annals contain virtual armies of roisterers who have survived the lifestyle, many of them for long enough to clean up.

Johnny Cash, for instance—country's Man in Black—is alive and well and religious at sixty-plus. Thirty years ago, though, he was a mess: booze-drenched and pill-addicted. When he achieved country and pop stardom with the crossover hit "I Walk the

Left: *Rick Nelson traveled far from the world of Ozzie and Harriet before the fatal plane crash that took his life in 1985.* **Below:** *Johnny Cash never let his personal life and habits get in the way of his rise to stardom; in his sixties at this writing, the Man in Black is perhaps the most respected figure in country music.*

Line" in 1956, he had been walking in Hank Williams' footsteps for years.

By the mid-1960s, Cash seemed all too likely to follow Hank all the way down the line. Busted in Texas for possession in 1964, he was holding an astonishing 688 Dexedrines and 475 tranquilizers; the next year, the Grand Ole Opry made it clear he would not be invited back to the show following an incident where the unsteady singer had stumbled and tripped onstage, smashing equipment in the process. In 1966 his first wife divorced him.

Then Johnny met second-generation Carter Family star June Carter. He also found God. After Cash and June married in 1968, he sobered up for the first—but not the last—time. Over the next several years, he became increasingly involved with evangelical Protestantism, often traveling and singing with evangelist Billy Graham.

Elected to the Country Music Hall of Fame in 1980, Cash cut an album called *Survivors* the next year with fellow Sun Records alumni Jerry Lee Lewis and Carl Perkins. His self-congratulation, however, had been premature; an accident brought drugs back

into his life in the form of painkillers, and he was off and running again—in the wrong direction.

But in 1983 Cash entered the Betty Ford Clinic for an extra-long stay and came out clean at last. Three years later, he published a book he had been writing for a decade: *The Man In White*, a novel about St. Paul. He still performs to standing ovations and sellout crowds; "survivor" is the right word now.

Meanwhile, show-business sobriety had become chic. Even most of the country "outlaws" of

Bob Wills was a genial man and a great fiddler, but his problems with alcohol and his many wives suggested that underneath his hat inner turmoil bubbled.

the 1970s turned in that direction in the 1980s, after years of excess and indulgence.

Waylon Jennings is a real survivor. Performing with the Crickets at the time, he missed death by a hairsbreadth back in 1959, when he gave up to J.P. Richardson—the Big Bopper—his seat in the plane in which Richardson perished along with rock pioneer Buddy Holly and Chicano rocker Ritchie Valens. Jennings lived to become the first of the outlaws; his *Honky Tonk Heroes* album defined the image in 1973.

In 1976 *Wanted: The Outlaws* (rereleased in its entirety in 1996), with Jennings and Willie Nelson, became the first million-selling country album ever. By the mid-1980s, both Jennings and Kristofferson had become clean and sober ex-outlaws. Kristofferson

straightened out after his marriage to singer Rita Coolidge fell apart in 1980, and Jennings followed suit in 1985.

For all those decades, the women of country led far more restrained lives, at least in public. In the 1970s superstar Loretta Lynn and Heartbreak Heroine Tammy Wynette both admitted shyly that health problems and stress had led them to take more pills than might have been good for them, but only recently, in the 1990s, do country women appear to have won equal rights in the hell-raising department.

In country's younger generation, stepsisters Carlene Carter and Rosanne Cash—the daughters, respectively, of June Carter and Johnny Cash by their first spouses—have both had serious struggles with alcohol and pills. They admitted the problems early and unself-consciously, long before they had done themselves the kind of damage their forerunners had done to themselves, and appear to have been victorious in their battles with addiction. And country's wild child, Tanya Tucker, has acquired major star status while generating as many tabloid headlines as any man in the business.

Tucker has, in fact, defied many stereotypes. Twice a mother, but never—so far—a wife, she is apparently part of a current rebellion against the old country tradition of marrying early and often.

In the past, the frequency with which Nashville's luminaries changed their legal partners gave a second meaning to the phrase "Tennessee Waltz." Like Hollywood's stars—and unlike rock-and-rollers—country stars appeared to be fearful of offending conservative audiences by merely changing mates and dancing without benefit of clergy.

In their rush to the altar, however, many have omitted legal steps necessary to shed previous spouses or otherwise skirted marriage laws, rendering their new bonds of dubious legality. Both of Hank Williams' wives, for instance (as noted previously), became bigamists when they went to the altar with Williams before the expiration of the waiting period required to finalize their divorces. And Jerry Lee Lewis, whose full story is told below, may have had only one legal divorce among his six marriages. But bigamy is rarely prosecuted, and no country performer has ever been charged with it in court.

Mere divorce and remarriage have never tarnished a country image. Even the venerable Carters—A.P. and Sarah—divorced, in 1933, and western swing bandleader Bob Wills, Waylon Jennings, and Willie Nelson are among the long list of luminaries who have been married at least four times.

Again, however, the level of tolerance has been somewhat different for women. Tammy Wynette's five marriages are notorious, although that may be as much because of the perceived incongruity of "Stand By Your Man" Wynette standing by five men, one after another, as it is because she is a woman. The man in the middle, her third husband, was George Jones, who was no slouch himself in the marriage department.

Wynette was eighteen and still known as Virginia Pugh when she married Euple Byrd in her native Mississippi. The unsatisfactory marriage was nevertheless fruitful: Gwendolyn Lee Euple was born in 1961, Jacquelyn Faye Euple (named after then–first lady Jacqueline Kennedy) in 1962, and Tina Euple in 1965. No one in Virginia's family had ever

Kris Kristofferson

Renaissance Cowboy

Kristofferson's career as an actor has obscured his impressive accomplishments as a songwriter and singer, mostly of country songs. His lonesome, tragic screen persona echoes the timbre of his musical catalog, which includes such mournful ballads of the dispossessed as "Me and Bobby McGee," "Sunday Mornin' Comin' Down," "Silver Tongued Devil and I," and "Why Me Lord?" His image as a scruffy, doleful, melancholy sort is also in sharp contrast to his early life as a Rhodes Scholar, an Army helicopter pilot, and a would-be instructor at West Point. The Brownsville, Texas, native has proven himself to be a jack of many trades and master of most of them, but his well-publicized problems with drugs and alcohol also show that the journey has not been smooth.

Kristoffer Kristofferson was born on June 22, 1936, into a military family (his father was an U.S. Air Force general). He was a model son, a Golden Gloves boxer, and a Phi Beta Kappa. He won the *Atlantic Monthly's* collegiate short story contest and went to Oxford University on a Rhodes Scholarship. Returning to the United States in 1960, Kristofferson joined the army, training and qualifying as a helicopter pilot; he also took up the guitar. When his tour ended, he reenlisted for a second three-year hitch and was sent to Germany, where other soldiers encouraged him to send some of his songs to Nashville. At the end of his second tour, Kristofferson returned to the States and contemplated a career at West Point.

Impulsively, and to the amazement and disapproval of his family, he instead moved to Nashville, arriving there with little more than the handful of songs he had written in Germany. The years that followed might just as well be taken from the story of any ambitious, would-be songwriter's biography; Kristofferson tended bar and even worked as a janitor at a Columbia Records studio as he tried to interest the reigning recording stars of the time in his material.

Roger Miller and Johnny Cash eventually responded to Kristofferson's persistence. Miller recorded "Me and Bobby McGee" and Cash made a #1 hit of "Sunday Mornin' Comin' Down," which in 1970 was honored as the Country Music Association's Song of the Year.

Cash and Kristofferson became friends, and with the star's encouragement Kristofferson signed a recording deal with the Monument label, making albums that were firmly rooted in folk and country music. In spite of chronic stagefright, his tours were well received and "Silver Tongued Devil and I" and "Why Me Lord?" went gold. At about the same time, Janis Joplin transformed "Me and Bobby McGee" into a rock classic and a blockbuster sales champ.

In the early 1970s Kristofferson went to Hollywood and began a film career, appearing in such movies as *Cisco Pike* (1971), *Alice Doesn't Live Here Anymore* (1975), *A Star Is Born* (1976), *The Sailor Who Fell From Grace with the Sea* (1976), *Semi-Tough* (1977), and *Heaven's Gate* (1980).

Kristofferson's marriage in 1973 to singer Rita Coolidge lasted only a few years, a period in which they toured the country as a country-pop duo and during which Kristofferson's drug and alcohol abuses worsened. His friendship and professional work with Willie Nelson and Waylon Jennings, themselves substance abusers, earned him recognition as one of country music's outlaws.

Kristofferson's life in the years following his divorce from Coolidge was difficult, but he managed to

Call them survivors: fellow "outlaws"—and humanitarians—Willie Nelson (left) and Kris Kristofferson.

kick his addictions. He gravitated back to country music and discovered that Cash, Nelson, and Jennings were also drying out. He joined them on a 1990 tour to promote the album *Highwayman 2,* which was released in 1991, and on a 1995 tour to promote *The Road Goes on Forever* (Liberty). Kristofferson continues to perform, promoting several humanitarian causes, and record.

Now married to attorney Lisa Meyers, Kristofferson continues to write and act; his 1987 solo album, *Repossessed,* was widely praised, as were his performances in the movies *Amerika* and *Trouble in Mind.* Kristofferson retains his hard-won reputation as a sensitive chronicler of the vagaries of lost love, loneliness, and despair, crafting his songs with the sophistication of a would-be novelist and taking life, as he told one interviewer, "one day at a time."

—P.B.

Rosanne Cash

The Woman in Black

Being the heiress to the throne of country music is not necessarily a blessing. In fact, in the case of Rosanne Cash (b. 1955), the inheritance led to an unsettled life, where recovering from near-death experiences, for instance, is more commonplace than one might think.

What Rosanne perceived as the common experience during her childhood would be considered tragic by most other people's standards. Only a toddler when her father, Johnny Cash, became a world-renowned country singer, Rosanne and her family lived in daily anxiety and confusion. Only months before Rosanne could walk, Johnny was simply an appliance salesman, the first generation of his family to work outside of sharecropping. This workingman's strapping son had a talent that would quickly push him beyond the world he understood. As Rosanne puts it, "Nobody's prepared for that kind of fame"—not the one who gains the fame nor the family he or she brings into it.

Rosanne's approach toward life—however hesitant she may be to admit it—was and is much like her father's. When things became too stable in their lives, the music in their minds began to stagnate. Recognition of this waning inspiration often led to drastic reactions. Father and daughter have both questioned the calm they have achieved for themselves, and in examining that feeling of stability, have taken steps to abolish it.

After the divorce of Rosanne's parents, the four Cash daughters went to live with their mother and her new husband, a police officer, in Ventura, California. As children often do in dysfunctional families, Rosanne, Cindy, Kathy, and Tara began acting out against every institution around them. Rosanne, in particular, was real trouble for her teachers in high school. At times she would drop her younger siblings off at school, pick up her boyfriend, and head for Tijuana. Trouble was a balm to the fury she had inherited.

Rosanne spent a year in London after high school and then attended Vanderbilt University for a while, until she moved to Los Angeles to study acting. Finally coming to terms with the fact that her talent—songwriting and singing—meant competing with her father and in a sense recognizing his influence on her, Rosanne moved to Nashville and began putting together a set with her future husband, Rodney Crowell, a gifted songwriter and guitarist who had made his name with Emmylou Harris. Rosanne Cash's first album, *Right or Wrong*, was a combined effort by Crowell and Cash.

As her father had after his first big success, Rosanne developed a drug addiction following the release of her album *Seven Year Ache*, in 1981. Rosanne, now out of control, was hospitalized by her family (as Johnny had been by his family years before) in the hopes of restoring the daughter (and wife) sadly displaced by fame. (She has since fully recovered.)

In 1985 Rosanne released *Rhythm and Romance*, which won her a Grammy that year for Best Country Vocal Performance, Female. *King's Record Shop*, a collection of songs that were for the most part made famous by other artists, paid homage to the music she loves. From that album came an astounding four #1 country singles.

In a break with the family tradition, second-generation country star Rosanne Cash got clean and sober while she was still young.

Since then Rosanne Cash has crossed over from country to rock and folk at Columbia Records, left her husband Crowell, and moved to New York City, doing what Cashes do best—shaking things up for the sake of a fresh start.

—A.H.

divorced; she would soon more than make up for that deficiency, but meanwhile she remained unhappily married to Byrd for seven years.

In 1966, however, she moved to Nashville, changed her name to Tammy Wynette, recorded her first hit ("Apartment No. 9"), and broadened her horizons. She ended her marriage to Byrd in 1967 and not long afterward married songwriter Don Chapel. Alas, marriage number two wasn't much of an improvement.

Then Wynette met Jones, at that point the reigning king of country; she, like legions of country fans, had idolized him for years. Jones had been married to his second wife for seventeen years. Like Tammy, he had had three children, a daughter from his first marriage and two sons from the current one. He was also as good at drinking as he was at marrying; at that point he was well on the way toward acquiring the nickname "No Show Jones."

Wynette and Jones fell irresistibly in love. They became a performing duo—one of the most popular in country—and moved in together in 1968, the same year she recorded "Stand By Your Man." (They announced they were married, but in fact she was still embroiled in a dragged-out divorce from Chapel.) In 1969 they made it legal and became Mr. and Mrs. Country Music; Tamala Georgette Jones was born in 1970.

Wynette's career soared, but all too soon Jones would be off on one of his increasingly frequent binges and she would have to perform alone when they were scheduled to appear together. And like so many of his colleagues, Jones was given to violence and gun-fondling when drunk. Once, when she locked the car keys away from him, Jones is reputed to have driven ten miles on a lawn mower for a bottle.

Wynette stood by Jones for as long as she could—six years. They separated in 1974 and divorced in 1975. It was over the next three years that she earned the "Heroine of Heartbreak" title.

Wynette started dating, virtually for the first time in her life; her beaux included actor Burt Reynolds. But a series of bizarre events began that would plague Wynette for the next several years. Vandals repeatedly broke into her Nashville home, at first merely leaving

Waylon Jennings

Highwayman at Large

Like his colleagues Willie Nelson and Kris Kristofferson, Waylon Jennings—here at Farm Aid V in 1992—gives time and money to humanitarian causes.

By the time Waylon Jennings (b. 1937) was twelve years old, he was a disc jockey for his hometown radio station in Littlefield, Texas, had sung in local talent shows, and was the frontman for his own band. His professional career began in earnest six years later with an introduction to Buddy Holly at the *Sunday Dance Party* radio show in Lubbock, Texas, where both were performing. Upon hearing Waylon, Holly immediately put him to work as the bass player for his band, the Crickets. In 1958 Holly helped secure a solo contract for Jennings and promised to produce and play guitar on Jennings' first single. That record, "Jole Blon," is now considered a Cajun classic.

In February 1959 Waylon gave up his seat to J.P. "The Big Bopper" Richardson on a plane chartered by Buddy Holly. In doing so, he saved his own life: the plane crashed in a cornfield, and all the passengers were killed, including Holly and Ritchie Valens.

Not until 1965 did Jennings again get the attention of a big label, when RCA brought him to Nashville to record his first single, "That's the Chance I'll Have to Take," which made it into the country top fifty. Three years later, Waylon finally made it into the country top five with "Walk On Out Of My Mind," and then to the #2 position with "Only Daddy That'll Walk the Line." It was around that time that he married country singer Jessi Colter.

By 1972 Waylon had tired of the clean-cut image that Nashville had assigned him. After a lot of negotiating, RCA finally allowed him to produce his own album, which resulted in a string of #1 hits, starting with "This Time."

If not for the 1976 collaboration of Jennings, Colter, Willie Nelson, and Tompall Glaser on *Wanted: The Outlaws*, the term "outlaw" probably would not have been so specifically associated with country music. The album went on to become the first Nashville-produced recording to be certified double-platinum.

Another Jennings collaboration would prove legendary. This time with Johnny Cash, Kris Kristofferson, and Willie Nelson, Waylon hit the charts in a big way with *Highwayman* (1985) and again with *Highwayman 2* (1990). Jennings continues to record (both by himself and with others, especially Willie Nelson) at this writing, releasing several successful original albums and best-of compilations, including *Too Dumb for New York City and Too Ugly for L.A.* (1992), a fifteen-volume collection of his work on the Bear Family label called *The Waylon Jennings Files*, and the follow-up album to *Highwayman 2*, *The Road Goes on Forever*.

With Jessi, Waylon established a telephone number so that their fans can hear the story of their lives and, at the same time, donate money to the Feed the Children project. Waylon Jennings also donates a portion of his time to promoting the national GED test.

—A.H.

George Jones

No Show Jones

George Jones' professional partnership with Tammy Wynette outlasted their turbulent marriage.

Very few country music lovers would dispute that George Jones (b. 1931) is one of the greatest country singers of all time. They would be talking not only about his voice and the way he sings a song, wrenching from it every smattering of emotion and nuance in a way that lacks guile or obvious theatricality, but also about his life, which has been a caricature of the brawling, hard-drinking, down-and-out, dissolute hero of so many country songs. Jones' life and career have teetered on the razor edge of oblivion more than once. His indisputable talent as a singer has repeatedly saved his professional life from the ravages of his personal life. In his time, Jones has lived through drug and alcohol addiction, arrests on drug and alcohol charges, a charge of armed assault, a near-fatal car crash, bankruptcy, and the nickname "No Show Jones," a title conferred upon him by countless concert promoters. But he has persevered, remaining an artistic inspiration to an entire generation of country performers.

The son of an alcoholic truck driver and a Pentecostal Baptist church pianist, George Jones was born on September 12, 1931, in Saratoga, Texas. When George was very young, the family moved from town to town, and his father eventually took a steady job as a pipefitter at the shipyards in Beaumont, Texas. Evidently George was frequently physically abused, and by the time he was fourteen he had left home, supporting himself by playing backup guitar with a variety of smalltime bands in Texas. By the time he was eighteen, he had married, and abandoned, his wife and first child. Following a three-year enlistment in the marines, Jones met a producer for Houston's Starday label in 1955 and recorded "Why Baby Why" and "You Gotta Be My Baby," both of which became hits. These were released at the time Elvis Presley, Carl Perkins, and other rockabilly singers were burning up the charts with their exciting new music; Jones saw the com-

mercial potential and recorded a string of rockabilly songs, which he hoped would prove as successful for him. He later came to regret this strategy, and as a successful country singer he tried to find and buy back his earliest recordings, saying that he wasn't at all proud of them.

Despite his false start, Jones soon began singing in a powerful honky-tonk style, and he was invited to join the Grand Ole Opry. Hits such as "White Lightning" (1959) followed; with these hits, fame and troubles with alcohol and drugs began to plague him. Jones became infamous for arriving too late for concerts, leaving them early, or missing them entirely. He was sued many times by promoters who had lost money on what turned out to be phantom events. Still, the early 1960s saw Jones recording such hits as "She Thinks I Still Care" (1961), "We Must Have Been Out of Our Minds" (a 1963 duet with Melba Montgomery), and the very popular crossover hit "The Race is On" (1964).

In the mid- and late-1960s, Jones' tumultuous personal life stabilized briefly when he began touring and performing with Tammy Wynette, whom he married in 1968. The two were extremely popular with audiences, and they scored big hits with tunes such as "Take Me" (1972) and "Let's Build a World Together" (1973). But Jones ultimately reverted to self-destructive behavior and he and Wynette were divorced in 1975 (they nonetheless continued their professional association in later years).

By 1979 the demands of creditors, mostly people suing him, had grown so great that Jones declared bankruptcy. He also checked into a hospital, hoping to dry out. This lull may have allowed him to collect himself enough to record the classic "He Stopped Loving Her Today" (1980), a spectacularly successful record and a performance that impressively showcased Jones' exceptional command of his craft. His personal demons had merely been beaten back, however, not exorcised. Another hospitalization in 1982

failed to prevent his 1983 arrest in Mississippi for cocaine possession and public drunkenness. Following his release from jail, he flipped his car, nearly killing himself in the wreck.

If 1983 was a low point in Jones' life, however, it was also the year that marked the beginning of his resurrection. He married Nancy Sepulveda, a woman he had met several years earlier at a concert in New York, and he credits her with helping him overcome his addictions. Moreover, he made a conscious decision to retake control of his career, and prohibited producers (such as Billy Sherrill) from soaking his music in the Nashville Sound. Jones returned to his roots as a honky-tonk singer, releasing such superb albums as *My Very Special Guests* and *Shine On*.

Acknowledged by most of today's neotraditionalist country superstars as a major influence, George Jones continues to perform at this writing in the style that brought him his greatest fame and that has touched the hearts and minds of countless fans.

—P.B.

behind nasty graffiti. Then the attacks escalated, culminating in a 1976 fire that left much of her house in ashes. Police were unable to find a perpetrator.

By her own account, Tammy reacted to the terror with the conviction that she needed a new husband to stand by and protect her. When the Burt Reynolds romance appeared to be going nowhere, she married a man on the fringes of the country business, Michael Tomlin. The attacks subsided, but the marriage had been a terrible mistake. Only two months after the wedding, she asked him to leave.

Plagued by ill health—she would have thirteen operations over the next several years—Wynette was at a low point. Sure enough, however, a new love blossomed, with long-time friend George Richey, who in 1978 became her fifth—and, so far, final—husband.

Two months after the wedding, Wynette hit the headlines one last time. She was kidnapped from a Nashville parking lot by a masked man who, she said, dragged her into his car at gunpoint, beat her, and drove her around for several hours. No one was ever arrested or charged and vicious rumors spread that the whole affair had been a staged publicity stunt engineered to boost her flagging career.

Since then, Wynette's life has quieted down. She has settled into her most enduring marriage with the man she says is the right one for her. She has even kicked the painkiller habit she acquired during the years of ill health.

Jones also found disaster after the end of their marriage, including bankruptcy, failed attempts to dry out, and a cocaine-related arrest. But he too appears to have won happiness with his fifth spouse, Nancy Sepulveda, whom he married in 1983.

Rhinestone Cowboy Glen Campbell holds a special place in the changing partners sweepstakes, a place won not by the number of his mates (a mere four wives), but by the number of his children (nine), the number of headlines accumulated during and between his marriages (innumerable), and the spectacular quality of his subsequent repentance.

Campbell began slowly, as a clean-cut country boy in the 1960s. In 1967, at the time of his breakthrough hit "Gentle on My Mind," he had been married to second wife Billie Jean, apparently happily, for

A moment of calm in a "sea of white powder": Tanya Tucker and Glen Campbell on their **Country Christmas** *television special in 1980.*

eight years (showing a taste even then for excess, he fathered three children during that marriage to add to the two he already had from his first marriage). His success spoiled that marriage, however, and Campbell and Billie Jean divorced in 1973. That was when he became the Rhinestone Playboy.

Campbell's amorous adventures seemed to culminate when he waltzed close friend Mac Davis' adored wife Sarah away from Davis' home and hearth and to the altar in 1977, but there was more to come. After all the heartbreak, his marriage to Sarah lasted only three years (just long enough to produce his sixth child). Then Campbell was off and running around again, this time with half-his-age Tanya Tucker.

By then, Campbell was deeply into drugs as well ("drowning in a sea of white powder," as he later described it). He also says he was trying to kick his coke habit at the time, but that "dating Tanya to escape cocaine was like jumping into a lake to avoid getting wet."

"THE WILDEST LOVE AFFAIR IN SHOW BUSINESS TODAY!" trumpeted *People* magazine, though *People* was too respectable to describe how wild it was. It took the tabloids to grapple adequately with the furniture-throwing, plate glass–breaking facts of the Campbell-Tucker romance.

Luckily for both, it didn't last long. They parted after only fifteen months, and in 1982 Campbell married Kimberly Wollen and found God.

Glen and Kimberly are still married. They've had three children (bringing Campbell's total to nine). His music and every other facet of his life are dedicated to Jesus now, he says, including his vigorous campaigns against other peoples' sexual freedom—he has become a prominent foe of both abortion and gay rights.

year—in fact, while visibly pregnant—Tucker was named Country Music Association Female Vocalist of the year.

Wynonna Judd, the former younger half of the spectacularly successful mother-daughter team the Judds, has recently elevated unwed motherhood to a hitherto-undreamed-of peak of respectability. Now a successful solo star, Wynonna is the proud mother of baby Elijah, though not the wife of Elijah's father. Naomi Judd, the baby's equally proud grandmother, drew a standing ovation at the 1995 Academy of Country Music awards merely by announcing that Wynonna was absent from the ceremony because she was home with the new baby.

Trouble with the law doesn't seem to have damaged many country luminaries either. More than one Nashville mansion rests on a rock-solid prison foundation, and some of the nation's most infamous penitentiaries, including California's San Quentin and Louisiana's Angola State, have country-icon alumni.

The most celebrated of the Nashville jailbirds is probably the Okie from Muskogee himself, Merle

Wynonna Judd (above), country's most famous unmarried mother, and Merle Haggard (right)— the Okie from Muscogee—country's most famous jailbird.

Yet, as sometime Nashvillean Bob Dylan once noted, the times they are a-changin'. The marriage rate in country music is plummeting, and even unwed motherhood seems to be no bar to block-buster record sales. Minor luminary Gail Davies became a single mother by choice in 1982, and since then, at least two superstars have won major honors while proudly showing off the fruits of their nonmarital unions.

Tanya Tucker bore Presley Tanita Tucker to Los Angeles actor Ben Reed in 1989. After another two years of the on-again, off-again relationship, she bore Beau Grayson Tucker in 1991. The same

Haggard (he was actually born in Bakersfield, California, to a family that had left Oklahoma for California's pastures of plenty only three years before). After his father's death in 1946, Haggard took to what was then just beginning to be called juvenile delinquency.

In 1957 Haggard reaped his reward: a one-to-ten-year sentence in San Quentin for burglary (or attempted burglary—sources differ). One chronicle places his cell there next to that of notorious murderer Caryl Chessman (presumably before Chessman, executed in 1960, was transferred to San Quentin's death row).

Whether it was Chessman's example or prison life in general, something in the San Quentin atmosphere persuaded the young convict to look for another line of work. During the two years Haggard wound up serving, he took up music and, once paroled in 1960, never looked back.

By 1964 Haggard was turning out such as hits "Just Between the Two of Us," a duet with his first-wife-to-be Bonnie Campbell Owens (who had been married to superstar Buck Owens). In 1967 and 1968, fans voted him the number one male country singer in the *Music City News* poll. The smugly self-righteous "Okie from Muskogee" lifted him to the top in 1969 and was followed by thirty-six more #1 hits over the next twenty years.

Neither David Allan Coe nor Johnny Rodriguez, whose backgrounds were similar to Haggard's, ever reached the heights that he did, but both went on from prison to solid careers.

Coe spent as much of his youth inside prison walls as out and was nearing thirty when he left Ohio State Penitentiary for the last time, in 1967. He drifted into the country orbit and released the aptly titled *Penitentiary Blues*; it sold well enough to get him a CBS contract as the Mysterious Rhinestone Cowboy in 1974 (a year before Glen Campbell's "Rhinestone Cowboy" hit the charts and went to #1). Coe joined the "outlaw" singers and wrote smash hits for other performers; Tanya Tucker recorded his "Would You Lay With Me (In a Field of Stone)" in 1975, and Johnny Paycheck made a blockbuster out of Coe's "Take This Job and Shove It" in 1977. (Paycheck's own

career was interrupted late in the 1980s by a term in Coe's alma mater, Ohio State Penitentiary.

Texas-born Johnny Rodriguez is reported to have been rescued from a life of early crime by a Texas Ranger who had arrested him for stealing a goat. (Rodriguez was caught red-handed barbecuing the animal). He went on to one bilingual hit after another, starting with "Pass Me By" in 1972.

Then there were the performers who actually served their time *during* (not before) their careers, among them the only woman in all country known to have a record, Aunt Molly Jackson. Actually, Jackson, although genuinely country in her roots, belonged to the folk-protest world of the Depression 1930s, a world that maintained a tenuous and uneasy connection to country at the time (the relationship would deteriorate in the 1960s). A union organizer from the coal-mining country of Kentucky, Jackson was jailed for ten days and then forced to leave the state. Along with her sister, Sarah Ogan Gunning, she was welcomed by the left-wing protest-music audience of the North.

Country's biggest Chicano star, Tex-Mex singer Freddy Fender (Baldemar G. Huerta) was moving up through minor hits toward the big time in the early 1960s when he was busted flat in Baton Rouge for possession of marijuana. He served three years in Louisiana's infamous Angola State Penitentiary. It took him twelve years to get back to where he had been, but he made the big time with "Before the Next Teardrop Falls" in 1975.

Of course, as country has moved from the margins of popular music toward its center, becoming a major industry in the process, the nature of its scandals has changed somewhat. None of its early stars, for example, could have owed the millions in taxes—$16 million, to be precise—that the U.S. Internal Revenue Service alleged Willie Nelson owed them in 1991. They proceeded to freeze various assets of Willie's, padlocking his recording studio in the process.

But the Red Headed Stranger was holding an ace or two—or rather, a tape or two—up his sleeve. The next thing the IRS knew, Willie had released a new album consisting of previously unreleased material he had salvaged from the freeze-out and titled *The IRS Tapes*. He threw himself on his fans'

mercy, as so many have thrown themselves on his (Nelson is among the most generous of country stars, especially with his time). No star of yore could have expected to raise the $16 million on the strength of one record, but Willie's many fans came through. Nelson remains an undimmed star, perhaps more beloved than ever for his troubles with the IRS.

One brilliant country career was finished in prison: that of western swing bandleader Spade Cooley, who was convicted of and imprisoned for murder in 1961.

It was a drunken, brutal murder, committed in front of a witness: in 1961 he reeled into his house, attacked his estranged second wife, Ella Mae, and beat her to death in front of their fourteen-year-old daughter, after having exclaimed, "You're going to watch me kill her." Days later, he expressed a sentiment common to many another wife-murderer when he wrote to a friend, "You know how much I loved her."

Cooley received a life sentence. Eligible for parole in 1969, he was allowed out of Vacaville Prison to hold a benefit concert; he collapsed and died during the performance.

The most famous penitentiary in country music—Folsom Prison—has never held a country star overnight. Johnny Cash has spent many an evening in the slam, singing to prisoners all over the country, but in all his long career, is known to have spent only one night inside, and that was in a local lockup, not Folsom or San Quentin. The judge who sentenced him after his massive pill-smuggling bust in 1965 gave him thirty days, but suspended the sentence, leaving Cash still innocent of prison. The next year, however, when he was picked up drunk, disorderly, and picking publicly owned flowers, he spent one night in jail.

Then there's the Jerry Lee Lewis story—not a single event, but the Killer's entire life and career. No one in all country music has been so consistently outrageous, endured so many tragedies, starred in so many farces, or garnered so many headlines inside and outside the United States. Jerry Lee has been on more rampages than Hank, had more spouses than Tammy, had more spouses die under

Spade Cooley enjoyed a brilliant career as a first-rate bandleader and fiddler until he killed his second wife in a drunken rage.

suspicious circumstances than Spade Cooley, and been arrested more often than anyone.

Lewis holds the headline record despite having begun with a handicap: his earliest escapades never made the papers because they occurred before anyone knew who he was. He had flunked out of religion school, married twice (the second marriage was bigamous), turned out his first two hits, and contracted a third (also bigamous) marriage all before he hit the headlines for the first time in 1958, at the age of twenty-two.

At that time, Lewis had been performing since he was fifteen. He had had a brief flirtation with another career, though; after high school, he had gone to the Southwestern Bible Institute of the Assembly of God, but he was expelled after three months for his diabol-

But the stories of the brouhaha that greeted Lewis' arrival in England with Myra Gale on his first tour outside the United States later that spring are not apocryphal. Though he tried to pass Myra off as sixteen, the Brits had learned the truth and they were appalled. Jerry Lee was booed on the streets and off the stages and had to cancel the tour and return home.

Lewis took out a full-page ad in *Billboard* and used it to apologize, but the damage was done. U.S. fans might or might not have been as judgmental, but the disc jockeys took no chances; it was the beginning of a ten-year radio blackout. Lewis continued to tour and record but got virtually no U.S. airplay. (Ironically, England was more forgiving; he had a triumphant return tour there in 1962, and his records returned to the British charts.)

Also in 1962 came the first of the tragic deaths that were to occur in Jerry Lee's life with startling frequency: three-year-old Steve Allen Lewis—his third child, Myra's first—drowned in the family's swimming pool.

The radio blackout ended in 1968, when deejays began to give Lewis' records airplay again. "Another Place, Another Time" and "To Make Love Sweeter for You" immediately climbed to #4 and #1, respectively, on the country charts.

Jerry Lee was no longer a kid. He was thirty-three and had settled in to a life of heavy drinking and pill-popping. Astonishingly, he was still married to Myra, but the marriage was on the rocks; she divorced him in 1970. This time the divorce was legal; Myra Gale saw to that.

Jerry Lee was so upset by the divorce that he cleaned up his act, briefly; he also married wife number four, Jaren Pate. They separated shortly afterward, though it was years before either of them attempted to end the marriage legally.

Then came a decade full of banner headlines. In November 1973, his oldest child, Jerry Lee Lewis, Jr., nineteen years old, was killed in a car crash. In September 1976 he shot his own bass player, Norman "Butch" Owens, in the chest during an argument (Owens survived and sued). Two months later Lewis was arrested twice in two days: on November 22 for driving his car into a ditch while intoxicated

ically inspired piano playing in chapel. (His cousin, Jimmy Swaggart, was more successful.)

So Lewis threw himself wholeheartedly into secular music and became a star, one of the first rockabilly performers, on the strength of 1957's "Whole Lotta Shakin' Goin' On" and "Great Balls of Fire." On December 12, 1957, he eloped from Memphis with his sweetheart, Myra Gale Brown, and married her in Mississippi.

Myra Gale, however, was a little more than his sweetheart, and a little less than ready to be a wife. She was his cousin, albeit a distant one, and on their wedding day she was thirteen years old (though some accounts say she had turned fourteen). And Jerry Lee had omitted—intentionally or not—a crucial prerequisite for the marriage: he had not yet divorced his second wife, Jane Mitcham Lewis, mother of his two sons. (In fact, he had never divorced his first wife, Dorothy Barton, either.)

One story from this period of the Jerry Lee chronicles is apparently apocryphal. Legend has it

The Killer, Jerry Lee Lewis, with wife number three, Myra Gale Brown, whom he married before she was fourteen years old—and before he was divorced from wife number two.

that when rock's first impresario, Alan Freed, demanded during a rock and roll extravaganza in early 1958 that Jerry Lee cede top billing to Chuck Berry, Jerry Lee pulled out all the stops during his set—the next-to-last of the evening—and then set his piano afire, challenging Berry to top the performance. According to biographer Jimmy Guterman, this did not happen; instead, Guterman claims that Jerry Lee merely did his usual, utterly outrageous performance and then, strolling jauntily offstage—leaving the piano unburned and intact—challenged Berry to "Follow that," adding a racial slur for good measure.

and on the next day for trying to force his way into Graceland with a gun (he said he had to see Elvis).

In 1979 a long struggle with the IRS was joined when the agency seized considerable portions of Lewis' property. In 1981 he was rushed to the hospital with a perforated stomach. The papers thought he was dying, but the Killer survived.

Jaren, however, died just a few years later. On June 8, 1982—they were at that point cross-filing for divorce—she was found dead in her swimming pool. But the biggest Jerry Lee scandal was yet to come.

Almost exactly a year after Jaren's death, Lewis married for the fifth time. His bride, Shawn Stephens, was twenty-five; Jerry Lee was forty-seven. After only ten weeks of marriage, Shawn told friends that she was going to leave him. A few days later, she died in their Mississippi home. County officials announced the cause of death as fluid in her lungs (a diagnosis approximately as informative as "cessation of heartbeat"). A Memphis coroner hired privately by Jerry Lee found methadone—the legal, prescription replacement for heroin—in her blood. A subsequent grand jury hearing, the records of which were sealed, found no evidence of foul play.

The next March—just after Jerry Lee had surrendered to federal marshals and pleaded not guilty to charges of tax evasion covering the years from 1975 to 1981—the most ominous news story of his entire career appeared in *Rolling Stone* magazine.

In *Rolling Stone*'s March 1, 1984, issue, journalist Richard Ben Cramer detailed a shocking account of the circumstances surrounding Shawn Lewis' death, alleging evidence that the body had been moved before the ambulance was called and that there were bloodstained clothes in the room where she had actually died and bloodstains and bruises on her body. No charges were ever filed. In June 1984 Jerry Lee married his sixth wife, Kerrie McCarver.

Lewis is nearing sixty now and has been battered by time and drink and drugs. Still a local celebrity in Memphis and Mississippi, he never reached the heights of stardom he was clearly headed for some forty years ago. There is, it seems, some quantity of scandal that can derail a country career.

There are still absolute no-nos in country music, too. You don't spit on the Bible, the U.S. flag, or motherhood. The continuing estrangement between the worlds of country music and its close cousin, folk music, is due at least in part to the fact that folkies were often a little too citified for country, but also because they were usually a little too far left.

Nor do country stars, by and large, come out explicitly for reproductive rights. The much-beloved Loretta Lynn generated a mild scandal with her 1975 hit touting "The Pill," and no tell-all autobiography (which in any case never tells all) has ever admitted to an abortion in a country star's past. Indeed, one factor in the increasing respectability of—not to say reverence for—unwed motherhood may well be the perception that every proud unwed mother strikes a blow against abortion.

But the area in which country audiences have so far appeared least tolerant is sexual orientation. Through all its transformations, country has been a world where men were men and women were women, and ambiguity or the appearance of ambiguity was impermissible. The only country performer ever to come out as homosexual is the Canadian k.d. lang, and the question of whether she could have succeeded in country after doing so was essentially rendered moot by her departure from the genre not long afterward.

It must be noted, though, that lang's 1991 coming out was attended by somewhat less publicity than was her militantly vegetarian "Meat Stinks" television spot the year before. The spot drew enormous fury from a cattle industry that still supports a considerable proportion of the country audience. A less eccentric open lesbian could yet become a country star.

Many boundaries are blurring in the 1990s. It may well be that ever-increasing sophistication and the integration of country into show business at large will broaden the country audience to even greater degrees of tolerance for law-breaking and convention-shattering behavior. At any rate, country stars will no doubt keep generating headlines and audiences will continue to enjoy hearing not just the music but about the stars' loves, losses, and excesses.

Jerry Lee Lewis with Kerrie McCarver, his sixth and—to date—last wife, whom he married after the shocking death of wife number five, Shawn Stephens, in 1983. Despite having had more than his share of troubles, Lewis has proven to be a survivor.

Bibliography

Allen, Bob. *George Jones: The Saga of an American Singer*. New York: Doubleday, 1984.

Bufwack, Mary A., and Robert K. Oermann. *Finding Her Voice—The Saga of Women in Country Music*. New York: Crown Publishers, Inc. 1993.

Cackett, Alan. *The Harmony Illustrated Encyclopedia of Country Music*. New York: Crown Publishers, Inc., 1986.

Cain, Robert. *Whole Lotta Shakin' Goin' On*. New York: The Dial Press, 1981.

Campbell, Glen, with Tom Carter. *Rhinestone Cowboy*. New York: Villard Books, 1994.

Cantwell, Robert. *Bluegrass Breakdown*. Urbana, Ill.: University of Illinois Press, 1984.

Carter, Janette. *Living with Memories*. Hiltons, Va.: Carter Family Memorial Music Center.

Chase, Gilbert. *America's Music: From the Pilgrims to the Present*. Rev. 3rd ed. Urbana, Ill.: University of Illinois Press, 1992.

Clarke, Donald, ed. *The Penguin Encyclopedia of Popular Music*. London: Penguin Books, 1989.

Country Music Magazine editors. *The Comprehensive Country Music Encyclopedia*. New York: New York Times Books, 1994.

Dellar, Fred. *The Country Music Book of Lists*. New York: Times Books, 1984.

———. *The Illustrated Encyclopedia of Country Music*. New York: Harmony Books, 1977.

Erlewine, Michael, Chris Woodstra, and Vladimir Bogdanor, eds. *All Music Guide: The Best CDs, Albums & Tapes*. 2nd ed. San Francisco: Miller Freeman Books, 1994.

Flint, Country Joe, and Judy Nelson. *The Insider's Country Music Handbook*. Layton, Utah: Peregrine Smith Books, 1993.

Flippo, Chet. *Your Cheatin' Heart*. New York: St. Martin's Paperbacks, 1989.

Fowler, Gene, and Bill Crawford. *Border Radio*. Austin, Tex.: Texas Monthly Press, 1987.

Ginell, Cary. *Milton Brown and the Founding of Western Swing*. Urbana, Ill.: The University of Illinois Press, 1994.

Goldsmith, Thomas. "Alison Krauss and Union Station, 1995." *Bluegrass Unlimited*, June 1995.

Grissim, John. *Country Music: White Man's Blues*. Philadelphia: Coronet Books Inc., 1970.

Guralnick, Peter. *Lost Highway*. New York: Vintage Books, 1979.

Guterman, Jimmy. *Rockin' My Life Away—Listening to Jerry Lee Lewis*. Nashville: Rutledge Hill Press, 1991.

Harris, Charles W., and Buck Rainey, eds. *The Cowboy: Six-Shooters, Songs, and Sex*. Norman, Okla.: University of Oklahoma Press, 1976.

Herzhaft, Gerard. *Encyclopedia of the Blues*. Fayetteville, Ark.: University of Arkansas Press, 1992.

Hopper, Phil. *San Antonio Rose: The Life and Legacy of Bob Wills*. (film in progress)

Horstman, Dorothy. *Sing Your Heart Out, Country Boy*. New York: E.P. Dutton & Co., Inc., 1975.

Ivey, William. Liner notes to *The Bob Wills Anthology* (CBS).

Jones, Jacqueline. *The Dispossessed*. New York: Basic Books, 1992.

Kochman, Marilyn, ed. *The Big Book of Bluegrass*. New York: Quill, 1984.

Koon, George William. *Hank Williams: A Bio-Bibliography*. Westport, Conn.: Greenwood Press, 1983.

Liebling, Rachel. *High Lonesome: The Story of Bluegrass Music* (film). Northside Films, 1991.

Logsdon, Guy. *"The Whorehouse Bells Were Ringing," and Other Songs Cowboys Sing*. Urbana, Ill.: University of Illinois Press, 1989.

Logsdon, Guy, Mary Rogers, and William Jacobson. *Saddle Serenaders*. Salt Lake City: Gibbs Smith, 1995.

Lynn, Loretta, with George Vecsey. *Coal Miner's Daughter*. New York: Warner Books, 1976.

Malone, Bill C. *Country Music, U.S.A.*. Rev. ed. Austin, Tex.: University of Texas Press, 1985.

———. *Southern Music, American Music*. Lexington, Ky.: University Press of Kentucky, 1979.

Morthland, John. Liner notes for *OKeh Western Swing* (Epic).

Nash, Alanna. *Behind Closed Doors: Talking With the Legends Of Country*. New York: Knopf, 1988.

Palmer, Robert. "Rock Begins." *The Rolling Stone Illustrated History of Rock and Roll*. Rev. 3rd ed. Anthony DeCurtis and James Henke, with Holly George-Warren, eds. New York: Straight Arrow Publishers, 1992.

Rinzler, Ralph. "Bill Monroe." *Stars of Country Music: Uncle Dave Macon to Johnny Rodriguez*. Bill C. Malone and Judith McCulloh, eds. Urbana, Ill.: University of Illinois Press, 1975.

Rogers, Roy, and Dale Evans, with Jane and Michael Stern. *Happy Trails: Our Life Story*. New York: Simon & Schuster, 1994.

Roland, Tom. *The Billboard Book of Number One Country Hits*. New York: Billboard Books, 1991.

Rosenberg, Neil V. *Bluegrass, A History*. Urbana, Ill.: University of Illinois Press, 1985.

The Rounder Collective. Liner notes for the Bailey Brothers' *Have You Forgotten?* (Rounder).

Stambler, Irwin, and Grelun Landon. *Encyclopedia of Folk, Country and Western Music*. New York: St. Martin's, 1969.

Thorp, N. Howard, with Austin E. and Alta S. Fife. *Songs of the Cowboys*. New York: Clarkson N. Potter, Inc., 1966.

Tosches, Nick. *Country: The Biggest Music in America*. New York: Stein and Day, 1977.

Townsend, Charles. "Bob Wills." *Stars of Country Music: Uncle Dave Macon to Johnny Rodriguez*. Bill C. Malone and Judith McCulloh, eds. Urbana, Ill.: University of Illinois Press, 1975.

———. *San Antonio Rose: The Life and Music of Bob Wills*. Urbana: University of Illinois Press, 1976.

Tribe, Ivan. Liner notes for the Lilly Brothers' *Country Songs* (Rounder).

Watson, Bruce. "This Here's All for Foot-Tappin' and Grin-Winnin'." *Smithsonian*, March 1993.

White, John I. *Git Along, Little Dogies—Songs and Songmakers of the American West*. Urbana, Ill.: University of Illinois Press, 1975.

Williams, Jett, with Pamela Thomas. *Aint' Nothin' as Sweet As My Baby*. New York: Harcourt Brace Jovanovich, 1990.

Wolfe, Charles K. Liner notes for *Altamont: Black String Band Music from the Library of Congress* (Rounder).

———. Liner notes for *Sixty Years of the Grand Ole Opry* (RCA).

Woods, Jeff. "Color Me Country: Tales from the Frontlines." *The Journal of Country Music*, Vol. 14, No. 2 (1992).

Wynette, Tammy, with Joan Dew. *Stand By Your Man*. New York: Simon & Schuster, 1979.

Photography Credits

AP/Wide World Photos: 28 bottom, 36 bottom right, 39, 47, 52, 120 bottom

Archive Photos: 8 left, 26 top left, 33, 56 right, 58 top; © Lee: 73 bottom, 92 bottom left, 100; Frank Driggs Collection: 34

Corbis-Bettmann Archive: 50 top left, 53 bottom, 56 center, 92 top right, 96 bottom

Everett Collection: 18 bottom, 55 bottom, 58 bottom, 61 right, 63, 69 both, 71 bottom, 74 bottom left, 80, 85, 86, 124 top left, 135, 136 both

Frank Driggs Collection: 13 top, 18 top, 26 bottom left, 30 both, 31 bottom, 40 both, 74 top left, 76 top, 78 left, 110, 111 both, 112 bottom, 113

Globe Photos: 83 center; NBC: 60 right, 124 bottom right, 134

Neal Peters Collection: 98 bottom

Photofest: 7, 8 right, 57 top, 59, 83 top, 90 top, 92 top left, 95 top, 97, 103 top, 106 left, 108 bottom right, 118 top, 119, 122 right

Retna: © Larry Busacca: 72; © Camera Press: 70; © Gary Gershoff: 132; © Beth Gwinn: 71 top and center, 84 bottom right, 90 bottom, 108 top left, 118 bottom, 123, 131; © Chris Kraft: 73 top, 133; © MJF/Redferns: 13 bottom, 89, 91, 114, 129 right; © Darryl Pitt: 129 top; © Michael Putland: 121; © Andrew Putler: 50 top right, 66, 67; © James Vita: 128

Reuters/Corbis-Bettmann: 68

Samuel M. Sherman Collection: 36 top left and top right, 41, 42 both, 43 both, 44, 45 both, 46

Showtime Archives: 2-3, 6, 10 all, 14 both, 15, 16, 19, 21, 22, 23, 26 bottom and top right, 28 top, 29, 31 top, 32, 35, 36 bottom left, 38, 48, 49, 50 bottom left and right, 53 top, 54 both, 55 top, 57 bottom, 60 left, 61 left, 62, 64, 74 bottom and top right, 76 bottom, 77, 78 right, 79, 81 all, 82 both, 83 bottom, 84 bottom left, 87, 88, 92 bottom right, 94 all, 95 bottom, 96 top, 98 top, 99, 101 both, 102 all, 103 bottom, 104 both, 105 both, 106 right, 107 all, 108 bottom left and top right, 112 top left and center, 115, 116, 117, 120 top, 122 top left and bottom, 124 top right and bottom left, 126, 127, 130, 137, 138

UPI/Corbis-Bettmann: 56 left, 65, 84 top, 139

Index